'… imagine if the plane crashed and we died.'
Star Zambia striker Kelvin Mutale aboard an
air force Buffalo on 22 April 1993.
Five days later, they did.

Zambia is the only country in the world
to lose its national football team in a plane
crash. This is the story and the aftermath.

To those we lost; and to those I lost while working on this project.

CRASH OF THE BUFFALO

CRASH
OF THE
BUFFALO

The Tragedy that Killed a Football Team
and Rocked the World

JAY MWAMBA

First published by Pitch Publishing, 2025

1

Pitch Publishing
9 Donnington Park,
85 Birdham Road,
Chichester, West Sussex,
PO20 7AJ

www.pitchpublishing.co.uk
info@pitchpublishing.co.uk

A CIP catalogue record is available for this book
from the British Library.

ISBN 978 1 80150 996 1

Typesetting and origination by Pitch Publishing

Printed and bound on FSC® certified paper in line with
our continuing commitment to ethical business practices,
sustainability and the environment.

Printed and bound in India by Thomson Press

Contents

Acknowledgements

CRASH OF THE BUFFALO was written on an emotional rollercoaster, and not because of the subject matter alone. Four of the sources I interviewed for the book passed on during the writing process. A fifth was tragically killed after the book's first edition was published. In addition, I lost my dad before completing the first draft, and suffered another shattering blow with the passing, in April 2022, of my brother Robert, whom I'd shared an apartment with since 1995. I persevered with the project determined to help perpetuate the memory and legacy of a fine crop of footballers (many of whom I knew and had travelled with) cruelly taken away from us. I'd like to thank those that made this project possible.

The late Dickson Makwaza, captain of Ante Bušelić's outstanding national team that established Zambia as an African power in the early 70s, was my first interview. He sadly died four months later aged 77. Ronnie Hollywood had arrived in Zambia in 1968 as an expatriate teacher from Newry, Northern Ireland. Retired in Newry now, he offered insight on the role the Zambia schools football programme played in moulding a strong national team. Nelson Sapi, a former international defender, offered a gripping first-hand account of the national team's first near-disaster aboard an air force Dakota plane in 1976, en route from an Olympic

11

qualifier in Sudan. He passed away aged 65, shortly after his contribution to this project.

Rupiah B. Banda, former president of Zambia (among the many senior positions he held in his storied lifetime), was a sports aficionado and long-time family friend. He shared many memories, including watching Zambia's twice-played 1974 Africa Cup of Nations Final with Zaire alongside boxing great Muhammad Ali. He died at 85 in March 2022. So did noted Zambian surgeon and professor Lupando Munkonge a couple of weeks later, also aged 85. Munkonge had led the medical team sent to Libreville to retrieve the remains of the Buffalo crash victims.

It took me a while to track down several sources. The retired Zambian Air Force (ZAF) Lt Gen Ronald (Ronnie) Shikapwasha was one. He was a commander at the time of the crash. When we finally connected, he was nothing but gracious with his time. He responded to all my questions in writing and reviewed the final text. He'd flown the ill-fated Buffalo plane days before it went down in Libreville. I landed in Lusaka on 15 January 2024, looking forward to meeting him for the first time, only to hear that he'd been mortally wounded in a shooting at his house. Aged 76, he went to the grave convinced that the Buffalo had been shot down. Winston Gumboh, vice-chairman of the Football Association of Zambia (FAZ) at the time of the crash, was another long-sought-after source. I traced him to Malawi, just to find out how much FAZ had paid to charter the Buffalo plane from ZAF.

Simon 'Kaodi' Kaushi and Jani Simulambo, among a handful of surviving members from Bušelić's pioneering 1973 Zambia squad, took me back to that era, as did Frederick Kashimoto and Peter Kaumba with memories of the 1980 Moscow Olympics and 1982 AFCON respectively. Kalusha Bwalya and Charles Musonda, meanwhile, shared their Zambia experiences before and after the crash.

Even before embarking on my research, I knew that Chanda Kristensen (known as Beauty Lupiya when on the *Times of Zambia* sports desk) would be key to retelling the story of the tragic team's last week. She'd travelled with the side to Mauritius, for what would be its final game, and returned with a harrowing tale, ominous of what was to follow. The players wanted her to cover the Senegal match as well, but her editor assigned someone else, saving her life. Thank you, Chanda, for agreeing to recall painful memories.

After the crash, there'd be claims by a few local players that they'd escaped death on the Buffalo only because they'd been dropped at the airport before departure. That was only true in the case of third-choice goalie Martin Mwamba and winger Andrew Tembo, both of whom were released from the squad hours before departure. Mwamba helped detail the team's last hours in Lusaka, including the last meal they ate.

Sonestone Kashiba, then acting director of sport, should have also been on the Buffalo, but work got in the way. He did, however, make it to the airport and saw the team off after boarding and disembarking from the plane. He was led aboard by coach Alex Chola, who pointed out where he'd have sat. Kashiba's story had not been told before. I thank him.

Times of Zambia reporter Chris Kachingwe was another 'survivor', as he termed those lucky souls who should have also been on the free flight but missed it at the last moment for one reason or another. He'd volunteered to relieve Beauty/Chanda on the Senegal leg, but along with the *Zambia Daily Mail*'s Goliath Mungonge, he was unable to obtain traveller's cheques in the few hours before the team's departure for Senegal. Simataa Simataa – sometimes aficionado, sometimes football insider – can also be counted among those unwittingly saved from death on the Buffalo. All three added their distinctive voices to the narrative.

Roald Poulsen was a key figure in rebuilding the Zambia national squad after the tragedy. It took a while to track him down as well in Denmark, but thanks to Chanda Kristensen I made contact. He shared his notes on the extraordinary task he'd accepted to undertake and the incredible fruits it bore. Ailing, he sent me this WhatsApp message in August 2024: 'Thank you from my heart, that you let me contribute telling about my experiences. Zambia and the people are deep in my heart.' It was his last missive to me. He died two months later.

It would have been impossible to profile, in detail, all 18 players who perished that awful night of 27 April 1993. So I did the next best thing, in my mind, by focusing on striker Kelvin Mutale, as representative of the young, exciting talent Zambia lost on the Buffalo. For the wistful details of Kelvin's tragically, albeit coruscating, short life, I thank his older brother Michael Chanda, and Noel Kawanu, Kelvin's team manager at second tier Nitrogen Stars.

My immense gratitude also goes to Emmanuel Maradas, former editor and CEO of *African Soccer Magazine*, and to Ponga Liwewe, one of his contributors; to Jerry Muchimba, Godfrey 'Ucar' Chitalu's biographer; to Patrick Kangwa, the only FAZ official in the delegation sent to retrieve the remains of the crash victims; and to Kaweche Kaunda, who accompanied his father, former president Kenneth Kaunda, to Libreville for the AFCON 2012 final that should have provided closure to the disaster.

Thank you, too, Hugh Molotsi and Chris Soto, for being such great sounding boards. I'm also greatly indebted to former *Times of Zambia* deputy sports editor Gerald Mulwanda for his reminisces of the fallen 18; to George Makulu, a former Zambia Airways executive; Khaled Al-Nasser, Al Ettifaq's former media and communications manager; noted Saudi sports journalist Dawwad Al-Musa; and to retired civil servant George Kateka.

I can't thank you all enough.

Jay Mwamba
New York
Spring 2025

Prologue

I MET Frank Taylor in Moscow back in September 1985. It was in the early days of Soviet premier Mikhail Gorbachev's transformative tenure and *glasnost* was in the air. Taylor, a motley collection of sports journalists and I were in the Soviet Union during the FIFA World Youth Championship, as it was then known.

A veteran British journalist who'd served in the Royal Air Force during the Second World War, he was in the USSR as president of AIPs, the world association of sports writers. Its meeting that year coincided with what's now the FIFA Under-20 World Cup. Short, portly and congenial with severely receding dark hair and a thin moustache, Taylor bore a striking resemblance to the American actor William Conrad, star of the detective series *Cannon* and *Nero Wolfe*. He had another notable feature: he walked with a limp. After a few days, my curiosity got the better of me. I inquired as to the nature of his disability. He explained almost matter-of-factly that he'd been on the ill-fated Manchester United plane that had crashed in Munich, West Germany, in February 1958, ultimately claiming 23 lives. He'd survived but only barely. I was stunned. I'd grown up reading British football publications *Scorcher and Score* and *Shoot!* and knew of the disaster that had so tragically decimated the Busby Babes, claiming the lives of eight players including the precocious Duncan Edwards, who'd lived just 21 years. And here I was travelling across the Soviet Union with the only journalist out of nine on the plane to survive the catastrophe. Little did I know that in less than eight years my own country would also be so awfully stricken. Two years after Munich, Taylor wrote a moving eyewitness account of the disaster. His book, *The Day a Team Died*, would become the definitive chronicle of one of the world football's most tragic events. Taylor lived for another 44 years after the Munich air crash, succumbing to lung cancer aged 81 in July 2002. Munich would be the precursor to another football catastrophe.

1

Quirk of Fate

TWO DAYS before his 41st birthday and 12 years after leading England to World Cup glory, Bobby Charlton suited up against African opposition for the first time in his fabled career. It was an autumn Monday evening in Shropshire, near the Welsh border, when he donned the blue and amber of Third Division title contenders Shrewsbury Town as a guest player at Gay Meadow on 9 October 1978. It would be one of his last games at organised level. The opposition? Zambia's national team in its first game on its first tour of Britain, the country the southern Africans had gained independence from 14 years earlier.

The Zambians were awed.

Skilful, dynamic and master of the thunderbolt shot, Charlton had brought glory to both club and country. As captain of Manchester United, the attacking midfielder had become the first English player to hoist the European Cup, forerunner of the Champions League, scoring twice in the 1968 final against Benfica.

A decade later, the enormous skills that had earned Charlton many honours, veneration and a world-class reputation may have diminished with the years. But they were still ample enough to beguile a team of talented but starstruck amateurs – at least in the opening 45 minutes during which Shrewsbury led 3-0.

In 2014, Vincent Chileshe, Zambia's teenage goalkeeper on that tour, recalled Charlton's scintillating display and attempted to exculpate his defenders. 'Sometimes it's [normal], where you find that if you are playing a player who's well known, the defenders are sometimes scared. That's how it is,' he said in Tampa, Florida.

Mesmerised was more like it, on what felt like an icy winter's night for the visitors from the tropics. Five years after leaving Manchester United with a then club record 249 goals, Charlton put on a clinic against opposition blindsided early by both his skills and the elements. The 40-year-old nodded in a dipping cross at the back post. A one-two with his striking partner split the Zambian defence and put him one-on-one with Chileshe; Vincent's next act was plucking the ball out of the net. Charlton would complete his hat-trick before the interval, beating the 19-year-old Chileshe with another header to add another match ball to his enormous collection.

'They were scoring through headers – you know how the [English] played,' recalled Chileshe, evoking the English game of that era, replete with long balls and crosses into the box. 'They'd go to the byline, square the ball and by the time, *mebbe*, you've covered the near post, they've put it in at the far post.'

At any rate, Zambia's pedigree would be more discernible on resumption, reported *Zambia Daily Mail* sports reporter Wellington Kalwisha, who accompanied the team. 'They showed great composure in the second half when they completely took charge, reducing their hosts to only one more goal despite the masterly distribution in midfield by the English maestro – the great Charlton, whose brilliant footwork delighted the crowd,' wrote Kalwisha.

The friendly, the first match of the Zambians' three-week, seven-game British tour, ended in a 4-0 drubbing.

Said Charlton to Kalwisha, 'I was greatly impressed by the natural ability displayed by your team. The skill is there but what they lack is the directness in front of goal. They have that fatal hesitation in front of goal but otherwise the approach is superb.'

At the final whistle, the Zambian players were predictably eager to shake hands with Charlton. It's likely that he shook hands with forward Godfrey Chitalu, a sometimes-fiery former boxer nicknamed 'Ucar' and, even then, Zambia's greatest player ever – based on his scoring and match-winning prowess. Six years earlier, Chitalu had struck a record 107 goals in one season for club and country. That remarkable tally would earn him posthumous global fame four decades later when his name was embroiled with Lionel Messi's in an impromptu debate on who had netted the most goals in a calendar year. Chitalu's idol was Charlton's former Manchester United team-mate Denis Law. That adoration had reportedly once earned the powerful Zambian striker – a precursor of the great Liberian George Weah in physique and style – a dismissal for his cheeky retort to a referee in a league match in 1967. The story, according to his biographer Jerry Muchimba, goes that warned earlier for rough play, Chitalu committed one infraction too many. Asked his name by referee Peter Bell, Chitalu responded, 'Denis Law.' Bell immediately ordered the striker off.

Decades later, Charlton's brief encounter with Chitalu could be interpreted for what it was: a quirk of fate. One of the most famous survivors of the tragic 1958 Munich air crash that ultimately claimed eight Manchester United players had just crossed paths with a future victim of an air disaster that would wipe out an entire national team.

Chitalu, then Zambia head coach, would perish along with his entire squad, and the crew of a Zambian Air Force transport plane, in Libreville, Gabon, on the night of 27 April 1993. Sir Bobby Charlton would live for 45 more years after his hat-trick against the Zambians, dying aged 86 on 21 October 2023.

A second, no less tragic participant in the Zambia-Shrewsbury encounter that autumn 1978 night was the Zambia boss and former Aston Villa player Brian Tiler. He'd die before Chitalu – the victim of a car crash after the Italy-Republic of Ireland World Cup quarter-final in Rome at Italia 90. A survivor in that doomed vehicle was one Harry Redknapp, then Bournemouth manager. Also quarter-finalists in Italy then were Cameroon, who'd made their World Cup debut at the 1982 finals in Spain. They'd returned to the big stage after spectacularly crashing out 5-2 on aggregate to Zambia in the 1986 qualifiers – several years after Tiler had left the Zambia job.

* * *

On a cool autumn morning in that part of the southern hemisphere, Zambians awoke to news of the worst aviation accident in its young history as an independent nation. It involved a utility aircraft manufactured by Canada's De Havilland company. Nine people, including eight of the southern African nation's best military pilots, had perished in the crash of a DHC-6 Twin Otter 300. The accident occurred during a demonstration flight for the Zambia Air Force (ZAF) on the morning of 3 May 1976, near Monze, a town 118 miles south-west of the capital Lusaka. Zambia was cast in mourning.

The plane reportedly came down a kilometre beyond the runway. The crash occurred during a demonstration of the Twin Otter's ability to recover from single engine failure on take-off. Going back to the Federation of Rhodesia and Nyasaland, it was the deadliest air disaster in what's now the Republic of Zambia since the mysterious crash of a Swedish Transair Douglas DC-6B operated by the United Nations in the northern city of Ndola. That tragedy, on the night of 18 September 1961, would ultimately claim the lives of all 16 people on board including Dag Hammarskjöld, the UN's charismatic secretary-general. They were flying to Ndola on a Congo peace mission when their plane dropped from the dark sky for reasons yet to be conclusively determined.

At any rate, the devastating loss outside Monze of some of its finest officers from the first cohort of ZAF pilots did not deter the Zambians from concluding a deal with De Havilland for the supply of new aircraft in 1976. They came in the form of seven recently developed De Havilland DHC-5D Buffaloes, the most advanced of the Buffalo series of short take-off and landing (STOL) utility transport turboprop aircraft originally developed from a 1962 requirement by the United States Army. The Americans would take delivery of four DHC-5s in 1965 and place no more orders thereafter. By 1966, the US Air Force was placed in charge of large fixed-wing transport craft and saw no need for the Buffalo.

Still, production of various variants of the Buffalo would continue even though only 126 planes would be manufactured over a 21-year period – with the last DHC-5D delivered to the Kenyan Air Force in December 1986. That's minuscule compared to most military aircraft. Lockheed Martin, for instance, has rolled out more than 2,500 of its popular C-130 Hercules transport plane, a workhorse of many militaries worldwide, since 1954. Add to that the more than 4,600 F-16 Fighting Falcon jets produced by General Dynamics as of 2018 and the nearly

11,500 Soviet-designed MiG-21 fighters, and the Buffalo output pales by comparison. Along with its capacity to carry 41 troops or 24 stretchers at a maximum speed of 290mph (467kp/h), the Buffalo's incredible ability to take off and land on unprepared airfields made it ideal for Third World nations. With a range of almost 700 miles (1,112km), the DHC-5D became popular with buyers from Abu Dhabi to Zambia. The Zambian Air Force's seven purchases put them only behind Brazil (24), Peru (16), and Egypt and Kenya, who each bought ten planes.

In addition to its primary military role for the ZAF, the Buffalo became the go-to transport for urgent civilian duties when needed. When opposition politician Simon Kapwepwe, a founding father of Zambia, died in January 1980, a Buffalo piloted by a young ZAF officer named Victor Mubanga flew his remains to Chinsali, in northern Zambia, for burial. Later, as Zambia's copper-based economy hit hard times and the country's football association struggled for funding, ZAF and its Buffalo fleet would become the national team's default air carrier. Neither the loss of two of ZAF's seven DHC-5Ds, in crashes between 1982 and 1990, nor several scary experiences over the years would deter Football Association of Zambia's interest in ZAF aircraft.

And even while the players may have griped about the plane's lack of comfort, in the increasingly tough economic times of the 80s and 90s, the relatively cheap to charter Buffalo with its lack of baggage restrictions (maximum take-off weight 49,200lb or 22,316kg) was a delight for football officials, according to ZAF pilots who flew the team pre-Gabon. Before the liberalisation of the Zambian economy, when luxury goods were at a premium, foreign trips doubled as shopping junkets of sorts for team members. Ironically, a De Havilland bid in the early 1980s to develop a 48-passenger Buffalo for civilian use, dubbed the 'transporter', came to naught. The programme was scrapped when the prototype crashed on landing at the 1984 Farnborough Airshow in the UK.

2

Ante Tonći Bušelić

A MINERAL-RICH region in the north-west part of the central African nation, the Copperbelt had been Zambia's economic and industrial hotbed long before independence from Britain on 24 October 1964. Located south of Katanga Province, and, like that incredibly wealthy part of the historically turbulent Democratic Republic of Congo, sitting atop veins of precious ores and metals such as copper and cobalt, it was the heartbeat of the newly independent nation. Copperbelt cities and towns such as Kitwe, Chingola, Kalulushi, Mufulira, Luanshya and Ndola were replete with social amenities for their employees, courtesy of the mining companies. That included football clubs with names such as Mufulira Wanderers, Rhokana United, Roan United, Bancroft Blades and Nchanga Rangers. Predictably, the sport, well catered for and fanatically supported, flourished in the mining communities, turning the Copperbelt into the epicentre of football in Northern Rhodesia and, after independence, Zambia. Inevitably, the Copperbelt became the assembly line for talent, rolling out generations of Zambia's top players. When the plane carrying the national team to a World Cup qualifying match in Senegal crashed moments after take-off in Libreville 29 years after independence, up to 13 of the 18 players who perished there had roots in the Copperbelt.

The Buffalo DHC-5D that plunged into dark waters off Gabon's Atlantic Coast shortly before midnight on 27 April 1993 carried no ordinary team from an obscure African country. The players on board were the greatest collection of footballers from one of the continent's powerhouses. Zambia had carried that reputation since coming a couple of goals short of qualifying for the 1974 World Cup in West Germany, and – four months later – reaching the Africa Cup of Nations Final on their debut. Fortunate to escape the Buffalo crash were the European-based trio of Kalusha Bwalya, Charles Musonda and Jonson (sometimes recorded as Johnson) Bwalya – all Mufulira products. How good was the doomed squad? It was the cream of a talented generation. Days after the unimaginable horror, Zambian football authorities decided to close ranks and continue with their World Cup quest. Incredibly, the rebuilt squad, inspired by the surviving captain Kalusha, would script one of the most remarkable fairy-tale stories in football history. Within an 11-month period of the unthinkable tragedy, the new side would come within one goal of qualifying for the World Cup and then storm into the Africa Cup of Nations Final – for the first time since 1974. They'd battle Nigeria's Super Eagles to the wire.

Still, outside the continent, the only other time Zambian football had made world headlines before that horrific nightmare was five years earlier when the Africans, in a seismic upset, had destroyed Italy 4-0 in a group match at the 1988 Olympic Games in Seoul. The masters of *catenaccio*, that concept of iron-clad defending and swift counterattacking they'd perfected, had been torn to shreds by a team of relative unknowns. It was the heaviest defeat by a senior Italian selection since the

4-1 loss to Pelé and Co. in the 1970 World Cup Final in Mexico City.

In Africa, Zambia's reputation had been established in the 1970s. Along the way, they'd picked up the tag of perennial bridesmaids after close calls for continental honours and World Cup qualification. But you underestimated Zambia at your own peril, such was the case in October 1971 when Congo-Kinshasa (later renamed Zaire and now the DRC Congo) came a-calling in an Africa Cup of Nations tie in Ndola. Crowned continental champions in 1968, the Congolese had regarded their southern neighbours as 'whipping boys' after a 10-1 mauling in their previous encounter. Another rout was anticipated at Dag Hammarskjöld Stadium, named for the UN secretary-general who'd died when his plane mysteriously plunged from the night sky on the outskirts of the city, while trying to bring peace to the Congo a decade earlier. Under the tutelage of their first professional coach, the Yugoslav Ante Tonći Bušelić, the Zambians, however, were about to signal the start of a new era. Midfielders Richard Stephenson and Peter Mhango both beat goalkeeper Robert Kazadi Mwamba with spectacular efforts to down the vaunted Congolese 2-1. It was a huge victory on many levels, far belying the narrow scoreline. Psychologically, Zambia had broken out of the shell as minnows of the African game.

Toni to his friends, Ante Tonći Bušelić was the mastermind of Zambia's meteoric rise from a middling side to African giants. Unbeknownst to Zambians, they had the illustrious coach Miljan Miljanić, of Red Star Belgrade and Real Madrid fame, to thank for that. Born in September 1931 in Makarska (in the present-day Croatia), an Adriatic sea coast town and popular tourist centre once famous for its 20,000 hotel beds in the old Yugoslavia, Bušelić starred at centre-half for top-flight side OFK Belgrade – albeit with no international caps – while a physical education student at the University of Belgrade. Cartilage trouble – once a scourge of footballers – in his left knee ended his playing career.

In 1956, Bušelić graduated with a degree in physical education and decided to do a two-year course in football coaching. An apt vocation, perhaps, for a man whose playing days had ended so prematurely. He was later appointed director of a national training complex in Makarska. It catered for the various Yugoslav national sports teams during the winter months when other parts of the country were covered in snow.

It was there that Bušelić met Miljanić, the future four-time Yugoslavia national team boss, and title-winning Red star Belgrade and Real Madrid coach. They bonded instantly and Bušelić would tell this writer in 1982, 'From the very beginning, we were together.' They worked together until 1968 when Bušelić left the national training complex. In 1971, seeking its first professional national coach, the Football Association of Zambia – chaired by businessman Tom Mtine – approached the Yugoslav FA. The Yugoslavs recommended Bušelić. On the advice of Miljanić, then managing Red Star, Bušelić acquiesced. Zambian football would never be the same again.

Bušelić's first order of business in Zambia, seven years after the country's independence from Britain, was to introduce the latest coaching techniques. 'I tried to implement the most modern methods of coaching. I don't believe in systems like 4-2-4 or 4-3-3 because they are very complicated,' he told this writer in a 1982 interview.

He believed the most difficult task in coaching was to find the right brand of football for a team to match the physical, tactical and mental quality of the players. He'd later concede that he found his job easier because, to his surprise, the quality of players he found in Zambia was on par with Yugoslav footballers. Of the players he found, Bušelić specifically lauded centre-halves Dick Chama and Dickson Makwaza, striker Godfrey Chitalu, link man Boniface Simutowe, and Peter M'hango. He'd sensationally convert M'hango from an attacking midfielder to an overlapping right-back. They and other young blood would all be instrumental in Zambia's rise as an African football power.

During Bušelić's tenure, Zambia morphed into a high-scoring team with an average of three goals per match. And that would include memorable conquests over some of Africa's biggest footballing nations.

Dickson Makwaza, a right-winger turned centre-half for Mufulira Wanderers, had been Zambia captain for four years when Bušelić arrived in 1971. In February 2019 – 17 months after Bušelić's death aged 86 – Makwaza, an elegant defender and team leader during that watershed period, recalled to this author what the Croat's masterstroke was: youth. 'Ante Bušelić brought in new blood,' said Makwaza. 'He retired the old *mudalas* [old-timers] and brought in former Zambia schools team footballers. That was his weapon.'

Assisted by George Sikazwe, Bušelić's decision to tap into Zambia's well-developed and largely Copperbelt-based secondary school football programme was a bold but ingenious move. Long before FIFA's world youth competitions had blossomed into proving grounds for future stars, the Zambia schools set-up had established an exchange programme with youth teams from top English clubs. From the late 1960s, youth sides from clubs such as West Ham United, Ipswich town, Nottingham Forest, Aston Villa, Newcastle United and Derby County would visit the country regularly for matches with Zambia schools select sides. The exchanges over the years would be a boon for the hosts whose best youth players would cut their international teeth early. Experience garnered from friendlies with visiting English and Brazilian sides, and tips from visiting coaches, would all be factors as Zambia morphed into continental giant killers.

In 2023, Ronnie Hollywood was happily retired in his hometown of Newry, Northern Ireland, 34 miles from Belfast. Just over half a century earlier, Hollywood, a graduate of Queen's University Belfast, had landed in Africa. He'd grown up with and was a close associate of Pat Jennings, the outstanding Northern Ireland and Tottenham Hotspur goalkeeper, whose 119 international caps were at one time a world record for goalies. Unbeknownst to Hollywood when he set foot in Zambia, he was about to become part of a group of expatriate British teachers who would play a fundamental role in Zambia's emergence as a football force in Africa.

Hollywood provided this modest recollection, 'I arrived in Zambia on 28 September 1968 and for my first three years taught in Roan Antelope Secondary School [in] Luanshya. When I began at Roan, one of our pupils, Emmanuel Mwape, was the national team goalkeeper.

'I wrote to my friend Pat Jennings, the Tottenham keeper, and he gave me some tips about goalkeeping. Bernard Chanda and Philip Tembo were also pupils at Roan and they (Emmanuel, Bernard and Philip) recommended me to Roan United and soon I was coaching Roan United although to be honest what I was doing could hardly be called coaching. I was very much a novice. Zambia Secondary Schools FA, later to become the Zambia Schools FA [ZSFA], was in its infancy and had been established shortly before I arrived in Zambia by Glyn Peters who was a teacher at King George VI SS in Kabwe.

'I first became involved when I helped in the organising of the 1969 tour of Zambia by West Ham United's youth team.

'In 1970, I was the coach in charge of the Copperbelt schools XI when we played an Ipswich Town team that included two players who went on to play for England – Brian Talbot and Mick Mills who captained England. Several other players had long professional careers and we, with the help of goals from Moses Simwala and Bernard Chanda, beat the cream of England's youth 4-3 in Mine Roan Stadium. Sir Bobby Robson, the Ipswich manager, who went on to successfully manage PSV Eindhoven in the Netherlands, Barcelona in Spain, and England, resided with me in Luanshya and gave us a bit more knowledge to pass on to Zambian footballers. I was beginning to get a totally unwarranted reputation as a coach with the success of my school team (the best in the country then) the Copperbelt team (it was the excellent players I had, not my coaching ability) and I was then offered a job by the manager of the NCCM [Nchanga Consolidated Copper Mines] in Kabwe to manage their football team Kabwe United.

'It was Glyn Peters, who was the secretary-treasurer of Kabwe United, who recommended me to Tad Moskva, the mine manager. By then I was the coach of the ZSFA XI. When I went on my first leave home to Ireland where I'd been born and reared in Newry, I was invited to Glasgow Celtic to get some more coaching tutelage under the guidance of the great Jock Stein. I returned to Zambia to begin my new job with Kabwe United and I was still the ZSFA coach and then I met Ante (Toni) Bušelić who began helping me with the schoolboys.'

The precocious talent produced by the Zambia schools set-up would rejuvenate the ageing senior national side that Bušelić had found. There were future standouts such as the aforementioned Emmanuel Mwape – later a star goalkeeper at the 1974 Africa Cup (in addition to Pat Jennings – via Hollywood – Mwape's early remote mentors would include Ray Wood, the former Manchester United and England goalie who'd miraculously survived the 1958 Munich crash with minor injuries). Bernard Chanda was another Zambia schools alum who added a vital spark to Bušelić's new side. Hollywood remembers him walking around Roan Antelope Secondary School calling himself Bernard 'Pelé' Chanda. And his skills may well have impressed the Brazilian superstar he idolised after an outstanding Africa Cup of Nations in Egypt. Other new blood in the national side included speedy right-winger Moses Simwala, cerebral midfielders Willie Phiri, Peter M'hango, Richard Stephenson, Jani Simulambo, and teenager wing wizard Brighton Sinyangwe on the left. Blending seamlessly with the trio of seasoned players retained by Bušelić – namely Makwaza, his defensive partner, the powerful and broad-shouldered Dick Chama, and Godfrey Chitalu – this proverbial blend of youth and experience would hit pay dirt for Zambia.

Fresh young legs were vital to Bušelić's tactics. As a former British colony, Zambian football was, predictably, moulded on the British game. It was fast, hard-running and physical with an added element: the jaw-dropping ball skills exhibited by generations of mesmerising dribblers. There was Samuel 'Zoom' Ndhlovu – Zambia's first football superstar – Chitalu (scorer of those 107 goals in 1972), Bernard Chanda and Alex Chola. Later, after the Bušelić era, Kalusha Bwalya, Charles Musonda, the tragic Kelvin Mutale and Gibby Mbasela would continue the lineage. Bušelić's most profound innovation, arguably, was the introduction of overlapping full-backs to a degree never seen before in Zambia. The new blood made it work, recalled Makwaza. 'When you have young ones, they have the energy. They liked the [overlapping] system.'

Centre-forward Bernard Chanda was a beneficiary of Bušelić's playing system. A solid 5ft 10in and, in the words of Hollywood, his secondary school coach, 'built like a well-honed super middleweight' prizefighter, Chanda was actually considered more technically gifted than his co-striker, the goal machine Godfrey Chitalu. 'He was quick, good in the air, even-tempered and tough. He could play anywhere but we used him as an old style centre-forward,' said Hollywood, the Bušelić collaborator and confidant. 'We simply gave him the freedom to express himself to the best of his ability. He liked to call himself Pelé and indeed he reminded me of Pelé when he played.'

The tactical freedom he was granted in attack allowed Chanda – first capped aged 19 in 1971 – to eke out a unique role for himself in the new Zambian side. With his incisive runs that often started on the left flank – almost like a second winger – and tricky dribbles as he cut inside, Chanda would today be dubbed a 'false forward'. He was an early exponent of the role; he performed it exceedingly well, earning recognition as one of the continent's best forwards in his one trip to the Africa Cup of Nations in 1974. He'd go on to net a documented 29 goals in 68 internationals, most of them during Bušelić's tenure.

As it transpired, Zambia's historic 2-1 win over the soon-to-be christened Zaire Leopards in Ndola would be the preamble to a remarkable run as Bušelić's charges gelled. Ethiopia, hosts of three Africa Cup of Nations tournaments between 1962 and 1976 and winners of the first of those, were the next powerhouse of that generation to fall to the emergent southern Africans. A 4-2 Zambian romp in Lusaka in April 1973 would decide a two-legged World Cup tie that had ended goalless in Addis Ababa. Skipper

Dickson Makwaza, the former winger turned centre-half, was among the scorers against the Ethiopians. He slammed in a 25-metre free kick to net the only goal of his nine-year international career. When Kenya's Harambee Stars were dispatched by the same 4-2 aggregate scoreline in the next round, Zambia were through to a three-nation play-off to determine Africa's sole representative at the 1974 finals in West Germany. It was a monumental achievement. In 24 months, Zambia had risen from minnows to one of the top three teams in Africa. They'd face Morocco and the Zaire Leopards (nee Congo-Kinshasa) for a ticket to West Germany.

But first Fluminense would drop by to test the Zambians in May 1973. The top-flight club side from Rio de Janeiro followed in the wake of a Brazilian under-22 squad that had toured Zambia the previous year. A highlight of the latter's visit was lanky 19-year-old striker Serginho equalising with a blistering shot that tore the net in a 2-2 draw with the senior national team in Chililabombwe.

Fluminense provided another test for the Zambians. Buoyed by a 4-2 victory in Kitwe the previous day, the Brazilians travelled 358km south to Lusaka, where they'd claw back twice to tie 2-2 on Dionísio's brace. Chitalu, wearing his favoured number ten jersey, was outstanding in that game at Independence Stadium. Tackled by a defender outside the box on the right, he'd retain possession of the ball while on the ground, his marker sprawled next to him. No foul called, Chitalu bested his man, got up and advanced toward the Fluminense goal. He juggled the ball with his right foot – once, twice, then a third time – like a player engaged in a keepie-uppie display. On the fourth juggle, Ucar, coming in diagonally from the right, lobbed the ball over the outstretched arms of the advancing Fluminense goalie. Racing in from the left, 19-year-old midfielder

Willie Phiri, another one of the former Zambia schools internationals capped by Bušelić, coolly tapped into the empty net to give Zambia the lead. Chitalu would score against the Brazilians as well.

Making his international debut that day against the Brazilians was another former schoolboy prodigy, link man Jani Simulambo, also 19. Eulogising Dickson Makwaza after the former Zambia skipper's death aged 77 on 29 June 2019, Simulambo recalled the occasion, 'It was in the [changing] room at Independence Stadium … Ba Makwaza, Ba "Sir" [Samuel] Zoom [Ndhlovu] and Dick Chama grabbed me, took me to a quiet corner, looked straight in my eyes, and said [in ChiBemba], "Iwe, uli wa bola, wi kwata u mwenso. Wala teya fye bwino." [You are a good footballer, don't be scared, you will play well.]'

Sure-footed, sturdy, with great passing range and vision, young Simulambo lived up to the three veterans' expectations. He held his own in the middle of the park against the skilful South Americans who duelled regularly against some of the best players in Brazil. 'Sure enough, I had an excellent game,' said Simulambo. 'Ante Bušelić gave me a nine out of ten score. During the match, I kept remembering the words of encouragement Ba Makwaza said to me.'

Acrobatic goalie Joseph Chomba was another Zambian hero on that afternoon as Fluminense laid siege on resumption. Still, Chomba could not prevent them from levelling twice. It was the first international game this future writer had watched. It was also the great Samuel 'Zoom' Ndhlovu's international swansong. He was Zambia's first football superstar, a dribbling wizard who 25 years later, with Makwaza as his assistant, would coach his country to its greatest victory – against Italy. His sacking as Zambia coach four months before the Gabon

Disaster would save his life. Zoom had been out of the international frame even before Bušelić's arrival. He was recalled against Fluminense for a formal farewell. Handed back the captain's armband he'd passed on to Makwaza, his Mufulira Wanderers club-mate, Ndhlovu thrilled the packed Independence Stadium during his brief cameo. The stadium would erupt with a deep throbbing roar of 'ZOOOM!' at his every touch. The ecstasy lasted some 15 minutes before he handed the armband back to Makwaza and was replaced by another one of Bušelić's teenagers, left-winger Brighton Sinyangwe.

The Fluminense tune-ups would augur well for Zambia ahead of three monster fixtures with giants of the African game. First up would be Nigeria. The newly crowned All-Africa Games champions had a two-legged date with the upstart Zambians. The winners would qualify for the eight-nation Africa Cup of Nations finals in Egypt in March 1974.

The Green Eagles, as they were then known, flew into Lusaka a highly confident bunch. They were led by German coach Karl-Heinz Marotzke, formerly with Schalke 04. In the Nigerian script, nothing short of a drubbing of their unheralded hosts would suffice. And it looked good for them when Iziebige handed them the lead inside 20 minutes. Zambia's response was ruthless. Bernard Chanda, quickly establishing himself as his country's biggest scoring threat after Godfrey Chitalu, sparked the fightback with the equaliser.

From second-tier Mufulira Blackpool, Congolese-reared substitute Simon 'Kaodi' Kaushi, on before the interval for the injured Chitalu, celebrated a sensational debut with a brace. Young Sinyangwe, spellbinding as always on the left, also struck twice. Nigeria could muster no response in a 5-1 thrashing. The Green Eagles would eke out a 3-2 result in Lagos two weeks later – Kaushi and Chanda on target again for the visitors. But it was academic. Zambia had qualified for its first-ever Africa Cup of Nations finals 7-4 on aggregate. The Green Eagles, meanwhile, were disbanded by the Nigerian FA as punishment.

Next up were Morocco, Zambia's sternest test ever. At a time when the World Cup was a 16-team tournament featuring only the crème de la crème, Morocco's appearance at the 1970 finals in Mexico had marked Africa's return to the World Cup for the first time since 1934. They'd been led to central America by the towering Blagoje Vidinić, a 6ft 6in former Yugoslav international goalkeeper with a Midas touch in Africa.

Under Vidinić, Morocco had raised Africa's stock appreciably in Mexico on the continent's return to the World Cup after a 36-year absence. The Atlas Lions took the lead against West Germany – losing finalists four years earlier – in their opening group match in León. Houmane Jarir needed just 21 minutes to solve the Franz Beckenbauer-marshalled German defence. They held out for over half an hour before the Teutons – being Teutons – did what they'd always done best in their illustrious footballing history. Uwe Seeler's leveller in the 56th minute was followed by the inevitable winner by 'Der Bomber' Gerd Müller in the 80th in a tough 2-1 Moroccan defeat.

Eventual quarter-finalists Peru, inspired by Teófilo Cubillas's brace, may have put Morocco back in their place with a 3-0 drubbing, but a 1-1 tie with Bulgaria in their last group match was proof positive that the African envoys were not completely out of their element. Forward Maouhoub Ghazouani cancelled out Bulgarian defender Dobromir Zhechev's 40th-minute goal to earn Morocco and Africa their first-ever FIFA World Cup point.

A year later in a friendly, the North Africans would edge Mexico 2-1 with goals by Moustapha Choukri and Boujemaa Benkhrif. That's the pedigree Zambia faced on a warm and bright Sunday October afternoon in Lusaka, in their first 1974 World Cup play-off match.

The tussle, three days before Zambia's ninth independence anniversary, was a mismatch.

Lithe and lethal on the left, teen star Brighton Sinyangwe fired a rocket into the Moroccan net minutes after kick-off. On the right wing, Simwala would also breach the vaunted visitors' defence before the interval to make it 2-0. Jani Simulambo and Bernard Chanda completed a 4-0 rout on resumption. For ecstatic Zambian fans, Lusaka's Independence Stadium, a bowl-shaped structure of steel and concrete hurriedly constructed for the independence celebrations in October 1964, had been transformed into a graveyard for Africa's big nations.

Morocco's bid for a World Cup encore had been dealt an early mortal blow. They'd lose 3-0 away to Zaire in their second play-off match. As they streamed out of Independence Stadium, all smiles and thrilled by the destruction of Morocco, not a single Zambian fan could have imagined that this was just the first battle of what would be an intense World Cup rivalry in years to come. By the time the two sides were drawn together again in that fateful play-off series with Senegal in 1993, Zambia and Morocco had met six times in World Cup qualifiers. The honours would be split evenly, with Zambia prevailing in Lusaka on all three occasions and Morocco victorious three times at home. But the 4-0 November 1973 rout by the Zambians would remain the biggest winning margin by any side in the rivalry.

Riding a crest of unprecedented success, knocking off one African colossus after another, and through to their first Africa Cup of Nations finals tournament, Zambia seemed certainties for the World Cup in West Germany. Not even the arrival of a formidable foe, now renamed Zaire, would change this notion. It would be Zambia coach Ante Bušelić's first encounter with his fellow Yugoslav and Zaire opposite Blagoje Vidinić, who'd been Morocco's 1970 World Cup boss.

As a player, Vidinić's greatest honour had been helping lead Yugoslavia to the inaugural UEFA European Championship Final in Paris in 1960. They lost 2-1 to the USSR after extra time. He'd also kept goal for the Yugoslav Olympic squads that had won the silver medal at the 1956 Games in Melbourne, Australia, and bagged gold at the Rome Olympics in 1960 – at a time when the Olympics was a purely amateur affair. Born in Skopje, Macedonia, Vidinić's playing résumé included club football with FK Vardar, Radnički Beograd and OFK Beograd in Yugoslavia. He also turned out for Swiss side FC Sion, before winding up his career in the United States in the late 1960s. There, there'd be stints with Los Angeles Toros of the National Professional Soccer League, San Diego Toros and St. Louis Stars.

Vidinić had taken charge of Zaire in 1972, a year after their stunning 2-1 defeat to Zambia in Ndola. In retrospect, he held most of the cards when the Leopards strutted on to the Independence Stadium pitch on 4 November 1973. In addition to his credentials as a player and coach, he had the more experienced and physical team. In the 24 months since the two neighbours' last clash, Bušelić had blooded a corps of former schoolboy internationals such as Sinyangwe, Simulambo, Willie Phiri and the Zambia Army FC duo of full-back Donewell Yobe and forward Obby Kapita. Yet his trump card against the Zaireans was expected to be the sensational newcomer Simon 'Kaodi' Kaushi, who'd struck three goals in the elimination of Nigeria. That's until the Zaireans raised a hue and cry.

Born in October 1950 in the village of Kwa Lukwesa, in Zambia's Luapula Province bordering the Congo, Kaushi had grown up in Élisabethville (the present-day Lubumbashi), Congo, where his father had sought work. It was a familiar tale during the colonial period – residents of the Northern Rhodesian regions bordering south-eastern Congo trekking across the artificial demarcations established by European colonialists at the 'Scramble for Africa' Conference in Berlin in 1884, in search of employment. Kaushi grew up in Lubumbashi playing for youth teams but never, by his own admission, garnering much attention. He returned to independent Zambia in 1970 and joined Mufulira Blackpool in the Zambian second division. Along with Butondo Western Tigers, the modest council-sponsored Blackpool played second fiddle to celebrated Mufulira Wanderers in the border town. At unheralded Blackpool, Kaushi blossomed into a skilful, rampaging forward with great finishing. At age 23, and despite plying his skills in the second tier, he caught the eye of Bušelić, who deemed him good enough to break into his high-flying national squad that was making noise in Africa. Kaushi would take the opportunity with both feet when handed his debut against Nigeria, at the injured Chitalu's expense. His brace against the Green Eagles would signal the birth of a new Zambian star.

When the Zaire Leopards arrived in Lusaka for the start of their World Cup campaign, a Zairean official recognised Kaushi from his Lubumbashi days and questioned his Zambian credentials. Playing it safe, the Football Association of Zambia withdrew the striker from the squad. Kaushi would be sidelined for the remainder of the World Cup qualifiers while FAZ verified his eligibility.

It was a blow to Bušelić's game plan, even with the great Chitalu back from injury.

As narrated to this writer by Obby Kapita in Miami years later, for all his brilliance and goalscoring abilities, Ucar Chitalu posed a dilemma for Bušelić. A skilful dribbler who could scythe through any defence on his day, Chitalu's individualism didn't always mesh with the Croat's tactics. 'So Bušelić brought me in to play with Bernard Chanda upfront when Simon Kaushi was unavailable,' said Kapita, who offered the coach a more direct option.

Still, on 4 November 1973, Bušelić would go with the Chitalu-Chanda combination. Early in the game, Chitalu broke through. He was thwarted at point-blank range by the Leopards' theatrical goalie Robert Kazadi Mwamba, voted best player at the 1968 Africa Cup of Nations that the Zaireans (then Congo) had won. It was a tense affair for the partisan 30,000-capacity crowd, including Kenneth Kaunda. The Zambian president was a lifelong football fanatic who rarely missed Zambia's home games. Until the end of his tenure in 1991, the national team would be known as the 'KK XI', a moniker coined by celebrated radio commentator Dennis Liwewe.

The pre-match protocol, after the national anthems, was always for Kaunda to shake hands with both squads and then have the match ball tossed at his feet. The president, to cheers from the crammed stadium, would juggle the ball, run a few steps with it and unleash a shot that invariably smashed into the visitors. That was construed as a good omen. Before the 3.30pm kick-off on 4 November, Kaunda's ceremonial shot smashed into the Zambia team. Bad omen.

And that's how it would unfold. Uncharacteristically out of sync, the Zambians failed to reproduce the form that had crushed other African giants at Independence Stadium. Zairean centre-back Lobilo Boba was imposing in defence and on the few occasions that the hosts found good positions, their efforts were – with one exception – off the mark. In the end, Kakoko Etepé's brace would carry the day for the Leopards – Zambia's attempted comeback effectively faltering with young Sinyangwe blasting a second-half penalty over the bar. It was Bušelić's first home defeat as Zambia coach since dropping a 1-0 decision to Ethiopia in an Olympic Games qualifier three months into his job.

Forty-six years later, Ronnie Hollywood provided an intriguing backstory to Zambia's defeat. For this writer, it then rekindled talk of the Leopards' mastery of the 'black arts' to subdue the Zambians. By 1973, Irishman Hollywood, who'd arrived as a school teacher in Zambia in 1968 and become involved with the Zambia Schools Football Association (ZSFA), had forged a close personal and professional relationship with Zambia national team coach Toni Bušelić. Hollywood's success with the talented Copperbelt secondary schools team had, in his modest opinion, earned him 'a totally unwarranted reputation as a coach'. This was parlayed into the manager's job with Kabwe United, the lesser of the Midland town's two football clubs – Godfrey Chitalu's Kabwe Warriors being the top dogs there. Hollywood still served the ZSFA, as chairman, and as such, along with secretary-treasurer Glyn Peters, sat on the FAZ council.

This is Hollywood's recollection of the Zambia-Zaire game: 'On 4 of November 1973, I was in the hotel in downtown Lusaka with Toni Bušelić and the Zambian team prior to the World Cup qualifier against Zaire at Independence Stadium later that day ... Toni asked me [if] I would like to accompany the team to the stadium on the bus. I declined as I intended to go straight back to Kabwe after the game. As an FAZ councillor, I had VIP tickets to the game but when I arrived at the stadium, the crowds were so vast I couldn't get in. I went round to the players' entrance and Toni came out and took me in. I was told to wait outside the changing rooms. The door was open and I could see the players inside.

'Shortly [after] the door closed and the door of the Zairean team opened and they came out and under the scrutiny of their Yugoslav coach, Vidinić, I watched in fascination as they did a very elaborate warm-up routine. They then returned to their dressing room, changed into their football boots, came out and went down to the pitch. I waited patiently for the Zambian team to emerge but they never did. It is now game time. I went over to the dressing room door but it was locked. I heard loud cheering from the stadium. As I exited the changing room area, I noticed a patch of foul-smelling liquid spilt on the entrance steps but thought no more about it. When I entered the stadium, the game was just kicking off. I was mystified how the [Zambia] team had got there but with the excitement of the game, I soon forgot about the incident.

'Zambia did not play well and were well beaten 2-0, and the dream of appearing as the African representative at the 1974 World Cup finals in West Germany was in tatters. I decided to go back downtown afterwards to the team hotel to sympathise with and console Toni. He was in despair. I asked him how had they got down to the playing area before the game without coming through the dressing room door. "That's what beat us" was his reply. The Zairean officials had spilt a foul-smelling magic potion outside the entrance door and the players were afraid to cross it as it would turn their legs to lead. They insisted [on climbing through] the dressing room windows so they wouldn't have to walk over the magic potion. Toni claimed the players were in such a state of nervousness they failed to play to their potential.

It wasn't the first time and [nor] the last when top players were psyched out!'

In November 2019, Zambia midfielder Jani Simulambo, who'd played in that game against the Zaireans five days before his 20th birthday, confirmed Hollywood's account of the Leopards' gamesmanship. 'Yes, it is true,' he told this writer. 'I was the only player who shot the ball on target,' added the devoutly religious Simulambo, from his retirement home in Port Elizabeth, South Africa.

With 14 days before the return leg in Kinshasa, a concerned Bušelić faced a dilemma he'd never encountered before in his coaching career – deeply ingrained cultural beliefs among some of his players. That level of superstition had never been part of European football. He had to act fast. The axe would immediately fall on Joseph Chomba, Zambia's acrobatic goalkeeper from the Zambia Army (later renamed Green Buffaloes FC) club. Legend, for years after that, would have it that in conceding Kakoko's two goals, Chomba was reported to have seen knives, and not the match ball, hurtling at him. He dived out of the way. Chomba would never play for Zambia again, allowing Emmanuel Mwape to reclaim the number one jersey and fame.

On 18 November 1973, Zambia and Zaire met again in the biggest event at Kinshasa's Stade du 20 Mai before the global boxing spectacle that would be forever remembered as 'The Rumble in the Jungle'. Fifty thousand fans, including a plane-load of Zambians, packed the stadium built by the Belgians – Zaire's colonial masters – in 1952. Zambia would kick off with a different mindset. 'We did not think about *ubwanga* [witchcraft],' Simulambo recounted in 2019. 'We just played our normal soccer.'

Bušelić's counselling had worked. And it showed even after the Zaireans had taken the lead. This time Bernard Chanda was unerring in his response as Zambia levelled.

Chanda then gave the Leopards an almighty scare by striking the woodwork. The match, and qualification to Germany, was up for grabs until Ndaye's second goal spelled the end of Zambia's World Cup dream. It ended 2-1 for Zaire. Vidinić would guide the Leopards to a 3-0 rout of his former side Morocco in their next game, sealing qualification to West Germany.

So close yet so far. The disappointment for a young fervid nation whose football dreams had been raised to unprecedented heights was palpable. Bušelić and his young side were gutted. But not for long. With their first Africa Cup of Nations ahead in the new year, there was no time for moping. Egypt beckoned. And with it, an opportunity to prove that the World Cup qualifying run had been no fluke.

3

Ali Encounter

FOUNDING MEMBERS of the Confederation of African Football (CAF) in 1957, Egypt had won the inaugural title in Sudan that year. There were only three participants that first time around – co-founders Sudan and Ethiopia being the others – after South Africa, conforming with the country's new Apartheid policy of racial discrimination, insisted on fielding an all white team. They were promptly barred from what would become a biennial event. Consequently, Ethiopia, who would have played the South Africans, got a bye to the final. There they'd succumb to an Egyptian side that had dispatched Sudan in their semi-final play-off. With most of the continent still under the yoke of colonialism, the same three teams met again in the second Africa Cup of Nations in Egypt in 1959. The hosts retained the title by defeating Sudan, this time in the final. The Egyptians were favourites to win a third title when they hosted the eight-nation AFCON in 1974. They were drawn in Group A with Ivory Coast, Uganda and new kids on the African block, Zambia.

Egypt were led by the pioneering German coach Dettmar Cramer – revered in Asia as the father of modern Japanese football for his work as technical adviser with the national team there before and during the 1964 Olympics. Cramer was an assistant to West Germany coach Helmut Schön at the 1966 World Cup in England, where the Germans lost 4-2 to Bobby Charlton and Co. in the final. And later in 1974, after the AFCON, Cramer would serve a two-match stint as United States national coach before his greatest managerial achievement: leading Franz Beckenbauer, Gerd Müller, Sepp Maier and that outstanding Bayern Munich side of the 70s to back-to-back European Cup titles.

For Cramer and the other coaches in Egypt, the ninth African Cup of Nations would be as much a test of endurance and mental strength for their players as it would be a battle of tactics and technique. Sixteen games were scheduled over the tournament's 12-day duration: 1 to 12 March. To be crowned African champions, the winners would have to play five games in just under two weeks and triumph in the last two. That's an average of a match every 48 hours in the group stages, and once every three days after that in the knockout round. In Zambia's case – with their first fixture against Ivory Coast scheduled for 2 March – it would mean exactly five in ten days if they reached the final.

By current standards, Zambia's preparations for that seemingly Herculean task were laughable. The debutants had a brief training camp at home and, remarkably, played no international friendlies ahead of the AFCON. The one significant game they played was against a Lusaka select XI. They lost 2-1 at Matero Stadium with striker Stanley Phiri, from modest Lusaka Tigers, scoring the winner.

There were no surprises in Ante Bušelić's travelling party to Cairo. Just the veterans of the recent World Cup campaign. But a big boost was the return of the Zairean-bred Simon 'Kaodi' Kaushi. The powerful forward, incredibly from the Zambian league's second division, had debuted against Nigeria, scoring three goals in those two AFCON qualifiers against the Green Eagles. He got to bully the Moroccans, too, in that 4-0 play-off rout – but was then sidelined for the remainder of the World Cup race after protestations by Zaire. Whatever issues were raised over his eligibility for Zambia by the Leopards were sorted out in time for the AFCON opener in Cairo. It was then that the Zambians realised how much he'd been missed in the World Cup quest. It took Kaushi just two minutes into Zambia's AFCON bow against Ivory Coast on 2 March 1974 to strike in the massive but near-empty 95,000-capacity Cairo International Stadium. Released on the left, Kaushi raced diagonally toward the Ivorian goal, a defender on his right shoulder. The Ivorian goalie sprinted out to narrow the angle only for Kaushi to deftly chip the ball over him and into the yawning net. Pure class. It quickly dawned on the Ivorian defence that they were in for a torrid afternoon. The only way to stop Kaushi was to get physical with him. Writhing in agony on the ground after one hit, Kaushi petulantly lashed out at his assailant with a kick to the face.

He became the first Zambia player to be sent off since big defender Dick Chama punched future Welsh international Leighton Phillips, then 20, in a friendly against Cardiff City in 1969. Godfrey Chitalu had been ejected earlier in that game, won 2-1 by the Welsh club in Ndola.

At any rate, reduced to ten men before half-time, Zambia had suffered a potentially devastating blow. But they held on to make a winning start on their Africa Cup debut.

Two days later, as Kaushi served a one-match ban, Godfrey Chitalu returned to Bušelić's starting line-up for Zambia's second game, against Egypt. Less than two years after netting those historic 107 goals in all competitions in the 1972 season, Ucar had been reduced to a peripheral figure in Zambia's recent games. The Egyptians were probably wondering why after Chitalu quickly cancelled out Abdel Azim's fourth-minute goal; it was 1-1 ten minutes into the first meeting between the two sides. The hosts would, however, score twice more to qualify for the semi-finals 48 hours after the start of the AFCON.

Zambia had to wait another two days to join them in the last four. Kaushi returned from suspension for the last group match, but it was Obby Kapita, the young and robust Zambia Army FC forward, who would score in a 1-0 victory over Uganda. Africa's second-best national side, based on their performance in World Cup qualifiers, Zambia had fulfilled expectations by reaching the semi-finals of the continental championship. Yet few expected them to go any further. Since Zambia were Group A runners-up (Egypt had defeated Ivory Coast 2-0 to top the group), they would play the Group B winners. That would be defending African champions Congo-Brazzaville, a side that even Zambia's nemesis, the Leopards, reportedly dreaded. En route to winning Group B, the Congolese had come from a goal down to edge Zaire 3-2 in a local derby of sorts by two nations whose capital cities – divided by the Congo River – were less than three miles apart.

Zambia travelled to the historic Mediterranean port city of Alexandria for their semi-final with Congo-Brazzaville. In an age before live televised matches in the country, Dennis Liwewe's breathtakingly dramatic radio commentary was the only real-time coverage of their team available to Zambian fans. But the radio connection to Alexandria cruelly failed that Saturday afternoon, leaving anxious Zambian fans in agonising suspense.

It was late evening when the news started spreading like the proverbial wildfire. Founded in 331 BC, Alexandria had seen youth stamp its mark early. Goals by Joseph Mapulanga, the injured Moses Simwala's backup on the right wing, and Bernard Chanda broke the first-half deadlock. But the African champions refused to go out without a fight. In a five-minute blitz, Paris Saint-Germain's François M'Pelé in the 76th minute and André Mbouta in the 81st erased Zambia's two-goal lead. The match went into extra time. At that point, conventional wisdom would have favoured the more experienced champions to prevail. But the younger legs of Toni Bušelić's Zambia would carry the day in the historic city. Chanda struck twice (97, 111) to complete a memorable hat-trick and shoot Zambia into the Africa Cup of Nations Final on their debut.

In 2020, Jani Simulambo remembered how Zambia lined up against the African champions. Tactically, it was quintessential Bušelić. 'Our main weapon was unity,' said Simulambo, then 20 and one of the youngest players at the 1974 Africa Cup. 'We employed the 4-4-2 formation in a diamond shape. On the wings we had Joseph Mapulanga [right] and Brighton Sinyangwe [left]. Our two attackers were Bernard Chanda and Simon Kaushi. We had two inside midfielders: [Simulambo himself] responsible to pass the ball very fast, to any one of our two attackers or to any one of our two wingers. Behind [me] was Boniface Simutowe, responsible for defending and to pass the ball forward, to any one of us five players in front of him.'

Ackim Musenge, on the left, and Edwin Mbaso, on the right, were the full-backs, and the two centre-backs were vice-captain Dick Chama and captain Dickson Makwaza. Chama, big, strong and with square shoulders, was the designated man-marker whose job was to shadow the opposing team's primary forward. 'Makwaza was in charge of covering mainly the centre zone of our defensive area,' said Simulambo, essentially describing the captain's *libero* or sweeper role perfected by players of that generation such as Franz Beckenbauer.

In goal for Zambia was Emmanuel Mwape who, via Ronnie Hollywood, had received some remote mentoring by the great Pat Jennings and Ray Wood, the latter a survivor of Manchester United's Munich air crash. Mwape would be one of the tournament's top goalkeepers.

'Zambia was very strong in both phases of matches – offensively and defensively,' said Simulambo. 'Because we had speed on the wings, we demolished Congo in the semi-finals. They were the defending champions but could not match our speed. We employed the element of surprise, which is paramount for any military operation to be successful,' added the former Zambia Army captain.

The stakes were raised when, in the other semi-final in Cairo, Egypt uncharacteristically coughed up a two-goal lead against the Leopards to bow out 3-2. The last four goals would come in an 18-minute burst. The form book had held and Zambia would face Zaire in the 1974 Africa Cup of Nations Final.

Seventy-two hours later, on Tuesday, 12 March, some 5,000 fans showed up at Cairo International Stadium to watch the third encounter in four months between Africa's two best teams. It was a sparse but enthusiastic turnout in the 95,000-capacity ground designed by the German Werner Julius March, architect of Berlin's storied Olympic Stadium, venue of the 1936 Games. The fans included two plane-loads of Zambians, members of the Bola Bola travelling supporters' club co-founded by the charismatic former diplomat and future Zambian president Rupiah Banda in the euphoria of the national team's World Cup run the previous year. They'd travelled to Kinshasa then for the 2-1 loss to the Leopards and a week later watched their heroes fall 2-0 to Morocco in Rabat. Within 24 hours of

Zambia's qualification for the final, Banda had rallied his Bola Bola compatriots and chartered two planes to Cairo – a British-manufactured BAC 1-11 and a ZAF Douglas C-47 Dakota transport plane.

On the flight deck of the Dakota – future top Zambian civil servant and member of the travelling Bola Bola party George Kateka recalled in 2019 – was a young air force pilot named Victor Mubanga. The Zambian fans were bubbling with confidence; they anticipated a successful Leopard hunt.

Before kick-off, Banda made his way up to the VIP section that his status as a top Zambian official and erstwhile ambassador – to Egypt at a youthful 27 and the United States, aged 30 – warranted. There he took a seat next to the most famous individual in the entire stadium, if not all of Egypt, that cool March afternoon: Muhammad Ali. It might have been the boxing legend's first and only international football experience but it wouldn't be his last Zairean encounter. Seven months later, after a prolonged 55 days in Kinshasa, Ali would, at approximately 4am local time, climb into a ring rigged in the centre of the Stade du 20 Mai pitch, where Zambia's 1974 World Cup dreams had been dashed. Before 60,000 delirious fans, he'd triumph in arguably the most historic boxing fight ever. A 4-1 underdog, the 32-year-old Ali would knock out a 25-year-old pulverising puncher from Texas named George Foreman to regain the world heavyweight championship in a fight that he'd famously dubbed 'The Rumble in the Jungle'. Ali was firmly in the orange-clad Zambians' corner when they kicked off against Zaire at Cairo International Stadium, recalled Banda 44 years later.

'We sat next to each other and he called me "brother – my brother from Zambia",' said Banda. 'He instantly took Zambia's side and enjoyed the match very much.'

So did the rest of the fans – from both teams. It was Zambia's fifth game in ten days and Zaire's fifth in an unbelievable nine days. But fatigue was the last thing on anyone's mind. Both were chomping at the bit. It was back and forth until five minutes from the interval. That's when the player the Zaire Leopards had claimed to be theirs – and successfully barred from the World Cup qualifiers – returned to haunt them. A long, searching ball from midfielder Boniface Simutowe found Bernard Chanda on the left. The forward skinned Lobilo Boba on the edge of the penalty box and lashed a shot that took a deflection before Kazadi punched the ball clear. It fell to Simon Kaushi, whose volley smashed into the net. Advantage Zambia. It was the first time the central Africans had led Zaire since that 2-1 victory in Ndola a distant three years earlier.

Then a nation of four million, Zambia had come to a complete standstill that Tuesday afternoon. Ears glued to transistor radios, fans hung on to Dennis Liwewe's every mesmerising word as his vivid and gripping commentary brought the tense final to life for millions of listeners the way no television broadcast could, such was Liwewe's gift that had earned the PR executive from a state-owned copper-mining conglomerate celebrity status, and a rep as the most exciting English-language radio commentator on the continent. He'd later work for the BBC.

Moments after the hour mark, Ndaye Mulamba equalised after Zaire had picked the Zambian defence apart with a succession of passes. The Africa Cup of Nations was up for grabs. There were chances for both sides but 90 minutes would not be enough this time to decide a winner in this epic third clash between the two central African neighbours.

Extra time was evoked – 30 additional minutes with a replay on the cards if no winner emerged. Post-match penalties were not on the cards then.

It was still 1-1 with barely three minutes of extra time left when the Zambians conceded a free kick outside the penalty box, at a very dangerous 90-degree angle. Ndaye stood over the ball with Kakoko. Zambia were surprisingly slow to organise a defensive wall and would rue it. Ndaye's low, hard shot sneaked through the poorly organised wall and past goalkeeper Emmanuel Mwape. It was a demoralising blow.

Zambian heads – both on and off the pitch – bowed in disappointment. To crestfallen listeners in Zambia, Liwewe's running commentary ceased. The only thing audible on the radio broadcast was the animated reaction of the fans. It seemed like a fleeting moment before there was an explosive roar. Suddenly, Liwewe was back on the air with a loud cry, 'GOOOOOAL!'

Zambia had equalised!

What had transpired before the eyes of Muhammad Ali, Rupiah Banda and the few thousand fans rooting for Zambia in Cairo was nothing short of miraculous. From the restart after Zaire had scored, Bernard Chanda had taken a long punt from the centre circle that had landed in the palms of Zairean goalie Robert Kazadi Mwamba. The Leopards quickly played out of defence but lost the ball to centre-back Dick Chama, who'd pushed into midfield. Chama would make the tournament's all-star team.

Zambia counterattacked, stringing together several passes before substitute Richard Stephenson, a goalscorer three years earlier in the shock defeat of the then Congo-Kinshasa, threaded a long ball to Brighton Sinyangwe on the left wing. Tricky and slippery as an eel, the speedy youngster turned the bigger Mwepu but had his heels clipped and went down. Zambia had a free kick some 25 yards out on the left, parallel to the penalty box. Simutowe cleverly chipped the ball into the box where

Bernard Chanda, several yards from the near post, skilfully plucked it from the ether with his right foot and let it roll to Sinyangwe. The little winger sprinted a couple of yards, tightening an already acute angle and then fired low and hard toward the near post. Kazadi had it covered but was still beaten by the velocity: 2-2. Zaire's lead had lasted a mere 98 seconds. There'd be a replay to decide the final.

With the miracle equaliser, Sinyangwe had atoned for his penalty miss against the Leopards in that World Cup qualifier four months earlier in Lusaka. The pro-Zambian fans, including the Bola Bola supporters who had flown in from Lusaka, were ecstatic. This was the stuff of *Scorcher and Score*, the famous British football comic magazine of that era. Nobody in the Cairo International Stadium that afternoon doubted that they'd just watched what still remains one of the most pulsating finals in AFCON history. A memorable initiation to football, too, for Muhammad Ali, for whom the apex of a phenomenal ring career lay ahead in Kinshasa. He had kudos for the team in orange before leaving the stadium.

'Muhammad Ali, when interviewed, praised Zambia for their fighting spirit,' recalled Jani Simulambo – noting something 'the Greatest' would have certainly found admirable.

Ironically, Ali's props, in retrospect, might have had the reverse effect on the Zambians two days later. Only a thousand fans showed up for the replay at Cairo International 48 hours later, on Thursday, 14 March. But Ali and his American entourage were back, too, perhaps anticipating another cracker. Alas, Zambia were a no-show, figuratively. They lacked the fighting spirit so admired by Ali two days earlier and a goal in either half by Mulamba (setting a still-unbeaten record of nine goals for the tournament) meant the Leopards would travel to the World Cup that summer as African champions. On the bench, it was yet another loss for Bušelić to his lofty Yugoslav compatriot Blagoje Vidinić.

'We lost in the replay due to over-confidence and complacency,' concluded Simulambo, at 20 the youngest player on the pitch that day. 'There was a lot of joy in camp that we had won the cup already.'

The Zambians were anything but losers back home. Welcomed back as heroes, they were feted by President Kaunda at State House and rewarded by the government with a trip to the World Cup – as tourists. They carried their football boots along on the $40,000 junket and squeezed in a few friendlies in West Germany. A German Army team was crushed 6-0, and a 3-1 loss suffered to Kaiserlautern – later a Bundesliga presence. They didn't watch any of Zaire's matches and missed nothing. The Leopards didn't exactly look out of their depth in a 2-0 debut loss to a strong Scotland side, whose manager Willie Ormond had promised to walk home if the Scots failed to pump five past Kazadi. But a 3-0 thumping to World Cup holders Brazil followed by a 9-0 shellacking by Yugoslavia left a sour taste in the Leopards' craw.

The rest of 1974 passed relatively quietly after the dizzying heights of the previous 24 months. But overall, it would be remembered as the year Zambia set a benchmark. They were now irrefutably one of the continent's elite teams and would remain so way after the horrific plane crash two decades in the future. Even during periods when they stuttered, Zambia, irrevocably, would always save their best for the best occasions.

4

Close Call

THE END of 1974 also marked the expiration of Ante Bušelić's three-year contract. As a first-former (eighth-grader) at Kabulonga Boys, this author recalls reading in the local papers of the physical education professor from socialist Yugoslavia demanding a then whopping $1,000-per-month contract to stay on. With another cycle of qualifiers for the 1976 Africa Cup of Nations in Ethiopia and Montreal Olympics ahead, expectations were high for more success, and the Football Association of Zambia was not about to let a good thing end. Bušelić got a two-year extension.

Returning with Bušelić was the core of his 1974 squad although skipper Dickson Makwaza would call time on his distinguished ten-year international career in June 1975. He'd captained Zambia since inheriting the armband from Samuel 'Zoom' Ndhlovu, his Mufulira Wanderers compatriot and the country's first football superstar, in 1967. It was Zoom who'd convinced Makwaza to switch from right-winger at Zambia's most celebrated club of the 60s and 70s to the heart of defence. The gambit worked, giving Zambia and Wanderers a skilful and elegant defender with Franz Beckenbauer-like abilities. Makwaza's debut as captain had been memorable: leading Zambia out against

Welsh legend John Charles's visiting select side. 'They beat us 2-1 in Lusaka – John Charles and his brother Mel scored,' Makwaza recalled from his Luanshya home in February 2019. The former Zambia captain would die four months later, on 29 June.

Makwaza's farewell international in 1975 was equally memorable for the veteran whose career had spanned Zambia's rise as an African power. It came in the Mozambican capital Lourenço Marques (rechristened Maputo in 1976), in a match to mark that country's independence. Zambia, Africa Cup of Nations runners-up the previous year, lost 2-1 to the newly independent nation. Eyebrow-raising perhaps, but not really surprising considering the footballing pedigree of the former Portuguese colony. The phenomenal Eusébio, once considered only second to his Brazilian contemporary Pelé, Mário Coluna, Carlos Queiroz and Abel Xavier were among the outstanding football personalities to emerge from Mozambique.

By the end of 1975, Bušelić and his charges had had a taste of that old adage about staying at the top being harder than getting there. Sure, there was a 9-0 aggregate rout of Indian Ocean Islanders Mauritius in the qualifiers for the 1976 Montreal Olympics. And equally nondescript Malawi had been dispatched 5-2 and 9-4 respectively in subsequent qualifiers for the Olympics and the AFCON. But the year had ended in disappointment with the shock elimination, 4-2 on aggregate, to Uganda in the Nations Cup. There would be no encore of Zambia's 1974 exploits at the tenth AFCON tournament in Ethiopia in 1976. And with the Zambia schools pipeline drying up, following the sudden death of Glyn Peters and departure of Ronnie Hollywood, Bušelić and assistant coach George Sikazwe had their work cut out to stay at the top. But missing the 1976 AFCON would be tempered by another major accomplishment.

* * *

Until the 1984 Los Angeles Games, the football competition played at every Summer Olympics – with the exception of 1896 and 1932 when the sport was excluded – had been a solely amateur affair. Footballers who received monetary compensation for playing or endorsing products or services were excluded. Invariably, that barred all the big names of the sport from the world's major leagues from the tournament. Even Zambia, whose clubs (with the exception of the Lusaka-based army-sponsored Green Buffaloes) trained after work hours, had to adhere to this strict International Olympic Committee (IOC) regulation. Although still a peripheral figure under Bušelić aged 28, the heralded Godfrey 'Ucar' Chitalu would be effectively eliminated from this new Zambian quest by the IOC's amateur requirement. Chitalu, whose documented 107 goals in 1972 had come in his second season with Kabwe Warriors, wasn't a professional player by conventional sense. But his popular 'Ucar' moniker was derived from his endorsement of a battery of that name produced by the American chemical concern Union Carbide. In the IOC's books that made him ineligible for the Olympics at that time.

The Chitalu situation addressed, the IOC would have been impressed by Zambia's adherence to the Olympic spirit, to the letter. 'We played for the [Zambian] flag,' said striker Simon Kaushi. 'We didn't get any allowances.'

You couldn't tell from the performances. Both Mauritius and Malawi were steamrolled in the 1976 preliminaries, with Zambia netting a combined 14 goals and conceding just twice. They'd draw 1970 AFCON champions Sudan in what would be a heart-stopping final qualifying round with a near-terrifying aftermath to boot.

When you are down 2-0 at home with some 15 minutes left in the first leg of a qualifying tie, chances are that your goose is cooked. That's the situation Zambia found themselves in against Sudan on 28 March 1976, in the third and final qualifying round for Montreal. Remarkably, this impending defeat was at Ndola's Dag Hammarskjöld Stadium where Zambia had never lost a competitive match. For the superstitious, the spirit of Dag Hammarskjöld, the Swedish-born UN secretary-general who'd perished in a plane crash over Ndola during a Congo peace mission in September 1961, had always had Zambia's back.

Dejected fans were streaming out of Dag, an 18,000-capacity multi-use stadium, when the proceedings got interesting. Zambia's disjointed attacks in the game had become more fluid and incisive in the dying minutes. They soon paid a dividend. Bernard 'Bomber' Chanda, whose post-1974 AFCON form had continued to live up to his reputation as one of the continent's best centre-forwards, pulled a goal back. The stadium erupted. Like a prizefighter needing a knockout in the final round to win the fight, Zambia opened up. Chanda struck again at the death to rescue the hosts. Dag sighed with relief. Under the circumstances, the 2-2 draw felt like a win that late Sunday afternoon. But Zambia were not out of the proverbial woods yet.

For all their success under Bušelić, Zambia's away record had been checkered at best with road wins only in Malawi and Mauritius. At a time when international games were decided on aggregate scores over two legs, the Zambian formula had always been to win big at home and limit the damage away. It played to Zambia's strength as a relentless attacking home team. Ironically, under the tutelage of a former centre-half, they knew only one way to play – going forward in waves, even when a defensive approach on the road was more prudent. Defeating the Sudanese in Khartoum in the return leg a fortnight later would be some feat.

Still, emboldened by the immense experience garnered since 1971, the Zambians strode confidently on to the pitch at the crammed 23,000-capacity Khartoum International Stadium where Sudan had edged Ghana 1-0 to win their first Africa Cup of Nations title six years earlier. It would be one of the best Zambian road performances at that time, as the delayed broadcast several days later attested. The away goals rule was way in the future and as the minutes ticked away with no goals, pressure mounted on the hosts, as well as the Zambian fans glued to their trusted radios and transistors nearly 3,000km south. That's until the elements permanently disrupted the transmission.

Yet again, torturous suspense gripped Zambian fans until news started trickling in that evening. Goalless after 90 minutes, the tie had gone straight to penalties where Zambia had triumphed 5-4. Defender Ackim Mulamata converted the winner, qualifying Zambia for the Summer Olympics in Montreal later that year as one of three African envoys. Nigeria and Ghana were the others. For Zambian football, it was a deserved consolation after narrowly missing out on the World Cup in West Germany two years earlier.

As a kid, Nelson Sapi had been more adept with his fists than his feet. A member of Kitwe's Rhokana ABC, his boxing skills were such that amateur officials tapped the diminutive youngster as a future Olympian. That's until he was kayoed in the classroom. 'My father curtailed my dreams in boxing [because] I had failed my first grade eight exams, which made me repeat the exams in 1966,' he wrote to this author in June 2018. Sapi passed on his second attempt and entered form one (grade eight) at Ndola's Mukuba secondary school in 1967. There a new sport beckoned: football. A natural athlete, Sapi's ball skills turned out to be as impressive as his discarded fistic talents. He was a standout defender for Mukuba and later made Ronnie Hollywood's Zambia schools squad for games against touring youth sides from Wolverhampton Wanderers and Ipswich Town – tussling with future England internationals Brian Talbot and Mick Mills in a 4-3 victory over the latter. Mills would go on to captain England at the 1982 World Cup in Spain. A prefect in his final year at Mukuba, Sapi later excelled at full-back for Rhokana United (as Nkana FC in the 80s, they'd dominate the Zambian league for more than a decade before being decimated by the Gabon plane crash). His Rhokana exploits eventually earned him a call-up to the national team during Bušelić's second tenure.

At age 22, he was in the squad for the Olympic qualifiers against Sudan. Forty-two years later, Sapi had aged gracefully. He was a successful businessman and was again involved in his first passion, as tzar of Zambia's professional boxing and wrestling board – and as the World Boxing Council's international secretary for Africa. That was all possible because en route from Sudan on the night of 4 April 1976, Sapi and the Zambian squad had narrowly escaped the fate that would befall the 1993 team aboard another Zambia Air Force plane.

They'd left Khartoum, the Sudanese capital, aboard a Second World War-era Douglas C-47 Dakota transport plane, one of up to nine in the ZAF inventory at that time. More than 10,000 of the sturdy US-built aircraft had been produced since the war. It had a maximum speed of 224mph (360km/h), a range of 1,600 miles or 2,575km, and could carry 28 troops.

In June 2018, Nelson Sapi shared his recollection of the Zambian national team's close call on the Dakota: 'After the match we hurried through our hotel and a cocktail [reception] where there was no alcohol being served; and knowing us Zambians, after such a big win, which qualified us to the 1976 Summer Olympic Games in Canada, and knowing that we had more than enough Mosi lager stocks on the plane, we rushed for the airport to fly back home. We arrived at the airport and quickly went through immigration formalities and then took off. I was sitting next to Ante Bušelić. It was after flying for an hour or so, as we were enjoying our beverages whilst singing our favourite Beatles songs, that we noticed that the ventilation started failing, and we noticed we had started sweating – and since I was sitting next to Ante, I noticed that he was sweating too. Within a short time, we noticed the lights went dim and that made us stop singing and take our seats.

'Next, the famous ZAF captain [Eddie] Lazaro left the cockpit and came into the cabin and we could all tell that things were not okay. The captain addressed us as follows, "Gentlemen, there are no women here. We are all men. You must have realised that the ventilation is failing and that some lights have gone off. The problem we have is that we have unfortunately lost one engine which has forced me to switch off the ventilation system and switch off some lights in order to save the limited power we are remaining with, and since we are now entering Ugandan airspace, we have to contact Entebbe Airport for an emergency landing. This is our only available option. so please start praying to our living God for a safe landing." And he walked back to the cockpit.

'We all went quiet and I could see that our coach [Bušelić] became very apprehensive and he was sweating even more, like his BP [blood pressure] had shot up.

'We abandoned our drinks because we started smelling death. I happened to be one of the youngest players in the team and this is why I was sitting with the coach because I could only take two beers unlike [the] other senior players. After some minutes captain Lazaro came back to tell us that he had managed to contact Entebbe Airport, who had said they had to get clearance from President Idi Amin since we were flying in a military plane. They said Amin was attending a dinner function at some hotel and that captain Lazaro had been told to wait for Amin's clearance. The captain then told us that he had brought the plane to a much lower flying level instead of maintaining a higher [altitude]. We took it to mean that we were flying at treetop level.

'When captain Lazaro finally got Amin's response, it was, "If you are flying a military plane then you proceed to Nairobi." And this is how captain Lazaro contacted Jomo Kenyatta International Airport in Nairobi, where we eventually landed safely. The plane was worked on and after six or so hours it was certified fit and we continued our journey back to Lusaka. It was only coach Ante Bušelić who refused to board the ZAF plane.'

Aboard the crippled Dakota, as delegation leader, was Musa Kasonka, the Zambian government's director of sport. A major in Zambia's military reserves, he'd led the Zambian contingent to the Munich Olympics in 1972 and had heard the gunfire from the terrorist attack on the Israeli team rooming near the Africans in the Olympic Village. Forty-two years after the Sudan flight ordeal, Musa Kasonka Jr. remembered his father returning home extremely shaken, 'He was traumatised because the [plane] could have dropped. It had to fly over treetops because there was a fault.' Kasonka Sr. would die in a single-car accident four years after that close call in the Dakota.

Exactly three months to the day he denied the crippled ZAF Dakota permission to land at Entebbe, Idi Amin would have no say when an Israeli commando team swooped on the International Airport there on 4 July 1976. Led by Lt Col Yonatan Netanyahu, its mission was to rescue the nearly 100 mostly Israeli hostages on a hijacked Air France Airbus A300. The older brother of future Israeli prime minister Benjamin Netanyahu, Yonatan was the only Israeli casualty in the otherwise successful mission that left all four hijackers and 45 Ugandan soldiers dead.

Sapi was one of five Rhokana United players who escaped death on the Dakota: Bernard Chanda, Moses Simwala, Ackim Mulamata and Brighton Sinyangwe were the others. As Nkana FC, 17 years later, the club would lose five stars in the Gabon crash: defenders John Soko and Eston Mulenga, wingers Timothy Mwitwa and Numba Mwila, and striker Kenani Simambe.

Spared that terrifying experience on the ZAF Dakota were future Gabon victims Godfrey Chitalu, whose endorsement of Union Carbide's 'Ucar' battery disqualified him from the Olympics, and a young, skinny, enthralling forward-cum-playmaker named Alex Chola. Born and bred in the southern Congolese city of Élisabethville (later Lubumbashi), where his Zambian father, like Simon Kaushi's, had sought employment, the player christened Alexander Chola had returned to Zambia in 1974. He tried out for Ndola United, then in Zambia's top flight, but was spurned on account of his slight build. It would not be the first time in what would be a sparkling career that managers would be deceived by his slender physique.

Chola had crossed paths with the older Kaushi growing up in Lubumbashi but they'd never played together. They finally teamed up at Mufulira Blackpool. The ball skills and trickery Chola honed at the second division side were uncanny. He'd redefine the relationship between player and ball – turning the latter into a wireless extension of his body, seemingly controlling it with Jedi-like mind power. Never the fastest player, speed was negligible for Chola when he could make the ball do his every bidding.

Years later, Kalusha Bwalya, a protégé of Chola's at Blackpool, recounted to this writer an incredible piece of ball control he'd witnessed Brazilian legend and then PSV Eindhoven team-mate Romário exhibit during training in the Netherlands. A corner was swung in and the diminutive Romário vaulted in the air, catching the ball on his chest and controlling it before it touched the ground. 'The only other player I'd seen do that was Alex Chola,' said Kalusha, who along with his older brother Benjamin broke into the Zambian league with much fanfare as teenagers late in 1981, bamboozling older full-backs with the dribbling skills learnt from Chola.

Emmie Musonda, Zambia captain in 1983, would also talk of seeing Chola – on more than one occasion – trap a goal kick of more than 50 yards with his instep before the ball touched the ground. Interest from English clubs in Chola in the late 70s was warded off by then Zambia coach Brian Tiler. The wiry magician would never survive in the physical English game warned Tiler. In Africa, Chola's often jaw-dropping moves, juggling and faking past opponents, would earn him admirers as far north as Egypt where he was reverentially known as 'Shola'.

He earned his first Zambia cap in 1975, easily the pick of new internationals a year after the Africa Cup of Nations in Egypt. Often playing as a deep-lying second striker whose dribbling befuddled defenders, he'd score five goals in the Olympic preliminaries against Mauritius and Malawi, setting up the final qualifier with Sudan that he missed through injury. Chola's exploits three seasons after being rejected by modest Ndola United would earn him the 1976 Zambian Footballer of the Year award.

There'd be another twist for the Zambians in this Olympic drama. They were drawn in what today would be termed a 'Group of Death' in the 16-team tournament in Montreal. Zambia's Group A opponents would include then world amateur powerhouse East Germany, Spain and a Brazilian squad that would feature future midfield star Léo Júnior. The Africans would warm up for the challenge with a training game against Olympic hosts Canada, which they'd lose 3-2. It would be Zambia's only match in North America.

A day before the opening ceremony in Montreal, Zambia and more than 30 other countries withdrew from the Games in protest against the presence of New Zealand. The Kiwis had established strong sporting ties with Apartheid South Africa. They further incurred the wrath of anti-Apartheid activists when their national rugby team planned a summer tour of South Africa despite the Soweto Uprising by black schoolchildren a month before the Olympics. The protests had been violently quashed by the police resulting in numerous casualties. African countries demanded that the International Olympic Committee ban New Zealand from the Olympics. When the IOC declined, arguing that rugby was not an Olympic sport, Zambia joined an Afro-Asian boycott of the Games.

Transformative as the boycott was – the *Montreal Gazette* quoted Canadian researcher Courtney W. Mason as saying it put the word 'Apartheid' on the front page of every newspaper in the world, 'and people started talking about the issue and pressuring their own governments' – it may also have altered the course of Nelson Sapi's life.

'I lost my chance of being signed on by the University of Akron [in Ohio) as a fully sponsored student [based] on my soccer ability,' he said, alluding to a scholarship offer from the NCAA Division I school that hinged on his Olympic performance. Noted Akron football alum in recent years have included US internationals Darlington Nagbe, DeAndre Yedlin, Wil Trapp and Darren Mattocks of Jamaica's national team, the Reggae Boyz. Instead Sapi, at 22 still one of Zambia's youngest players in Montreal, returned home with the rest of the Zambian contingent. He finished his career with Rhokana United. Sapi owned a chain of schools in Lusaka when he died on 25 February 2019. He was 65.

5

Ucar Resurrection

THE FIRST major boycott of the modern Olympics in 1976 would start a chain reaction. The next two Olympics would also be marred by boycotts. Four years after Montreal, the United States led a Western boycott of the Moscow Games in retaliation for the Soviet invasion of Afghanistan in December 1979. Ironically, Zambia would benefit from this bit of Cold War gamesmanship. To woo African support, US president Jimmy Carter turned to a figure insanely popular on the continent: Muhammad Ali. The former three-time world heavyweight champion, famous for boycotting the Vietnam War, was dispatched as a special envoy to urge African nations to join the boycott. Egypt – where Ali had watched his first international football game – did. Zambia, who'd thrilled Ali with their fighting spirit in that 1974 Africa Cup of Nations Final in Cairo, didn't. They replaced the Egyptians in the 1980 Olympic football competition. By now Zambia's bogey team, the Pharaohs had eliminated Zambia 5-2 on aggregate in the final qualifying round for Moscow that April. A 4-1 rout in Cairo, after sensational newcomer Peter Kaumba had levelled within three minutes of Egypt's opener, effectively decided the tie. Alex Chola scored in a 1-1 draw in Lusaka as the Zambians failed to beat Egypt on their fifth attempt since their first meeting in 1974.

A fillip to Zambia's return to the Olympics – albeit by the back door – would be the inclusion of the suddenly eligible Godfrey 'Ucar' Chitalu. His previous commercial endorsement of batteries no longer an impediment, Chitalu finally found himself on the biggest stage of his career. Approaching his 33rd birthday that October, he was in the twilight of his dazzling, if at times controversial, career. But, ironically, the scorer of 107 documented goals eight years earlier had been in blistering form the previous three seasons as he incredibly enjoyed a new lease on life. In 1980, that coincided with the ebbing form of some of Zambia's other top forwards who had confined Chitalu to the bench during the Ante Bušelić era – namely Bernard Chanda, Simon 'Kaodi' Kaushi and Obby Kapita.

Chitalu's resurgence began after Bušelić's departure in 1976. In January 1977, stand-in coaches Brightwell Banda, a major in the Zambia Army, and Freddie Mwila had called up the forgotten Kabwe Warriors striker for his first competitive international match since the 1974 AFCON. Then 29, Chitalu would announce his international resurrection in devastating fashion, in a tricky World Cup second-round qualifier against Uganda on 27 February 1977.

The Cranes had eliminated Zambia from the AFCON two years earlier. They'd flown into Ndola fancying their chances of another conquest after nicking a 1-0 result in the first leg of the World Cup qualifier in Kampala. It got better for the visitors 12 minutes in when they doubled their aggregate lead. Abdullah Nasur probably couldn't believe it when a defensive error gifted him the opportunity to silence the jam-packed crowd at Dag Hammarskjöld Stadium.

A year after the close call with Sudan in the Olympic qualifiers, the Zambians were facing another dire crisis at Dag. Watching from the bench, his 107 goals four coruscating seasons earlier now a wistful memory, was Godfrey Chitalu. No doubt that he was eager to join the fray. To his immense relief, and to the delirious delight of the 18,000 fans in the stadium, his number was called a minute after Alex Chola had slammed in the equaliser.

The enormous roar when he entered the game in the 27th minute might have been a giveaway. But hardly anyone fathomed that an epic was about to unfold, and the defining role Chitalu would play in it. It would inspire Zambia's first vinyl football record, featuring excerpts of celebrated radio commentator Dennis Liwewe's play-by-play account of the game and Chitalu's heroics.

The resurgent striker's introduction sparked the home side. Ten minutes later, Bernard Chanda connected from a corner to put Zambia 2-1 up, levelling the aggregate tally. Away goals still in the future, the World Cup qualifier was now all square. Beseeched by their country's dictator Idi Amin in a pre-game telegram to 'conquer or die', as recounted by radio commentator Dennis Liwewe in his book *Soccer in Zambia*, the Cranes were not about to go out without a dogfight.

Down the stretch of a testy second half, Denis Obua equalised, putting Zambia back in arrears. It was 3-2 now on aggregate in Uganda's favour. Runners-up on the continent in the play-offs for the 1974 World Cup, the Zambians now had 20 minutes to avoid elimination in the second round on this occasion. There were five minutes left when Chitalu ended a sweeping move involving Alex Chola and Willie Phiri with a well-struck shot that restored Zambia's lead.

The 3-2 Zambian victory in regulation time meant extra time to break the 4-4 aggregate tie. Extra time was a nail-biting affair. First, Polly Ouma, scorer of the Ugandan goal in Kampala, rattled the crossbar, as Zambian hearts missed a collective beat.

Then Chitalu took over.

His innate individualism on the pitch had not always endeared him to former coach Ante Bušelić. In the final third at least, Ucar was more wont to latch on to a pass and run at defenders than play off his fellow attackers. With Bušelić gone and time running out at Dag, Chitalu instinctively resorted to the individualism that had kept him out of the national team for so long. He received a pass from midfielder Jani Simulambo, turned, and went at the Ugandan defence.

The packed stadium roared with every dribble. Chitalu slalomed past defenders. Goalkeeper George Mukasa came rushing out and suffered the same fate as his back line. Chitalu's finish produced the most dramatic international goal in Zambian history at that point. His superb brace had sealed a 4-2 extra-time victory, carrying Zambia into the third and penultimate round of the African qualifiers for the 1978 World Cup finals in Argentina, to face Egypt.

Fans were agog. Chitalu was carried off the pitch like the conquering hero that he was. He'd claimed redemption after winding back the clock to his free-scoring years. 'They had me buried on the international scene so I had to come back in style,' he told the *Zambia Daily Mail*.

Brightwell Banda, in the first of his several stints as one of Zambia's most successful indigenous coaches, claimed some credit for the renowned forward's virtuoso performance. 'I deliberately put Chitalu on the bench and started with Burton Mugala so that he could tire the Ugandan defence before introducing "Ucar",' said Banda.

'One of the greatest soccer matches ever played!' declared Dennis Liwewe, never one to spare a hyperbole.

Thirteen months later, Uganda went on to stun Morocco 3-0 and Nigeria 2-1 en route to their first and only appearance in the Africa Cup of Nations Final. They lost 2-0 to hosts Ghana in the 1978 championship game.

Chitalu's international resurrection would continue in June 1977. Four months after he'd eviscerated the Cranes, the nation looked up to him again after Zambia returned from Algiers with a 2-0 deficit in a 1978 AFCON qualifier. Ucar did not disappoint, connecting once in each half in a 2-0 victory in Lusaka. There was no extra time. For the second time in a year, Zambia had to win a penalty shoot-out to qualify for a major tournament. And like in Khartoum the previous year, they were flawless from 12 yards, prevailing 6-5 in the sudden-death shoot-out to reach the biennial AFCON for only the second time. Brightwell Banda, who had Chitalu on the pitch from kick-off this time, was back as interim coach after what amounted to a cameo by an enigmatic German named Ted Virba. Hired as Zambia's second foreign coach following the World Cup triumph over Uganda, Virba had a huge act to follow after Bušelić's success. But his tenure lasted just one match, the 2-0 road loss in Algiers, before he was swiftly sacked for undisclosed reasons.

Virba's sudden departure – like his arrival months earlier – caused nary a ripple among Zambian fans. He'd been unknown, untested and had not bonded with the fans the way Bušelić had. And besides, Chitalu was back in devastating form, as Uganda and Algeria had both found out.

Zambia hoped to bank on Ucar big time one more time in 1977.

Three weeks after dispatching Algeria to qualify for the AFCON, stand-in coach Brightwell Banda took Chitalu and Co. back to the scene of Zambia's greatest near-triumph: Cairo. Standing between them and a return to the World Cup Africa zone play-offs were the inscrutable Egyptians. Alas, the Zambians left the Egyptian capital with a 2-0 defeat. Could Chitalu inspire an improbable comeback in the return leg?

At half-time, solid defending by the Egyptians had kept Zambia at bay at Independence Stadium in Lusaka. Four years after a similar change had worked magic for Bušelić against Nigeria, Banda sent on Simon Kaushi for Chitalu in the second half. Given Ucar's amazing form that year, the switch was baffling. There would be no Kaushi encore. The Egyptian defence remained impregnable in a goalless draw that advanced them to the three-nation play-off from which Tunisia would qualify for Argentina. Nigeria was the other team in the play-offs.

For the next three years before the Moscow Olympics, Chitalu would continue to deliver for Zambia. He starred under Brian Tiler, the former Aston Villa and Wigan Athletic defender who was 34 when appointed national coach for a two-year stint in 1978. The Englishman, who'd later manage Wigan, and Portland Timbers in the US, gushed over his talismanic forward. 'I rate him high and the one thing with Godfrey is that he's hard-working,' said Tiler. Chitalu starred under Dick Chama too, the erstwhile Zambia defensive kingpin, vice-captain and later captain, who succeeded Tiler in 1980. Chama's assistant during his tenure as national coach was his former skipper Dickson Makwaza.

Injury limited Chitalu to less than 90 minutes over two games at the 1978 AFCON. There'd be no goals, just a rare assist that set up Obby Kapita's early first goal in Zambia's 2-1 loss to Ghana in the tournament opener. It was Zambia's only defeat in the toughest group of the eight-nation tournament – a group so competitive that not even a 2-0 win over Burkina Faso on matchday two followed by a 0-0 draw with old rivals Nigeria could avert the Zambians' first-round elimination. It would be Chitalu's last AFCON appearance. Ironically, Africa's all-time top scorer at international level would retire having played just one full game in the continent's premier tournament. Only one of a documented 79 goals for Zambia, from his debut in 1968 to his swansong in 1980, came in the Africa Cup of Nations finals.

Still, Chitalu would get one more shot at redemption on the big stage. It came in the boycott-marred Moscow Olympics in the summer of 1980. At the Games by invitation after Egypt's withdrawal, Zambia had flown to the USSR without two key players, in the experienced link man Jani Simulambo and the lanky flying left-winger Peter Kaumba, who were both injured. Even then, their odds seemed better than good after landing in a dream group of sorts. If the Soviets were as formidable a proposition as any European host could be, Chitalu and Zambia surely fancied their chances against the other Group A members Cuba and Venezuela: two baseball-crazy nations then on the outer fringes of the football universe. Like Zambia, the Venezuelans were stand-ins, late replacements for the boycotting Argentines. Chitalu and right-winger Moses Simwala were the sole survivors from the Zambian squad side that had almost conquered Africa in 1974. In addition to the injured Kaumba, Simulambo, Bernard Chanda, Simon Kaushi and Obby Kapita were also absent. And like in Egypt, six years earlier, Zambia would be required to play a game every other day – three matches in five days starting with Cuba on 20 July 1980.

A capacity crowd of 100,000 mostly curious Soviet fans packed the Kirov Stadium in Leningrad (now St. Petersburg) to watch a rare encounter between a Caribbean island – then more renowned globally for its revolutionary zeal, world-class amateur boxers, baseball and cigars than its football – and an African side on the frontlines of the liberation struggle in southern Africa. Pedigree alone might have made the Zambians favourites that Russian summer evening. But whether it was stage fright before the largest crowd they'd ever played before, or simply one of those aberrations common in the game, the Africans would succumb 1-0. Andrés Roldán, a diminutive 5ft 6in midfielder capped only 35 times by the Cubans between 1971 and 1981, notched the solitary goal in the 58th minute.

If he was smarting over that debacle, Chitalu chose the right occasion to vent his football anger two days later, before an 80,000 sellout crowd at Moscow's Luzhniki Stadium. This was the one game in the group stage that everybody had probably anticipated a Zambian defeat. The Soviets' amateur status was on paper only. Winners of UEFA's inaugural European Championship in 1960, runners-up in that competition in 1964 and 1972, and fourth-place finishers in 1968, they were a bona fide European power that had also advanced to the semi-finals of the 1966 World Cup in England.

No surprise then that nine minutes into the Zambia-USSR encounter, Vagiz Khidiyatullin, a fresh-faced 21-year-old defender from Spartak Moscow, struck the first goal in the expected rout. But that was just the cue for 32-year-old Chitalu to go into his act. In the biggest game of his career, against the toughest opposition he'd ever faced, the Zambian icon would give Soviet fans in the crammed Luzhniki a glimpse of the scoring prowess that had produced 107 goals eight years earlier. Four minutes after Khidiyatullin's strike, Zambia counterattacked. The ball found Chitalu. Next, Ucar did what he'd always done.

It was how he'd always played, the way his football brain was wired.

Thirty-nine years later, Frederick Kashimoto, a diminutive defensive midfielder on the Zambian bench at the Luzhniki, recalled what unfolded next: 'Godfrey got the ball in the centre circle. He beat one defender and went to the left wing. He beat two other players and then went inside into the [18-yard box] and beat another defender.'

At that point, Ucar found himself in the six-yard box with Soviet goalie Rinat Dasayev dashing out to narrow an already acute angle at the near post. It was an impossible shot to make, but Chitalu did. Adept with both feet, and a believer of power over finesse when striking the ball, his low and hard shot zoomed past Dasayev and into the net. Zambia were level after four minutes. It was undoubtedly the best goal of his international career. It was also the first competitive Zambian goal scored outside Africa and – perhaps deservedly – it had been scored by the country's greatest striker who'd go on to net a still-record 79 goals in 108 international appearances, between 1968 and 1980.

The next 38 minutes of football, covering both halves, would burnish a gusty and intelligent Zambian performance in the lion's den that was the Luzhniki Stadium that night. Rattled by Chitalu's equaliser, the Soviet juggernaut stepped it up. They attacked relentlessly and methodically – perhaps too methodically – and found the Africans tough to crack. 'They were building slowly from behind,' recalled Kashimoto, an unused substitute in the game. 'We defended well, packing the midfield to stop them and [counter] attacking when we had the ball. When we lost the ball, we dropped into midfield, all the players.'

The tactic frustrated the Soviets for the rest of the half. And into the early second half. That's until the young defender Khidiyatullin unbelievably struck again, restoring the USSR's lead from a free kick in the 51st minute. Three minutes before Syrian referee Marwan Arafat blew the final whistle, Fedor Cherenkov notched a third Soviet goal. Zambia were beaten but not bowed. Chitalu, above all, had shown his pedigree against a European power.

How dominant were the Soviets in Group A? They'd beaten Venezuela 4-0 before besting Zambia and would batter the Cubans 8-0 in the final game to decide the group winners, after Cuba had edged Venezuela 2-1. Two years later, Soviet coach Kostantin Beskov took ten members of that Olympic squad, including Khidiyatullin and Dasayev, to the FIFA World Cup in Spain, where they led Brazil before succumbing 2-1 to brilliant strikes by Sócrates and Éder. It would be the first of goalkeeper Dasayev's three World Cup tournaments. He'd earn the sobriquets 'The Iron Curtain' and 'The Cat', along with a reputation as the USSR's second-best goalkeeper ever after the great Lev Yashin. He'd also play in the 1988 European Championship Final in Munich, where he'd be beaten again from an impossibly acute angle – this time by Marco van Basten in a 2-0 Dutch victory.

Godfrey Chitalu shone again in Zambia's last group match. He scored off an Alex Chola pass with 17 minutes left to give the Africans a 1-0 lead against Venezuela in Leningrad. Four minutes from time, Zambia seemed headed for their maiden victory outside Africa. Defeat at that point was utterly unimaginable. Alas, there'd be another shock for Chitalu and Co. at the Kirov Stadium. A sudden collapse in those four traumatic minutes allowed Iker Zubizarreta and Robert Elie to nick a stunning result for baseball-mad Venezuela.

Although they'd return home from the Olympics winless, Zambia's inspiring performance against the

Soviets, and Chitalu's undiminished scoring form, gave fans massive confidence ahead of the national team's next major assignment in 1980. It would be against an old foe.

A month before the Moscow Olympics, Zambia had thrashed Ethiopia 4-0 in Lusaka to finish off a World Cup Africa zone first-round qualifier whose first leg – like in the same competition in 1973 – had ended goalless in Addis Ababa. Chitalu connected twice. Next in the bid for a place at Spain in 1982 would be another familiar World Cup rival. Seven years after first locking horns in the play-offs for the 1974 finals in the then West Germany, Zambia had drawn Morocco in the second round. This encounter, unlike the first back in 1973 and unlike the next three in the future, would be a knockout affair over two legs. The first leg would take the Zambians to the historic north-eastern Moroccan city of Fez. There, Dick Chama and his technical staff would match wits with a World Cup legend.

The 1958 World Cup in Sweden was memorable not just for the emergence of a precocious 17-year-old Brazilian with jaw-dropping skills named Pelé. It was also the tournament at which the Moroccan-born son of a French father and Spanish mother shot the lights out, scoring a still-World Cup finals-record 13 goals – and in six games for that. Born in Marrakech, Just Fontaine began his career as an amateur at USM Casablanca but would make a name for himself in his father's homeland. He'd netted a hat-trick on his France debut, an 8-0 annihilation of minnows Luxembourg in December 1953. He'd go on to score 30 goals in 21 international appearances – almost half of them in those six matches in the 1958 World Cup. Fontaine's international career ended two years later. He prolonged his club career for another two years until injury forced him out of football in 1962, just shy of his 29th birthday. He had a two-match stint as French national team manager in 1967, losing both games. He'd not coach another national side before taking charge of Morocco in 1979.

In March 1980, Fontaine led Morocco to third place at the Africa Cup of Nations in Nigeria – a tournament Zambia missed. The Moroccans had lost 1-0 to the hosts in the semi-finals (Nigeria went on to lift the trophy for the first time). In the dreaded third-place 'heartbreak' match, Fontaine saw his charges maintain their traditional dominance over Egypt with a 2-0 decision – between 1961 and 2017, Egypt had won only three of 29 encounters with Morocco.

Then came a chance for Fontaine to return to the World Cup finals; as a manager this time. But first he had to negotiate past a difficult Zambian side drilled by former defensive stalwarts Dick Chama and Dickson Makwaza. Both had played in the 4-0 destruction of Morocco in Lusaka in 1973, which, until April 1985, was Zambia's finest performance in a World Cup qualifier. A new addition to the Zambian coaching staff was technical director Theodore 'Ted' Dumitru, a Romanian with coaching experience in his country, Turkey and the United States. Stateside, Dumitru's employers had included the Rochester Lancers and New York Apollo, both in the defunct American Soccer League.

Zambia's game plan at the Hassan II Stadium in Fez on 17 November 1980 was no secret. The ubiquitous Dennis Liwewe, for a decade then the eyes and ears of Zambian international football fans before the advent of live television broadcasts in the 1990s, had announced it in his pre-match reports. Inspired by the team's defensive display in Moscow where they'd defied the USSR at length before succumbing 3-1, Zambia were confident of pulling off a similar feat in Fez against slightly less formidable opposition – even an attack-minded one coached by the deadliest single tournament scorer in World Cup history.

It didn't go well.

Against the slow-building USSR, choking the midfield with players had worked well for Zambia. When the tactic was applied against Morocco, the Moroccans, playing at a much faster tempo than the Soviets, lobbed balls into the spaces left behind by the Zambians. 'We were a bit slow in marking, so Morocco, playing fast and long balls, had the advantage,' said midfielder Frederick Kashimoto.

After 45 minutes, Morocco led 2-0. During the interval, the Zambian brains trust of Chama, Makwaza and Dumitru decided to discard the game plan. Zambia reverted to their traditional attacking game on resumption and the match changed. But there would be no more goals. Critiquing his rivals' performance ahead of the return leg in Lusaka, Just Fontaine pointed out that Zambia were 'no good in the first half, but they improved in the second half'.

If Fontaine and his Atlas Lions were bullish over their chances of completing the job in Lusaka two weeks later, Zambian fans hadn't read the memo. The earnest belief then by the locals – the draw with Egypt in 1977 notwithstanding – was that any two-goal advantage by visitors to the southern African nation was never safe against Godfrey 'Ucar' Chitalu and Co. There was a particularly heightened expectation for this game, and not because Morocco had been demolished 4-0 on their last visit to Independence Stadium.

The second leg was scheduled for Sunday, 30 November 1980 – punctuating a massive week in Zambian sports, during which the nation's top athletes would be pursuing glory in three major international events. While its ace footballers sought to overturn that 2-0 deficit against Morocco in the World Cup, a Zambia 'B' national side had battled its way to the semi-finals of the regional CECAFA

Cup – Africa's oldest international football competition dating back to 1926 – against hosts Sudan in Khartoum.

In San Diego, California, prizefighter Lottie Mwale, the highly talented light heavyweight king of both Africa and the British Commonwealth, would square off with the tough American Matthew Saad Muhammad for the World Boxing Council championship. Legendary for their eternal optimism, Zambians were by midweek dreaming of an unprecedented sporting trifecta.

Zambia B were first in the spotlight, in Khartoum. Giving a glimpse of the uncanny depth of local talent later highlighted after the Gabon crash, the squad of second-string players had topped a group in the preliminaries comprising Kenya, Malawi and Zanzibar. That earned them a date in the last four with the runners-up in the other group, contested by hosts Sudan, Tanzania and Somalia. Surprisingly, that would be the Sudanese. Zambia B and Sudan met in the semi-finals on Tuesday, 25 November 1980. Sudan prevailed 2-1 and went on to beat Tanzania 1-0 in the final. Zambian disappointment was compounded on 27 November by a 1-0 loss to Malawi, who they'd beaten 3-2 in the group stages, in the third-place match.

In Lusaka, with the preparations against Morocco intensifying, the senior Zambian squad was undaunted by news of their second unit's setback in Sudan. In the wee hours of Saturday, 29 November, Frederick Kashimoto and his team-mates, like most Zambians with television sets then, woke up at 3am local time to watch a live boxing fight from the United States. In an hour's time the wildly popular Lottie 'Gunduzani' Mwale, whose stature in Zambian sport equalled Godfrey 'Ucar' Chitalu's, would become the first Zambian to challenge for a world title in any sport.

Like Chitalu, Mwale, then 28, grew up in Kitwe, was charismatic and possessed world-class skills in his calling.

He'd missed an excellent opportunity to showcase his enormous talent before the world when Zambia's Olympic contingent withdrew from the 1976 Summer Games in Montreal at the 11th hour. Dashed were hopes of a possible dream match-up between Gunduzani and the classy Michael Spinks, a future world light heavyweight and heavyweight champion in the paid ranks. The American would cruise to Olympic gold in the middleweight division. Spinks had a bye and two wins by walkover before minting gold with two subsequent victories. Mwale turned pro in 1977 under a management group that included Rupiah Banda, the former diplomat, football fanatic and future Zambian president. Shortly afterward, the German industrialist Wilfred Sauerland assumed management control of the boxer.

Fighting out of trainer George Francis's Wellington Stables in London, Mwale was 21-0 with 17 KOs when he challenged Matthew Saad Muhammad for the WBC 175lb belt. Their scrap was scheduled for 15 rounds at the Sports Arena in San Diego. Muhammad was a battle-tested fighter with a record of 27 wins, three losses and two draws. Out of that old American boxing hotbed of Philadelphia, he was two years younger than Mwale but had turned pro three years earlier than the Zambian, in 1974. He epitomised all the qualities of the legendary Philly fighter and was in his prime. Still, more than a few fight experts gave the challenger a chance against the slow-starting Muhammad. Tall and wiry with tremendous upper-body movement, Mwale was a classical boxer-puncher. In May 1978, he'd stunned British boxing in his seventh professional fight with a devastating one-punch first-round KO of undefeated future world middleweight title contender Tony Sibson – who at the time had a record of 24-0-1 – at De Montford Hall, Leicester. In his next fight, Mwale comprehensively outpointed American Marvin Johnson over eight rounds at the Red Star Stadium in Belgrade, Yugoslavia to improve to 8-0 with six KOs. Johnson would recover from that defeat to win three world light heavyweight titles.

Huddled around a black-and-white TV set, Frederick Kashimoto and his enthusiastic Zambia national football team-mates would cheer on their countryman that early Saturday morning in late November 1980. From the first bell, Mwale went at the intimidating Saad Muhammad who'd entered the ring in a long black cowl and black trunks. To the rhythmic beat of African drums in the hands of a small group of travelling Zambian fans, including Rupiah Banda, Mwale edged the first two and a half rounds with quick and hard combinations. Muhammad took the punches that had levelled lesser fighters. He later conceded that Mwale could bang. Then late in the third round, a counter left hook to the jaw by the sturdy Muhammad rocked the challenger, turning the fight around. The champion opened up but Mwale, trapped in his own corner, was saved by the bell. Between rounds, George Francis, whose other notable charges would include John 'The Beast' Mugabi and Frank Bruno, worked frantically to revive the Zambian. The trainer's efforts were not entirely in vain. Mwale was fighting back in the fourth stanza and landing punches. That's until he was flattened by a decapitating left uppercut flush on his whiskered chin. Zambia had suffered its second major sporting defeat in four days. It was left to Godfrey Chitalu and Co. to lift Zambian spirits in the next day's must-win World Cup qualifier against Morocco.

The two teams took to the pitch at a packed Independence Stadium shortly before 3pm local time. There was no standing room left, neither in the 30,000-capacity stadium nor on 'Humanism Hill', a rocky ridge overlooking the western end of the stadium that offered non-paying spectators a view of part of the pitch below. The day was overcast and the turf sodden after overnight rains. Zambia went on the attack from the first whistle. They had 90 minutes to erase a two-goal deficit and, in the process, salvage a thus far disastrous weekend for Zambian sports. The pressure was undoubtedly crushing.

For World Cup scoring legend Just Fontaine in the Moroccan dugout, it was a different view of a team he'd seen struggle in the opening 45 minutes in Fez – one that he might have admired. Morocco was under the cosh from kick-off. The Zambians were in their element. In midfield, Alex Chola was among those orchestrating the moves.

A feint here and a fake there would send Moroccan markers slipping on the moist turf. Up front, Chitalu and long-striding left-winger Peter Kaumba led the charge. But Morocco held out until half-time. Keeping the rampaging Chitalu and his team-mates off the scoreboard was alone a feat for Fontaine's men.

Zambia kept up the heat on resumption and were duly rewarded. A corner was swung in and Emmy Musonda, from national coach Dick Chama's army-sponsored Green Buffaloes club, sprinted into the box.

The robust defender's bullet header beat Morocco's 21-year-old goalkeeper Ezzaki Badou. The ball violently shook the net, eliciting a deafening roar from the crammed stadium. Zambia had a goal back. They went for the jugular. Morocco were pinned back as the Zambians attacked the way they always did at home – in unrelenting waves. Inevitably, the second goal came. Bizwell Phiri, a speedy young right-winger, was the scorer; Morocco's two-goal lead had been erased. Zambia were on the verge of another remarkable fightback. Chola, Chitalu, Kaumba and Phiri pressed on. But Morocco would not concede a third goal. Level at 2-2, the tie would go straight to penalties.

For the third time in four years, Zambia would have to rely on their proficiency from 12 yards to pull off a major victory. They'd beaten Sudan 5-4 on penalties in Khartoum to qualify for the 1976 Olympics. Algeria had also been dispatched 6-5 in a sudden-death shoot-out in 1977 to book Zambia's return to the Africa Cup of Nations. Would the Atlas Lions be next?

Between the posts for Zambia was Kenny Mwape, the young brother of Emmanuel Mwape who'd enhanced his reputation at the 1974 AFCON. Kenny was beaten four times from the penalty spot. So was the fledgling Ezzaki Badou, who failed to stop shots by Jani Simulambo, Alex Chola, Peter Kaumba and Michael Musonda.

Morocco then converted their fifth penalty. It was now up to Willie Phiri to keep Zambia in the World Cup race. Significantly, Chitalu was not among Zambia's designated penalty takers – he never was. The packed stadium watched with bated breath.

Later a standout goalkeeper with Mallorca in Spain's La Liga, Badou pulled off the most important save of the afternoon for the visitors to deny Phiri. There was indescribable anguish as Zambia bowed out 5-4 on penalties. A week that had begun with so much promise had ended in bitterly numbing disappointment. The Zambia B team defeated in the semi-finals of the continent's oldest tournament; boxer Lottie Mwale knocked out in his bid for the world light heavyweight title; and now Zambia eliminated from the World Cup qualifiers on a missed penalty. Until the air crash 13 years later that would claim the lives of Chitalu and Chola – and a new generation of football talent – this would be the darkest moment in Zambian sports.

* * *

Postscript: ten months later, Zambia and Morocco would clash again in the final qualifying round for the 1982 Africa Cup of Nations in Libya – with some changes. Brightwell Banda, now an army lieutenant colonel, was back as interim coach in place of Ted Dumitru. Elevated to head coach after the World Cup elimination by Morocco, the Romanian's role had amounted to a cameo. He was let go when the Football Association of Zambia was dissolved by the Ministry of Sport in June 1981 – at a time before FIFA barred government interference with its affiliates. FAZ's crime was defying a ministerial order to reschedule a friendly with Zaire at Lusaka's residential Woodlands Stadium that coincided with an international boxing show at Independence Stadium. In another change, Godfrey Chitalu's illustrious career had ended weeks earlier when, for the third time as a player, he'd broken an arm in a league game for Kabwe Warriors. He retired with an official 79 goals in 108 international appearances between 1968 and 1980 – a tally that would no doubt have been higher if not for his absence from the national side during coach Toni Bušelić's two-year second stint in charge.

6

Bušelić Reunion

ZAMBIA'S FUTURE now lay in the twinkle toes of midfield maestro Alex Chola, first capped after the 1974 Africa Cup of Nations and Chitalu's striking partner since 1977. Stepping up as Chola's wingman, reprising their phenomenal partnership for Welsh-born Arthur Davies's Kitwe-based Power Dynamos club, was the 23-year-old Peter Kaumba. The winger with dribbling skills and a deceptively slow take-off, Kaumba had another talent – a knack for goals beyond conventional wingers.

New skipper Jani Simulambo, who'd made his international debut in 1973 aged 19 against Brazilian club Fluminense, led Zambia back to the Hassan II Stadium for the AFCON first-leg qualifier against Morocco. There was no defending this time, just an open game that would pay a dividend when Chola fired Zambia ahead. Morocco replied in kind twice, allowing them to take a precarious 2-1 lead to Lusaka.

If the Atlas Lions were trepidatious over the second leg, it was for a good reason. Twice earlier, they'd failed to score in regulation at Independence Stadium. Indeed, goals by Peter Kaumba and Jack Chanda – the latter a newcomer with blistering pace, a low centre of gravity, a lethal right foot and the hybrid qualities of both winger and lighting-fast centre-forward – saw off the Moroccans 2-0. The result qualified Zambia for their third African Nations Cup, 3-2 on aggregate.

It also set the stage for a brief and happy reunion.

In the more than five years since Ante Bušelić's departure as national coach at the end of 1976, Zambia's association with expatriate trainers had been flirtatious at best. Only Brian Tiler had spent more than a year on the job. Following Zambia's qualification for their third AFCON, to be hosted by Libya in 1982, the Ministry of Youth and Sport, in a nostalgic move, decided to recall Bušelić to assist Brightwell Banda in Libya. The Croat was still highly venerated in the country for moulding Zambia into an African powerhouse. To everyone's delight, Bušelić agreed.

The 1982 AFCON was the first continental tournament to be played on synthetic turf. Africa's eight top nations were drawn equally in two putative 'groups of death'. Hosts and first-time participants Libya were in the Tripoli-based Group A alongside Ghana's Black Stars, Roger Milla's World Cup-bound Cameroon and Tunisia, who four years earlier in Argentina had defeated Mexico 3-1 to record Africa's first World Cup victory. Zambia ended up in Group B in Benghazi with defending champions and old foes Nigeria, Africa's other España 82 World Cup envoys Algeria, and tournament pioneers Ethiopia. The Zambians' third Africa Cup campaign opened against – on paper at least – the best team in the tournament: an Algerian side led by Rabah Madjer, Lakhdar Belloumi and Salah Assad, players who would later make international news at the World Cup in Spain that summer.

Hitherto team captain Jani Simulambo had been surprisingly dropped after leaving his long-time army club, Green Buffaloes. And Alex Chola, Peter Kaumba, midfielder Willie Phiri and defender Michael Musonda aside, it looked like it would be a baptism of fire for the new Zambian caps against the Algerians. It was. Coaches Bušelić and Banda watched as Zambia were pinned back for the better part of the game. This was a souped-up version of the Algerian side beaten 2-0 by Godfrey Chitalu's brace nearly five years earlier in Lusaka. Rachid Mekhloufi, a French-Algerian ex-professional who'd spent the 1950s and 1960s on the books of Servette FC and AS Saint-Étienne before retiring at Bastia, had moulded a swift, organised and incisive side that would soon shock world football. Still, it took Rabah Madjer and Co. 85 minutes to end Zambia's resistance. Chaabane Merzekane was the solitary scorer.

Zambian resilience was epitomised by rookie right-back John Kalusa from Nkana (nee Rhokana United). Quick, nimble and standing barely 5ft 4in, Kalusa was the smallest man to play for Zambia at that time. But he was gargantuan and tenacious in defence, as the 5,000 fans at the March 28 Stadium in Benghazi on the night of 7 March witnessed. The tiny Zambian chased and harried the swift Algerian attackers, making goal-saving tackles and clearances. In the process, he earned the sobriquet 'Libya' from Zambian fans faithfully glued to their transistor radios back home.

In their second match, Zambia laboured to a 1-0 victory over an Ethiopian side thrashed 3-0 earlier by Nigeria. Godfrey Munshya, earning the second of his three international caps, scored in the 68th minute. In the other group fixture, Salah Assad's winner in a 2-1 defeat of cup holders Nigeria – a rematch of the 1980 final won by the Green Eagles – qualified Algeria for the semis. And with their final game to come against eliminated Ethiopia, topping Group B was almost certain for the Desert Foxes.

That left the Zambia vs. Nigeria winner to dispute the other semi-final berth, most likely against hosts Libya in Tripoli.

Nine years had passed since the Green Eagles' 5-1 mauling in Lusaka in the first Zambia-Nigeria encounter. While the two nations ranked among the continent's best, Nigeria's AFCON victory in 1980 had certainly edged them ahead of Zambia. That, in addition to their innate confidence, made them – in their own minds at least – favourites to reach the semi-finals. The West Africans were so confident of beating Zambia that they'd already booked their hotel rooms and flight to Tripoli in advance of a potential semi-final clash against the Group A winners – expected to be Libya.

Nigeria's cockiness would be their undoing. Not even a 3-0 drubbing by a Godfrey Chitalu-inspired Midlands select side in a friendly in Lusaka the previous year had tempered the Eagles' confidence. They'd forgotten the cardinal rule that you underestimated Zambia at your own peril.

Peter Kaumba, Zambia's first-choice left-winger since scoring on his debut in April 1979, a 2-0 away win over Malawi aged 21, remembered how one of the most stunning encounters at Libya 82 unfolded.

'The game was very important to us, so everybody put in their best,' Kaumba said from his retirement home in Kitwe, 38 years later. 'We had an advantage because Nigeria thought they'd just walk [over] us – they were overconfident. They'd booked their flights from Benghazi to Tripoli, their hotels and everything – in the end they were disappointed.'

Nigeria were chasing the game from the moment Kaumba struck in the 25th minute. 'I scored a header from around the 18-yard [box]. It was a cross,' recalled the lanky winger, who'd come to prominence in the Zambian league playing alongside the mesmerising Alex Chola at Power Dynamos FC.

A titanic battle ensued as the defending African champions, marshalled by legendary defender Stephen Keshi and midfielders Mudashiru 'Muda' Lawal and Henry Nwosu, attempted to stave off defeat to the plucky, quicker and more cohesive Zambians. It lasted until ten minutes from time when a double strike 60 seconds apart killed off the Eagles. First, diminutive wing-back Aaron Njovu made it 2-0 after the Zambians had pried the tiring Nigerian defence apart. Then, in a singular feat 16 months after his botched effort from 12 yards against Morocco had resulted in Zambia's World Cup elimination in a penalty shoot-out, midfielder Willie Phiri scored one of the rarest of goals in football: an 'Olympic Goal'. Direct from a corner.

It was another thrashing of Nigeria, as African champions, by Zambia. And for the second time in as many attempts, Ante Bušelić – in tandem with Brightwell Banda this time – had led his old side to the last four of Africa's premier competition.

The Tripoli hotel rooms reserved earlier by the Nigerians were turned over to the Zambians. They'd meet Libya in the semi-finals.

From playing before relatively subdued crowds of approximately 5,000 in each of their three group matches in Benghazi, Zambia suddenly stepped on to the big stage. A raucous 50,000 crowd turned out at the June 11 Stadium on the night of 16 March for the Libya-Zambia semi-final. The southern Africans, despite their checkered away record, were hardly intimidated. Having eliminated the defending champions (this time Nigeria) – like they'd done to Congo-Brazzaville in Egypt eight years earlier – they'd come to Tripoli prepared for a fight.

Kaumba underscored that as he continued to script his African Nations Cup legend. Latching on to a pass from Alex Chola, he slammed the ball into the net on the half hour. The goal put Zambia ahead, stirring a hornet's nest. Midfielder Abdel Razak Jaranah led the Libyan fightback. Between the posts, Ghost Mulenga, aged 28, a sensational late bloomer who'd not conceded a goal since making his debut against Ethiopia in Zambia's second match, kept the Libyans at bay.

That's until the shot-stopper from Zambia Air Force club Red Arrows took a knee to the head. He was stretchered off, face bloodied. Michael 'Spinks' Bwalya, from rival Zambia Army side Green Buffaloes, replaced Mulenga. Bwalya had made his international debut in the 1-0 opening defeat to Algeria.

Zambia defended doggedly. But intense Libyan pressure paid off before the interval. Forward Ali Al-Beshari levelled. The semi-final was now reduced to a 45-minute contest. It was tooth and nail until six minutes from regulation time when Al-Beshari scored again. Zambia went down fighting. But there would be a shot at redemption of sorts for Kaumba and Co. in the third-place play-off. It would be against the most unlikely of opponents.

Seconds before the end of their own semi-final, Ghana's Black Stars, with a 17-year-old Abedi Pele on the bench, trailed Algeria 2-1 after goals by Djamel Zidane and Salah Assad. Then Samuel Opoku Nti equalised, forcing extra time. In the 103rd minute, George Alhassan, on his way to winning the Golden Boot as top scorer with four goals, snatched a surprising Black Stars winner.

Algeria would not travel to the World Cup as African champions. Instead, their last competitive match – a little less than 90 days before their España 82 bow against West Germany in Gijón – would be the dreaded heartbreak match with Zambia for third place. Peter Kaumba was dazzling once again.

The winger, a natural right-footer who terrorised full-backs on the left flank, outshone Algerian aces Lakhdar Belloumi, Salah Assad and Rabah Madjer that afternoon, starting with a superb individual goal two minutes into the game. 'I just dribbled them and shot on goal' was Kaumba's recollection of his early dagger against the Desert Foxes. 'I think there were two [defenders]. I came from the wing, [cut] in and shot into the net.'

Midway through the first half, the burly Godfrey Munshya, winning his third and final international cap, put Zambia up 2-0. He later made way for Alex Chola, who'd started on the bench in the consolation match watched by a meagre 2,000 at the June 11 Stadium. It was Zambia's second major scalp of that AFCON after dethroning Nigeria. Overall, the third-placed finish affirmed that Zambia were still one of Africa's crack sides.

For disappointed Algerian fans, the loss to Zambia would be a distant memory three months later. At approximately 7.15pm local time on 16 June 1982, at Estadio el Molinón, Gijón, in Spain, Peruvian referee Enrique Labo Revoredo blew the whistle, signalling the end of what, until eight years later, would be the most earthshaking African victory at the World Cup. Three goals in an 18-minute second-half spell climaxed a gripping affair between then two-time World Cup winners West Germany and African newcomers Algeria.

Algerian speed and ingenuity had prevailed in a 2-1 result. Lakhdar Belloumi, still regarded by many as Algeria's greatest player, tucked in the 68th-minute winner from a low Salah Assad cross, a minute after German skipper Karl-Heinz Rummenigge had cancelled out Rabah Madjer's 54th-minute strike. In the end, the

Desert Foxes saw a surreal World Cup debut come to a cruel conclusion.

The Germans rebounded from their Algerian awakening to thrash Chile 4-1. Then they'd be principal actors in the World Cup's most controversial match of the last half century, one remembered as 'The Disgrace of Gijón'. Playing a day after a 3-2 Algerian win over Chile, the Germans knew that a victory by a one-goal margin over Austria in their final group match in Gijón would see them through to the next round. The Austrians led Group 2 with four points from results over Algeria (2-0) and Chile (1-0), at a time when a win only earned you two points.

Ten minutes into the German-Austria derby, Horst Hrubesch effectively settled the game with a stooping header. It was all the Germans needed. What followed was 80 minutes of insipid play that guaranteed both teams' qualification to the second round, at Algeria's expense. The fallout was universal. Most significantly, FIFA, after a postmortem, ruled that all final first-round group matches would be played on the same day and at the same time.

For Zambia's star performer in Libya, his first and only Africa Cup of Nations would be the apex of a cruelly short career. Peter Kaumba made the tournament's all-star team for his wizardry on the left wing – becoming the first Zambian attacker voted the best on the continent. He was the tournament's second-top scorer with three goals, one fewer than Ghana's George Alhassan's four.

Kaumba's Libya exploits caught the attention of AS Cannes in the French second tier and a long courtship ensued. After trials on the French Riviera in 1983, the club that would later launch the careers of Zinedine Zidane and Patrick Vieira offered Kaumba a contract. Enter the towering Simplice Zinsou, an Ivorian journalist turned businessman. He owned glamorous Ivorian club

Africa Sports and was plotting to conquer football on the continent. In the end, it came down to dollars and cents as Africa Sport hijacked Cannes' bid for Kaumba.

'I was told they offered a better deal [than Cannes]. It was about $3,000 per month, tax-free and free accommodation,' affirmed Kaumba.

Measly as that may sound for a professional player today, it was a king's ransom then, in Kaumba's context. An amateur by status, Africa's best left-winger was before his departure a $207-a-month records clerk for a utility that provided power to the copper mines. Africa Sports' professional contract amounted to a massive salary bump.

Alex Chola, Zambia's Congolese-born, French-speaking midfield maestro, was also part of Zinsou's ambitious plan to conquer African football. A horticulturist, professionally, he got the same offer. Chola and Kaumba joined Africa Sports in December 1983, teaming up there with two other signings from Ghana's triumphant 1982 Africa Nations Cup squad – midfielder Kofi Badu and veteran goalie Joseph 'The Cat' Carr. Africa Sports' bid for glory with a squad of continental *Galácticos* was an anticlimax. Shockingly, neither Kaumba nor Chola, Badu nor Carr could get AS past the first round of the 1984 African Cup of Champions Clubs competition, in its bid for the continent's biggest club prize. They bowed out 5-4 on aggregate to modest Togolese side Semassi. Africa Sports' quest was suddenly over. Kaumba and Chola's Ivorian experience lasted just eight months. Kaumba's career would end shortly on his return to Zambia. He blew the anterior cruciate ligaments in his right knee, in a cup game for Dynamos in August 1984. He was only 26.

With the ageing Alex Chola approaching a decade as a Zambian superstar, Kaumba's career-ending injury in 1984 meant that the baton had to be passed on to a new icon. The heir apparent was no surprise to Zambian fans. They'd flocked to stadiums in droves every weekend to watch his mesmerising skills as his notoriety with Mufulira Wanderers spread in the league. He was a left-winger too, one with so much intoxicating promise that on his international debut a year before Kaumba's career-ending injury, the star was deployed on the right flank, where he was equally comfortable. His name was Kalusha Bwalya – a name that would become synonymous with the most triumphant and tragic moments of Zambian football.

The son of an FAZ committee member, Kalusha together with his older brother Benjamin Bwalya Jr. had been mentored in their teens by a revered team-mate at modest Mufulira Blackpool: Alex Chola. Years later the brothers would both acknowledge learning some of their mesmerising skills from the ball-juggling Chola. Although born two years apart, the siblings were, skill-wise, like two peas in a pod. Out-and-out wingers at the onset, any differences were merely physical. Kalusha, a six-footer, tormented full-backs – to the enormous delight of fans – on the left. Benjamin, a couple of inches shorter than his kid brother, did the same to defenders on the right. To be a full-back playing against Mufulira Wanderers – Blackpool's celebrated neighbours whom the young brothers had joined in 1980 – meant 90 torrid minutes on the park.

Wanderers had unleashed the whiz kids on the league at the tail end of 1981. They were exciting enough to be considered by selectors for the 1982 Africa Cup of Nations in Libya that March. Benjamin, 20, made the initial cut but was dropped when the final squad was announced. In its final training game, the Libya-bound squad played a friendly in Kitwe with a Mufulira select side. Kalusha was in the latter.

'Buchi stadium was packed. I was playing on the left. Who was marking me? ... I think Milton Muke in that match, and Jack Chanda I think was number seven [right-winger]. So, I think in the first 15 minutes I had them pinned; both the number seven and number two [right-back] were following me. I dribbled them. Emmanuel Mwape was in goal. Ah! It was a beautiful game. We were leading, they equalised and I think they beat us 2-1 or something like that,' he recalled.

Restored on a short contract for the Libya assignment, Ante Bušelić was impressed by the insanely gifted albeit skinny 18-year-old Kalusha. The Croat had banked on a talented corps of young ex-Zambia schools internationals to mould Zambia into African titans during his first stint as coach and might have had flashbacks watching this emergent star.

'Bušelić after the match said, "No, this young man, we have to take him to Libya," but then [other] people said he's too thin! So, that was my introduction in 1982,' said Kalusha.

At any rate, Zambia would finish third in that AFCON in Libya, won by a Ghanaian side, that would introduce a teenage prodigy of its own – one Abedi Pele.

Kalusha and brother Benjamin, meanwhile, would have to wait until Zambia's first post-AFCON engagement, a two-match jaunt to Egypt that October, for their first international call. Then their careers would diverge.

A couple of weeks before reporting to the Zambia camp, Benjamin – 'Boga' to his family and friends – suffered a knee injury in a league match. It seemed innocuous at first but its ramifications would alter his career, leaving his young brother to blossom alone as the country's next superstar. Benjamin stayed home while Kalusha travelled to Cairo with a Zambia squad under the temporary tutelage of Wanderers boss Samuel 'Zoom' Ndhlovu and Power Dynamos technical adviser Bill McGarry. The latter was a former English international midfielder who'd managed Wolverhampton Wanderers and Newcastle United.

The results were stellar from the Zambian perspective. But Kalusha was no happy camper, despite a first victory over Egypt, and a rout at that.

He recalled, 'I made the squad and went to Egypt for two friendlies in October 1982. Bill McGarry was there. Zambia won that first match 5-3 and the second match was a draw [0-0]. And I remember that I was very upset. I still remember the hotel where we were staying, I think it was the Meridien hotel or something and I didn't play one minute, I was on the bench.

'I think we were on the seventh floor and everyone was there trying to get their allowances before we could fly out the following morning. And Bill McGarry comes in and he could see that I was very upset because I thought that I had trained well and I deserved a minute or two in the two matches but alas! He looked at me and I was looking upset. He said hello to everybody, then he came to me and pulled me aside and said I know that you are upset that you have not played. I thought you have trained well but, unfortunately, I could not use you. But then he said to me one [thing] that I will never forget my entire life. He said you will play more games than everybody who's here – in the Zambia national team – that's what he said. So I said, yeah, OK!'

McGarry's words would prove prophetic. Capped months later aged 19 against Sudan on 24 April 1983, when Kaumba, a naturally right-footed player who'd made his legend on the left wing for both club and country, was made to start on the right flank just to accommodate the new cap, Kalusha would wear the Zambia jersey for 19 years – half of them as captain. His documented 87 caps over the nearly two decades would not necessarily reflect his longevity. But that's only because once he'd made the switch to Europe in 1985, FAZ, like it would do with its European-based pros later, would only call on him for the big matches, relying on home-based players for other games, for financial reasons.

No other Zambian player has come close to matching his international longevity, nor his record of never being substituted. His 39 goals for his country remain third on the all-time scorers list behind record holder Godfrey 'Ucar' Chitalu's 79 from 111 appearances, and Alex Chola's 43 from 102. And it should be noted that Chitalu was an out-and-out striker.

Kalusha's move to Belgian side Cercle Brugge for a $25,000 fee in 1985 finally opened the door to Europe for Zambian players. The country's first European-based pros in the late 1960s, midfielders Freddie Mwila and Emment Kapengwe, had spent what amounted to a cameo with Aston Villa. This time, the best Zambian player of his generation would pique European interest in his country's young talent.

At the end of Kalusha's first season in Belgium, Cercle Brugge would tour Zambia with their new African star and return with another precocious talent on their books: midfielder Charles Musonda, Kalusha's erstwhile Mufulira Wanderers team-mate. Musonda would also cost Brugge $25,000.

The next year, Power Dynamos right-winger Lucky Msiska – an early pioneer of the stepover in the local league – and live wire centre-forward Stone Nyirenda from Nchanga Rangers would both head to Belgium, to KSV Roeselare and KRC Harelbeke respectively.

For Wanderers and Zambian fans in general, their greatest consolation after Kalusha's departure to Belgium was the emergence of Johnson Bwalya (no relation to Kalusha). Squat, fleet-footed and just 19, he slipped in almost seamlessly on Wanderers' left wing, to the horror of many a right-back anticipating some relief after Kalusha's wizardry. The revelation of the 1986 season was that Johnson would be crowned Footballer of the Year, and promptly signed by Swiss side FC Fribourg for an undisclosed fee.

In 1989, Johnson was joined at Fribourg by Geoffrey 'Free Joe' Mulenga, a slender left-footed player from Nchanga Rangers. And after his older brother Kalusha had joined Guus Hiddink's European Cup-winning PSV Eindhoven side – boasting Dutch goalie Hans van Breukelen, Belgian defender Eric Gerets, Dutch full-back Berry van Aerle and Brazilian goal poacher Romário – Joel Bwalya accepted Cercle Brugge's overtures in 1991.

Belated as it was – considering that by then many African nations above it, geographically, had scores of established professionals in Europe – this minor exodus would be a boon for Zambia.

7

'The Black Pearls'

BY JANUARY 1988, Zambia had gelled around Kalusha Bwalya and Charles Musonda. The duo, whose attacking partnership was nurtured at Mufulira Wanderers, had become the heart and soul of this latest Zambian squad.

Kalusha's reputation as Zambia's top player had been confirmed in the autumn of 1985 when Cercle Brugge, Belgian Cup winners that season, had paid Wanderers $25,000 for his signature. He became the first Zambian to sign professional terms for a European club since Freddie Mwila and Emment Kapengwe's brief stints with Tommy Docherty's Aston Villa in 1969. Before the start of the 1986/87 season, Kalusha was joined at Brugge – also for a $25,000 fee – by the precocious Charles Musonda. Belgian fans would dub them 'The Black Pearls' for their skills.

Musonda was a special talent from the beginning. And his rise was meteoric. He'd been introduced to league football by Mufulira Wanderers aged 15. His tremendous vision, incisive passing, and uncanny calm and control on the ball were light years beyond his age. Those qualities earned him the sobriquet 'Charlie Cool'. He'd played just a handful of games when he received a call-up to the national team in November 1985. The assignment was a four-nation tournament in Kinshasa also featuring the Zaire Leopards, Ivory Coast and Egyptian club side Ismaily, Musonda recalled. The Zambian squad flew to the Zairean capital in a Zambia Air Force Buffalo; not the first time – nor the last – that they'd used that transport plane. Their first game in Kinshasa would be against Zaire, and young Musonda would be pleasantly surprised when coach Brightwell Banda called his number. The teenager was to partner the experienced and cerebral Nkana link man Jericho 'Tanker' Shinde in the engine room. Not even a starter for Wanderers in the Zambian top flight the previous year, here was the teenage Musonda earning his first international cap against the dreaded Zaire Leopards. It would be a dream debut.

'So, we started playing against Zaire, [and] I went into the corner, on the right side,' Musonda remembered. 'Now I want to make a cross [but] the ball swerves into the goal. I hit a straight right [shot] two metres from the corner flag and [it] beat the goalkeeper who was at the near post.'

It was the only goal of the match and it set records. At 16 years, two months and 28 days, Musonda became the youngest-ever scorer for the Zambia national team. It also earned Zambia their first victory in Zaire (now DR Congo) against their most feared nemesis of the 70s.

After the match, Musonda recalled Ivory Coast's then French-based captain – whose name he couldn't remember – telling him and goalkeeper Efford Chabala that they ought to be playing in France. 'You must play in France. I play in France! You are too good! You and Efford Chabala. You are the best players in Zambia,' said the Ivorian.

Musonda riposted that it was his Zambia debut.

The captain would get a first-hand taste of Zambia's overall quality three days later: Jack Chanda was the scorer in Zambia's 1-0 victory over the Elephants. The only stain on the Zambian visit was a 3-1 loss to Egyptian club Ismaily

– the only known match between the Zambia national side and an African club team.

Six months later, Musonda caught Cercle Brugge's eyes. At the end of Kalusha's first season with Cercle, they took their first tour of Africa to Zambia – an ode to their great signing in Kalusha. They played three games – one against Kalusha's former club Mufulira Wanderers and two against the Zambia national team. Musonda played in all three games against the Belgians – all losses. But Brugge were smitten and would offer him a professional contract.

Swedish superstar Zlatan Ibrahimović once defined footballers as being of two kinds: those who 'play football' and those who 'think football'. The latter, the goalscoring colossus noted, were better players because 'the guys that play football, they are trained to play football. The guys that think football, they are made to play football. That's a big difference.'

Musonda belonged to the latter class. He made football seem so simple – easily validating Leonardo da Vinci's axiom of simplicity being the ultimate sophistication. For such a young player, he came seemingly preloaded with all the nous, vision and skills other top midfielders take years to develop. And it was perhaps no surprise that when the renowned Georges Leekens left Cercle Brugge in 1987 to manage Belgian giants Anderlecht he took Musonda, then 18, along.

What most Zambian fans didn't know in 1988 was that there was a tactical difference between Anderlecht's Musonda and the Charlie Cool who starred for the national team. The former was a ball-winning defensive midfielder tasked with breaking up attacks and distributing the ball, with that uncanny vision, to strikers. For Zambia, Musonda was a creative playmaker, whose defence-splitting passes, through balls and – when the opportunity presented itself

– mesmerising moves resulted in goals. He'd pull off the latter against the Black Stars with a bit of ball trickery his predecessor in that midfield role, Alex Chola, would have been proud of.

Playing under their former Mufulira Wanderers mentor Samuel 'Zoom' Ndhlovu, an exponent of the free-flowing football they'd been weaned on, Kalusha and Musonda crafted Zambia's resurgence as an African power in devastating fashion. After dispatching Botswana and Uganda, Zambia were drawn against four-time African champions Ghana in the final qualifying round for the 1988 Seoul Olympics. The two-legged affair that January would be only the second competitive encounter between the two nations after the Black Stars' 2-1 victory in the 1978 Africa Cup of Nations opener in Accra. Ghana had gone on to win that tournament 2-0 over Uganda; the first of two African titles they'd add to their ledger in the next four years.

The Black Stars were indeed a formidable proposition, even if they arrived in Lusaka for the first leg on 17 January without the phenomenal Abedi Pele. But Samuel Opoku Nti, on the books of the Ottmar Hitzfeld-managed Swiss side FC Aarau and considered Ghana's best player before the emergence of Abedi, was there. And so was the powerful future Eintracht Frankfurt and Leeds United cult hero Anthony Yeboah, then 21.

For their part, Zambia had their two game-changers: Kalusha and Charles Musonda. They would be the difference at another jam-packed Independence Stadium that Sunday afternoon. The following excerpt is from the author's match report published in the *Zambia Daily Mail* on Monday, 18 January 1988: 'It was the hard-fighting Zambians' individual flair, as expected, triumphing over a sleek and well-greased side that even in defeat kept the Ghanaian flag flying high. Wisdom Chansa, playing at centre-forward for the first time for Zambia, rammed in the ice-breaker five minutes into the second half, after the ingenious Charles Musonda from Belgium's Anderlecht, had cracked the Black stars' defence with a solo ball-juggling act. Thirteen minutes later, Kalusha Bwalya, recalled from Cercle Brugge, also in the Belgian league, stunned the Ghanaians with a spook goal that left goalkeeper Muhammad Odu motionless. The exciting Kalusha could have added a spectacular third in the 85th minute. He hit a dipping banana shot with his magical left foot, which just flashed past the crossbar.

'In a torrid opening 15 minutes, the Zambians stamped their mark on the game with mesmerising movements, particularly by the professionals, Kalusha, Musonda, Lucky Msiska and local midfielder Derby Makinka. The Black Stars were given the run around and would have fallen behind as early as the fifth minute when Makinka released Kalusha outside the penalty box. As Kalusha, in full flight, lined up [his] shot, a timely tackle by sweeper Aseidu Kwabena put the ball out for a corner. It was not until the 22nd minute that Ghana made a threatening attack, the dangerous left-winger Anthony Yeboah breaking through before skipper Fighton Simukonda felled him centimetres outside the penalty area. There were few chances created after that on both sides. The game clammed up and degenerated into a chess-like spectacle with both teams making probing moves but to no avail. However, Ghana nearly stole the lead when Yeboah clipped the upright with a powerfully driven low shot in the 40th minute.

'In the opening minutes after the break, the Black Stars took the initiative to attack, pushing forward with determination. Winger Ebo Smith came close again in the 47th minute, shooting wide from a dangerous position. In response, Zambia counter-attacked and came much closer to scoring than the visitors when full-back Kwesi Appiah fluffed a clearance and allowed Lucky Msiska, the fourth professional in the Zambian side, to shoot from an acute angle, albeit centimetres off target.'

It was goalless after an hour when Musonda trapped a high ball on his left thigh. He was in the Ghanaian third, his back to goal and a big defender breathing down his neck. He juggled the ball twice with his thigh, turned sharply to his left and, without the ball touching the ground and while in full stride, lobbed it to the versatile Chansa, Zambia's makeshift centre-forward on the day. A hard-running midfielder for Power Dynamos, and Kalusha's closest international mate, Chansa was another Zambian of his generation who could play in several positions. The ball from Charles Musonda had scarcely touched the ground when Chansa beat his marker Edward Aboagye and thumped a shot past Odu from close range, to thunderous approval from the crowd. Zambia had drawn first blood.

And like was always the case whenever they scored at home, the Zambians went for the jugular. The ensuing pressure paid dividends when Kalusha, coming in from the left, weaved past two defenders and fired a low and hard diagonal shot into the far corner. They would take a 2-0 lead to Accra for what everyone expected to be a hellacious return match before 40,000 fervently passionate fans of one of Africa's most successful national teams. The Black Stars had eliminated Senegal and a Roger Milla-led Cameroon in the previous rounds. They would not go out without a dogfight. Getting to Ghana, however, would be a harrowing tale of its own – an ominous warning again of the perils of using military aircraft for international fixtures.

Left-back Manfred Chabinga had turned 22 years old two months before facing the Black Stars in Lusaka on 17

January 1988. The tall Nchanga Rangers defender played his part as Zambia kept the African giants off the scoreboard. The job half done, Chabinga and his compatriots knew that they'd just stirred a hornets' nest ahead of the second leg in Accra. What they didn't know was that getting there would be just as terrifying.

In an era when it was much easier to book a commercial flight to Europe than to most African destinations, Zambia Air Force served as the Football Association of Zambia's default carrier. That was the case when the national team had to fly to West Africa to defend the 2-0 lead against Tony Yeboah and Co. ZAF laid on a Canadian-manufactured De Havilland DHC-5D Buffalo utility transport, one of six such aircraft in ZAF's inventory then. A red flag – the first of several leading to 27 April 1993 – went up even before the team's departure from Lusaka.

In an interview with this writer, Manfred Chabinga recollected that the Buffalo's flight path to Accra included refuelling stops in Congo-Brazzaville and Cameroon. However, ZAF – rather crucially – had neglected to obtain clearance to fly over Zaire (now DR Congo), then under the rule of the dictator and former military officer Mobutu Sese Seko, until the last minute. It wouldn't be the first such ZAF oversight, and it would result in the team's late departure, with consequences.

Said Chabinga, 'From Lusaka … I remember at that time the pilot trying to get permission so that we could use the Zaire airspace. Permission was granted, [but] by the time we reached DRC, the unfortunate part [was that], the one who was communicating with [the pilot] had already knocked off, so we had a problem. He never left a message that there would be a plane from Zambia, a military plane, carrying the players, so the plane was intercepted, so we were in trouble.'

It was 2am local time when the Buffalo was approaching Kinshasa, on its descent to its first scheduled refuelling stop, in Congo-Brazzaville, some 4.76km from the Zairean capital across the Congo River. It had been an uneventful flight to that point. But when the Buffalo was ordered to land in Kinshasa or risk being shot down, a nightmare ensued.

'The plane was uncomfortable – it was noisy, there was no air con when we landed [in Kinshasa], we nearly suffocated. We were struggling to breathe. It was hot,' recalled Chabinga. 'In the air it was cool, but [not] on the ground. It was a terrible experience.'

On board the Buffalo were coach Samuel 'Zoom' Ndhlovu and his entire squad for the return leg with Ghana. Having scripted the victory in Lusaka, Kalusha Bwalya and Charles Musonda had not been called back for the second leg and were not on the aircraft. But Zambia's three other European-based professionals then were. These were right-winger Lucky Msiska of Belgian club Roeselare, utility winger Johnson Bwalya with Swiss club Sion, and forward Stone Nyirenda from Harelbeke in Belgium. The French-speaking Bwalya would be a key player for the Zambians in the unfolding drama, acting as interpreter.

On the tarmac at Kinshasa's main airport, the green-camouflaged Buffalo was quickly surrounded by soldiers curious at the 'unannounced' military transport with close to two dozen young, athletic-looking passengers. That alone was a red flag to a jaundiced military regime in the eternally troubled former Belgian colony, always on alert because of a history of attempted coups and insurrections.

'The plane was searched,' recalled Chabinga. 'They couldn't believe that soccer players were using a military plane. They were saying, "No, we don't understand why you are using a Buffalo plane, a military plane – no, you are not soccer players – these are soldiers.'"

With Johnson Bwalya doing the French translation, team manager Godfrey 'Ucar' Chitalu was asked to hand over the players' passports in his possession. As team manager then (not to be confused with his head coach role later), Chitalu's role was more administrative than technical. One of his responsibilities was keeping the squad's travel documents and checking them in, as a group, on flights and in hotels.

What followed next was a bit of mind-baffling cultural shock mixed with an ample dosage of paranoia on the part of the Zairean inquisitors when they leafed through the passports.

'So, they didn't understand, why in Zambia we could have three names, as in [goalkeeper] Efford Chabala,' said Chabinga. 'David Efford Chabala? No … no … no! This guy is a crook! We have to detain this one! We can release the other players but this one, we have to detain him. How can he have three names?' A Zairean soldier protested to Johnson Bwalya interpreting for his Zambian compatriots.

Ironic, since the soldier's own commander-in-chief and head of state, born Joseph-Désiré Mobutu, had changed his name to Mobutu Sese Seko Kuku Ngbendu Wa Za Banga.

Fortunately for the Zambian contingent, according to Chabinga, the Zaireans were finally convinced by Johnson Bwalya's explanation that it was not uncommon for Zambians to have more than two names. 'He explained to them and then they understood,' said Chabinga.

Still, Zairean suspicions on the identity of the Buffalo's nearly two dozen athletic-type passengers lingered. That would mean confinement on the aircraft on the sweltering Kinshasa airport tarmac, nearly 300 miles (480km) south of the equator, for 12 hours with no food.

'We were there, I can say from 2am, and I think it was 2pm when we were released,' said Chabinga. 'It was uncomfortable on the plane. It was hot. It was a terrible experience.'

They were also out of food, having exhausted their packed meals aboard the craft before departure from Lusaka. Appeals to leave the steaming Buffalo and seek relief in one of Kinshasa airport's air-conditioned lounges were rebuffed.

'Johnson requested if we could go to the lounge and relax there, but still they were saying, "How can you go there? We don't know who you are … we think you guys are soldiers. If you want to go to the toilet, you have to be escorted." They were saying we don't trust you guys. You can do anything.'

The horrible ordeal for the players mistaken for a small invading commando force by the military regime finally ended around 2pm local time – with some fanfare. Still incredulous about the tracksuit-clad contingent in a Canadian-built military plane, the Zairean Air Force launched a jet fighter before allowing the ZAF turboprop craft to refuel and take off. The jet escorted the Buffalo as it departed Zairean airspace headed for Douala, Cameroon, 700 miles north-west.

The Buffalo flew over Congo-Brazzaville, its initial refuelling stop, and Gabon before landing without incident in Douala. There the Zambians spent the night reflecting on their Zairean ordeal. The big takeaway by the players was that flying on a military aircraft was extremely risky.

'What I can remember is that we were talking about it,' recalled Chabinga. 'We were saying that one day this plane will be shot down. It was dangerous as football players to use a military plane, we concluded. We were putting our lives at risk.'

Those concerns were soon forgotten in Accra where the Zambians had to defend a two-goal lead against an African giant with a berth at the Seoul Olympics at stake. A plane-load of Zambian fans and media – including this writer – had landed in the Ghanaian capital on a chartered Zambia Airways Boeing 707 a day before the 31 January match. The 200 or so Zambians in the crammed 40,000-capacity Accra Sports Stadium amounted to nary a bucketful in the raging Atlantic barely two miles away. So, not surprisingly, it was the home fans on song from the first whistle as the Black Stars made a rapid start.

Ghanaian confidence and strategy might have been bolstered by the absence of Kalusha Bwalya and Charles Musonda for the second leg. Chabinga recalled striker Samuel Opoku Nti, a member of the Black Stars' 1982 Africa Cup of Nations-winning squad, coming into the Zambian locker room with the Ghanaian inspection team before kick-off and enquiring about the duo.

'I can't see Kalusha Bwalya and Charles. Where are they,' asked Nti, who'd played in the first leg in Lusaka and had a first-hand look at the Zambian duo as they scripted the Black Stars' downfall.

'Are you hiding them?'

'They were scared of Kalusha and Charles,' said Chabinga.

Predictably, the absence of the erstwhile Mufulira Wanderers duo didn't help the visitors. The return leg was everything the Zambians had dreaded. Under pressure from kick-off, it would be another Mufulira product that would excel on the afternoon, his heroics earning him immediate notoriety in the former Gold Coast.

At the post-match reception at the Zambian team hotel, goalie David Efford Chabala was accosted by a lanky Ghanaian who proceeded to engage him in a lengthy conversation. The stranger happened to be a goalkeeper from a local club. Curious, this writer approached Chabala and inquired as to the nature of their chat. According to Chabala, the Ghanaian, impressed by his heroics against the Black Stars, wanted him to share the 'juju' or magic that made him so good.

I asked Chabala what his response was. 'Kuiposafye,' Chabala replied in ChiBemba (literal translation: you just have to throw yourself).

Chabala had done that spectacularly against the Black Stars earlier that day, producing one of those coruscating performances that by April 1993 had established him as the best goalkeeper on the continent. It started from kick-off with Ghana – sans Abedi Pele once again, but led by Tony Yeboah again – going at the visitors like an unrelenting tornado. The absence of Kalusha and Charles Musonda was a boon to the Ghanaians, and their young, bull-like striker Yeboah in particular. Built like an NFL linebacker, he'd been threatening in Lusaka, where Kalusha and Musonda had controlled the game. Almost 6ft of muscle and bone – Yeboah would repeatedly torment the Zambian rearguard built around lanky, 6ft 4in captain Fighton Simukonda and his central defensive partner, Ashols Melu, a robust former goalscoring midfielder.

'Chali fina! [He's heavy!],' Chabinga recalled Melu's cry to his team-mates at Yeboah's incredible strength, after the Zambian defence's early encounters with the Ghanaian wrecking ball.

Fourteen minutes into the match, the 22-year-old Chabinga, reprising his role at left-back, was drawn into the penalty box by another Ghanaian attack. He leapt high for a header, making contact with Yeboah and unbalancing his much bulkier opponent. Yeboah went sprawling and the referee pointed to the spot.

Penalty duty fell to Kofi Abbrey. In January 1988, Abbrey was a team-mate of George Weah – the future World Player of the Year and Liberian state president – at Cameroonian club Tonnerre Yaoundé. Abbrey had also been a hero in the 7-6 penalty victory over Libya in 1982 that had earned the Black Stars a then-record fourth Africa Cup of Nations title. The left-winger, who'd given Zambia right-back Peter Mwanza a torrid time, stepped up hoping to halve Ghana's deficit 16 minutes into the game.

But Chabala had Abbrey pegged.

'Ninjikata, nika ma left!' Chabala shouted to his defenders in ChiBemba. The translation in today's urban parlance being: 'I've got this. He's a leftie.'

Having long played and trained with a world-class left-footer named Kalusha, the seasoned Chabala was confident of plotting and impeding the trajectory of Abbrey's penalty even before the winger's foot made contact with the ball.

The hero of Zambia's first tournament victory when he saved three penalties in the 1984 East and Central African Challenge Cup, against Malawi, Chabala was so sure of stopping Abbrey that he told his defenders to be ready to clear the rebound.

Zambia skipper and fellow Wanderers club-mate Ashols Melu echoed Chabala's warning as Kofi Abbrey prepared to shoot. But the other defenders were still incredulous, conceded Chabinga. That's until Chabala dived to his right to block Abbrey's effort, just as he'd said he would. The ball was hastily booted out of play, 30 years later, Chabinga would swear that the referee got his next decision wrong.

'It was a throw-in, not a corner kick after Chabala's penalty save,' argued Chabinga. 'We almost confronted the referee, but Chabala said, "No, no, no. This is West Africa. Let's just fight until the 90 minutes."'

From the corner, Yeboah powerfully headed into the net. The packed Accra Sports Stadium exploded. Chabala and Zambia had 73 minutes to prevent a second goal. The odds looked daunting. It was pretty much one-way traffic after that.

'We were under pressure throughout,' said Chabinga.

It seemed a matter of time before the Black Stars – with Yeboah bullying Melu and Fighton Simukonda, and Abbrey still tormenting right-back Peter Mwanza – would level the aggregate score. Yeboah, big, thick-set yet nimble and quick, would score numerous spectacular goals in his illustrious career, including a wonder strike from at least 35 yards for Leeds United against Liverpool in the Premier League on 21 August 1995. But Chabala would parry, punch and block everything directed his way that gripping Sunday afternoon in Accra. Zambia would lose 1-0 but prevail 2-1 on aggregate to qualify for the Seoul Olympics.

After the post-match reception, where Chabala had been accosted by the awestruck, juju-seeking local goalie, the travelling Zambian supporters and media left for the airport. As the chartered Zambia Airways Boeing 707 taxied down the runway, several fans including this writer caught a glimpse of the ZAF Buffalo that had brought the national team to Ghana. The distinctive Zambian flag – fish eagle, wings spread out and hovering over a red, black and orange rectangular block against a green background – was visible on its tail rudder in the dim light outside. The Buffalo's long hopscotch flight back to Zambia would be uneventful.

'We used the same route flying back,' said defender Manfred Chabinga, the highlight of his young career a few months ahead in South Korea. 'Ghana to Cameroon then Kinshasa. [This] time we had no problems.'

8

Seoul Exploits

THE 16-TEAM football tournament at the Seoul Olympics had enough talent to rival many a World Cup. Brazil alone had goalkeeper Cláudio Taffarel, Jorginho and the trio of Romário, Mazinho and Bebeto, who six years later would perform one of the most memorable World Cup celebrations ever – the spontaneous 'three men and a baby' revelry en route to victory at USA 94. West Germany had Jürgen Klinsmann. Italy boasted Stefano Tacconi, Ciro Ferrara, Mauro Tassotti and Gianluca Pagliuca. There was Davor Šuker, Srečko Katanec and Dragan Stojković from the former Yugoslavia – with midfielder Stojkovic, two summers later, making the World Cup all-star team at Italia 90. And from Nigeria came the gentle giant Rashidi Yekini, who would make an early mark at USA 94 with the Super Eagles' first World Cup goal and an unforgettable net-shaking celebration. These were players who would make many a football headline in the years to come. It was a milestone competition, in retrospect, as Olympic football morphed from amateur status to a fully professional event. The 1984 Games in Los Angeles had begun that process. For the first time in Olympic history, professional players, regardless of age, albeit with less than five senior caps, were allowed to participate. Four years later in Seoul, the latter rule was relaxed. It allowed emerging stars such as Klinsmann, fresh from West Germany's UEFA Euro 1988 campaign, on to the Olympic stage.

Italian centre-half Ciro Ferrara – another Euro 1988 veteran – and this rendition of the *Azzurri* would be Zambia's first competitive European opposition since Godfrey Chitalu and Co. faced the USSR at the Moscow Games in 1980. But first Kalusha Bwalya and Zambia would make their bow – in a Group B that also included Guatemala – against Iraq on 17 September. Nearly 30,000 curious fans packed the Daejeon Hanbat Stadium in Daejeon, 140km south of Seoul, to watch the early evening clash between the African and Asian confederation envoys. They would not be disappointed.

Coached by Samuel Ndhlovu, his country's first football superstar as a master dribbler for Mufulira Wanderers in the 1960s, Zambia – with a spine comprising current and former Mufulira Wanderers players – had arrived in Seoul in top form.

'The most important thing we did for the Olympics was prepare well. And I think Zambia was in top form,' recalled Kalusha, then on Cercle Brugge's books in the Belgian top flight.

Other European-based professionals in the Zambian squad included midfielder Charles Musonda, then with Anderlecht, right-winger Johnson Bwalya from Swiss side FC Sion, and the KSV Roeselare duo of striker Stone Nyirenda and winger Lucky Msiska. They all joined Zambia's pre-Olympics camp in Lusaka in August, fresh from their respective clubs' pre-season training. With the Zambian domestic season, which ran from March to November back then, approaching its final stretch, the home-based players were also in peak form. Ndhlovu's intense camp fine-tuned the cohesion between the pros and the local players.

The local preparations ended with two friendlies against nettlesome neighbours Malawi a week before departure for Seoul. The visitors were blown away 4-1 in Kitwe and 7-1 in Lusaka.

'The team was playing some fantastic, fantastic football before we left,' said Kalusha. 'The kind of football we played was incredible.'

It showed in spots in Zambia's opener against Iraq in Daejeon on 17 September, after Ahmed Radhi – later voted 1988 Asian Footballer of the Year – beat Efford Chabala from the penalty spot in the 36th minute. Stone Nyirenda equalised a minute before the interval as the Zambians rallied back. Then the game took a turn, providing a rare insight into the Zambian camp.

In 2018, left-back Manfred Chabinga recounted what transpired as the game approached the hour mark at the 20,618-capacity Daejeon Hanbat Stadium. 'The floodlights were very powerful, then they dimmed them,' he said. That posed a quandary for coach Samuel 'Zoom' Ndhlovu on the Zambian bench. Zoom's relationship with Efford Chabala went back to his days as Mufulira Wanderers coach and he was one of a few privy to the outstanding goalkeeper's only known Achilles heel. Chabala's night vision was less than 20/20. Luckily, it was never an issue in Zambia where all but the odd game kicked off at 3pm local time.

'So, Ba Zoom assumed that since Efford was known to have poor vision at night, they should make a change,' Chabinga recollected. 'It didn't come from Efford; he never complained that he couldn't see.'

And so, for the first and only time in his international career, Chabala was substituted. On came Richard Mwanza to earn his first Zambia cap after five years then as Chabala's understudy. What no one knew is how risky the change was with only two goalies in the 20-man Zambian squad. Unbeknownst to his team-mates and coaches, Mwanza was nursing a swollen finger injured in training. He didn't tell Zoom of his discomfort even when summoned off the bench.

Still, six minutes after Mwanza's entry, Kalusha scored to put Zambia ahead. The lead lasted for just five minutes – or 11 minutes into Mwanza's debut. Chabinga recalled the injured Mwanza being beaten by a powerful drive from the centre circle, in what would be midfielder Karim Allawi's last goal in 91 caps for the Iraqis. It ended 2-2.

That was the final straw for the enraged Chabala, on the bench where he'd been consigned. Peeved by his substitution and then incensed by the Iraqi equaliser, he exploded in ChiBemba. 'You know *abene* Efford, *tabatemenwe ukulusa* [he didn't like losing],' said Chabinga, before launching into an impersonation of the incandescent goalie's locker room rant. 'What's this?! I was fine! I didn't say that I couldn't see! I always say when I can't see! I could see fine and you took me out. See, they've equalised!'

All would be forgotten 48 hours later, and with no hard feelings.

Chabala was back between the sticks against Italy at the Gwangju Mudeung Stadium in Gwangju, 268km south of Seoul, on 19 September. It was a strong Italian side Zambia faced in front of 9,800 fans. By 1988, Juventus stopper Stefano Tacconi had won all but one of the international club competitions recognised by UEFA. His accolades included the European Cup, the UEFA Cup Winners' Cup, the UEFA Super Cup and the Intercontinental Cup. Two years after Seoul, Tacconi became the first goalie to win all the international club competitions when Juve lifted the UEFA Cup.

Against the first and only African opposition of his illustrious career, Tacconi would shift four goals – the most conceded by an Italian team since the 4-1 Pelé-scripted rout in the 1970 World Cup Final. Kalusha Bwalya, in the greatest virtuoso performance by an African player against a European side at national level, would bag a hat-trick against the masters of *catenaccio*.

Tacconi would get his fingertips to Kalusha's first effort, a hard grass-cutter from the left that would nestle in the Italians' bottom-left corner. Charles Musonda's through ball had released Kalusha on a quick break initiated by Wisdom Chansa in the Zambian half.

Kalusha got his second goal from a clever free kick some 25 metres from goal on the left side of the penalty box. The Italians set up a loose two-man wall, but from Tacconi's positioning near his left post, he evidently expected a high ball into the box. Before taking the free kick, Kalusha pointed to the same far-post area, as if telegraphing his shot. Instead, the left-footed wizard brilliantly curved the ball around the wall from the left side and into the gaping net on Tacconi's right, leaving the goalkeeper stranded.

Tacconi was beaten again, spectacularly, for Zambia's third goal. It was a long-range Johnson Bwalya effort with the trajectory of a ballistic missile. It was set up by Charles Musonda who made a square pass to Johnson and darted to the right flank, taking a defender with him. That created space for the squat and explosive Johnson to accelerate into after deftly swerving past his marker. From no less than 30 yards, Johnson, aged 20, unleashed a fierce shot that first soared high then began to drop. Left arm outstretched, Tacconi leapt high to parry the ball, but it dipped just beyond his reach and into the net.

Kalusha completed his hat-trick – and Charles Musonda his third assist – after another through ball by the latter with the outside of his right foot like the Brazilian greats of old used to do. One-on-one, Kalusha had all the time to wrong-foot Tacconi. Zambia had slain a footballing giant 4-0.

Reflecting on that unforgettable victory three decades later, Kalusha credited it to a prime Zambia team playing its best football. 'The core of the team had been together for a long time – let's say since 1984 when we won the East and Central African Challenge Cup with coach Brightwell Banda,' he said.

A year later, in 1985, Banda's squad would eliminate Cameroon from the 1986 World Cup qualifiers 5-2 on aggregate after the shell-shocked Indomitable Lions – sans a few of their European-based stars – had left Lusaka 4-1 in arrears. At full strength in Yaoundé two weeks later, Roger Milla and Co., who'd gone unbeaten at the 1982 World Cup in Spain despite bowing out in the first round, could only salvage a 1-1 draw.

That was the level of football – with relatively new blood in Derby Makinka, Charles Musonda, Johnson Bwalya and Stone Nyirenda – that Zambia reproduced at the Seoul Olympics.

Proving that the rout of Italy was no fluke, Zambia returned to the Gwangju Mudeung Stadium 48 hours later to post another 4-0 victory. Guatemala were the victims this time in another first-time encounter between the two nations. Goalless at half-time, the Zambians exploded in the second half, the 23-year-old Makinka and Kalusha each notching a brace. It was methodical, as Kalusha recalled.

'[Goalkeeper] Efford would get the ball, throw it, and the build-up would start from the back. And the team had such talented midfielders; so strong, ball winners, passers of the ball, and runners up front. We could shoot, we could score, we could do everything, dribble. If you look at the tapes, especially the game against Italy, it was incredible that we were able to play that kind of football,' Kalusha reminisced.

A little more than two hours after Kalusha and Co. had seen off Guatemala in Gwangju to win Group B, West Germany – with a core of Bundesliga veterans and new star Jürgen Klinsmann up front – kicked off against Sweden in the Group A finale in Daegu. After romps over PR China and Tunisia, the Germans led Sweden by a point.

A draw against a Swedish side that included defender Roland Nilsson, winger Anders Limpar and forward Martin Dahlin would seal the group. But the Teutons surprisingly lost 2-1 when Leif Engqvist and Peter Lönn cancelled out Fritz Walter's opener. That meant that the Swedes topped Group A and would have to face Italy in the quarter-finals. Germany, as runners-up, got Group B winners Zambia. It was a match-up that *Die Mannschaft*, coached by 1970 World Cup veteran Hannes Löhr, would have relished anytime.

Zambia, meanwhile, were confident of claiming another major scalp. Perhaps too confident.

Reflecting on the Zambia-West Germany quarter-final more than three decades later, Kalusha said, 'I think that we should have changed tactics, you know, when you [think back]. I thought that we should have employed another tactic,' mused the slayer of the *Azzurri*. 'Let's put the ball in the "mixer" because we had such intelligent midfielders – especially Charlie and Derby, they were always where the ball was – so we'd get the second ball and then play to the front, which was our strength, going forward. And, so when you think about it now, after analysing – after many years and with the experience we have, we should have adopted a different tactic.' They didn't and paid the price.

But based on full-back Manfred Chabinga's recollection, Kalusha's observation was a generous critique of what went wrong and why. Chabinga pointed the finger squarely at coach Ndhlovu who surprised his players at the pre-game tactical meeting hours before the game.

'He said no long balls,' recalled Chabinga. 'So, you have to start from the back [with short passes], from the back to the midfield and then to the attacking third.'

Basically, Ndhlovu wanted Zambia to play out of defence throughout the game. The players were incredulous. That was not their style. Charles Musonda, then playing for Georges Leekens at Anderlecht, was the first to protest. Chabinga remembered him saying, '*Ba Coach aba basungu, balatusepa. tiyeni tuteye bola yesu* [Coach, these are Europeans. They will beat us. Let's just play our usual game]. These people are able to read the game quickly. I know them. *Ba la tusepa* 4-0 [They will beat us 4-0].'

Further rattling the squad ahead of Zambia's biggest game outside Africa yet was dynamic right-winger Johnson Bwalya, 5ft 6in of pure power and pace, raising his hand and saying that he wasn't ready for the game. The 20-year-old from FC Sion had scored that spectacular goal against Italy but announced that he'd only play the first half against the Germans. He didn't elaborate why.

Giving his take on the pre-quarter-final kerfuffle in a separate interview with this writer, Musonda said, 'What the coach [Ndhlovu] decided was let's try to build up from behind, but then we argued that they [were] going to kill us because we are going to be losing the ball every three passes. We'd rather play long balls, the strikers can hold [the ball] and we can join them. But we couldn't convince the "Big Man" [Ndhlovu] so we ended up playing the short passes and we were losing the ball every two or three passes and they'd score. By the time it was half-time, the game was out of hand.'

The first-half damage was wrought by the emergent Jürgen Klinsmann, then on VfB Stuttgart's books and less than two years away from helping West Germany win their third World Cup with his three goals at Italia 90. He'd earned the first of his 108 international caps for his country in 1987, in a 1-1 draw with Brazil. Against Zambia, Klinsmann notched a brace after Wolfgang Funkel's 18th-minute penalty.

The half-time team talk was predictably muted, Chabinga recalled. What could Ndhlovu say after his tactics – questioned by his European-based stars – had backfired spectacularly? So, in the second half Zambia went out and played their usual football. Those 45 minutes were more competitive until the last minute when Klinsmann completed his hat-trick and a 4-0 rout.

'We were demoralised about the strategy,' said Chabinga. '*Twale itina sana li Zoom* [We feared Zoom very much].'

'Any other team, and Zambia could have probably come back,' said Kalusha. 'But Germany [had] Klinsmann, and he took advantage. And for every mistake Zambia made, he punished us heavily. So, we were already [down] quite early in the game. So not taking away anything that Zambia had done at this juncture at the Seoul Olympics, I think Zambia was probably the first team from Black Africa to beat a big team convincingly, playing good football.'

The Zambians placed fifth overall out of 16 teams on the honours table – behind gold medal winners the USSR, silver medalists Brazil, the Germans and Italy in that order. Personally, it was a career-changing tournament for Kalusha. The former out-and-out left-winger had announced his world-class skills – and Zambia their potential. Kalusha's six goals tied him in joint second with the USSR's Igor Dobrovolski on the scoring chart. Brazil's

Romário, 22 but lethal even then, was the Golden Boot winner with seven goals. Kalusha's Seoul exploits would earn him not only the 1988 African Footballer of the Year award, but also a move from modest Cercle Brugge – who'd paid Mufulira Wanderers $25,000 for his signature more than two years earlier – to defending European champions PSV Eindhoven. There he teamed up with Romário under Guus Hiddink in 1989 – winning two Dutch titles and one KNVB Cup.

9

Group of Death

THE JÜRGEN Klinsmann-inspired drubbing in Gwangju would be Zambia's first defeat with erstwhile Mufulira Wanderers and Cercle Brugge team-mates Kalusha Bwalya and Charles Musonda both on the pitch for 90 minutes. The duo that Belgian fans had dubbed 'The Black Pearls' would only lose two more games with Zambia, when starting and finishing together. And that would be against some of Africa's top sides.

Their second loss together would be against Morocco four months later, when forward Abdelfettah Rhiati's 39th-minute goal edged the Zambians 1-0 in Rabat in a World Cup qualifier. There would be one more defeat with the dynamic duo in tandem for an entire match – also 1-0, also in a World Cup tie later that year – and then no more.

That initial setback to Morocco in Rabat on 8 January 1989 marked the start of Zambia's 1990 World Cup campaign. It was the second round of the African qualifiers. And Zambia – after Rwanda withdrew in the first round – ended up in the dreaded 'Group of Death' that's ubiquitous to most qualifying competitions in football. Morocco, Zaire and Tunisia – who'd all previously qualified for the World Cup when Africa had just one spot – were Zambia's opposition in Group D. Buoyed by their Olympic exploits, Zambia beat them all at Lusaka's Independence Stadium.

On 22 January, two weeks after the Rabat loss, the Zambians reproduced their Seoul Olympic form against an old rival. They downed Zaire 4-2 in the first competitive encounter between the two neighbours since the Africa Cup of Nations Final replay in Cairo 15 years earlier. Once Zambia's bogey team, the Leopards trailed 3-1 at the interval after an early mauling.

It was 3-0 some 25 minutes in, with the KSV Roeselare duo of Stone Nyirenda and Lucky Msiska netting in the tenth and 17th minutes respectively. Home-based link man Derby Makinka added a third in the 25th minute. But the Leopards' Eugène Kabongo, a free-scoring forward on his stints with French clubs RC Paris, Lyon and Bastia, pulled one back on the half hour. Physically imposing, Kabongo struck again three minutes after Kalusha had put Zambia 4-1 up after 75. It was Zambia's most emphatic victory in a competitive match over their northern neighbours.

Five months later, on 11 June, Tunisia, the first African nation to triumph at the World Cup when they rebounded from Vázquez Ayala's penalty to beat Mexico 3-1 in a Group 2 match at the 1978 finals in Argentina, were the next to fall. Makinka's long-range strike with his left foot from the right side in the 73rd minute being the only goal of a tense encounter.

Then another old foe came a-calling. On 25 June, Morocco made their third visit to Independence Stadium for a World Cup tie. And like the first time in November 1973, the Atlas Lions arrived in Lusaka with a seasoned squad of World Cup veterans. Three years earlier at Mexico 1986, they'd become the first African team to top a World Cup group and advance to the knockout round. In a Group F comprising 1966 World Cup winners England, 1966 World

Cup semi-finalists Portugal and 1974 semi-finalists Poland, Moroccan goalie and skipper Badou Zaki, and compatriots Mohamed Timoumi, Aziz Bouderbala, Abderrazak Khairi and the Merry brothers Krimau and Mustafa tore up the form book.

Drilled by Brazilian José Faria, Morocco, with Zaki superb, played both Poland and England to goalless draws. Then like a predator pouncing on the perceived weakest of the group, the Atlas Lions mauled Portugal 3-1 in their last match to top the group. Khairi bagged a first-half brace while Krimau Merry got the third, in the second half.

Morocco continued to run the gauntlet in the second round. Two days after the Atlas Lions had beaten Portugal in Jalisco to win Group F, Group E favourites West Germany, losing finalists in 1966 and winners in 1974, slipped 2-0 to Denmark in Querétaro. Defeat meant the Franz Beckenbauer-coached *Die Mannschaft* finished second to the talented Danes – a side boasting Manchester United phenom Jesper Olsen, Liverpool midfield workhorse Jan Mølby and the emerging Michael Laudrup. A fortuitous loss perhaps, once again, for the Germans as that meant a second-round date for them with Morocco while the Danes' reward was a run-in with Spanish predator Emilio Butragueño, aka *el Buitre* – 'the Vulture'.

West Germany vs. Morocco was a rematch of the two nations' first World Cup encounter in Mexico 16 years earlier. Gerd Müller's late goal had snatched a 2-1 victory then. This one would be just as close. It was goalless after 87 minutes at the Estadio Universitario in Nuevo León with Badou Zaki in incredible form. That's when German skipper Karl-Heinz Rummenigge was fouled. Lothar Matthäus, in the second of his five World Cup tournaments, drilled a low flying shot with his right foot from a 25-yard free kick. The ball eluded a three-man wall, took a hop and nestled in the net. The Germans had nicked it once again and would go on to reach the final.

That was the pedigree Morocco brought to Lusaka. They were led by Zaki, whose World Cup heroics had earned him the 1986 African Footballer of the Year award and a move to Spanish club Mallorca. Still, they'd fall behind before the interval when Charles Musonda slammed in Kenneth Malitoli's lay-off, punctuating Zambia's first-half dominance. The lead held until the 73rd minute of an absorbing encounter that featured three of the last four African Footballer of the Year winners. From a 25-yard free kick, Mohamed Timoumi, then on Belgian side KSC Lokeren's books, levelled. Up and over a six-man wall went the powerfully struck ball before it dipped past Efford Chabala's salmon-like dive to the right and into the net.

But what Africa's 1985 Footballer of the Year could do, 1988's Kalusha could also – and in crunch time too. There were three minutes of regulation time left when Malawian referee Bestor Kalombo awarded Zambia a free kick a good 30 yards out. The distance was further than Kalusha's set piece against Stefano Tacconi and Italy in Gwangju the previous summer. And Zaki, who'd conceded just two goals in four games at the 1986 World Cup, was better positioned on the goal line than Tacconi had been. So Kalusha went for power, smashing the ball low and hard with his gem of a left foot. It curved around the Moroccan wall, bounced some four yards in front of the diving Zaki and beat him at the foot of the far post. Zambia had won it late with a Kalusha masterpiece eerily similar to Matthäus's winner in Nuevo León. It wouldn't be Kalu's last dagger against the Atlas Lions.

What it was, however, was the apex of Zambia's Italia 90 qualifying campaign. Atop Group D with six points from four games (when two points were awarded for a win), Zambia's old road woes would return to haunt them. They'd slip 1-0 in Kinshasa to Zaire in their penultimate qualifier. And needing just a point to hold off second-placed Tunisia and advance to the four-nation knockout round, the Zambians went to Tunis without the injured Kalusha. They succumbed 1-0 to midfielder Mohamed Ali Mahjoubi's world-class free kick from the penalty arc 15 minutes from time. Another World Cup campaign that had promised so much had ended in bitter disappointment.

A year later, a sense of what might have been likely gripped many a Zambian fan as they admiringly watched old rivals Cameroon, who'd defeated Tunisia 3-0 on aggregate to qualify for the World Cup, light up Italia 90. The Indomitable Lions would stun Diego Maradona and his defending world champions Argentina 1-0 at Milan's San Siro thanks to François Omam-Biyik's stooping second-half header in the tournament opener.

Five years earlier in Lusaka, as a lanky 19-year-old, Omam-Biyik had nodded in Cameroon's consolation goal in a 4-1 rout by Zambia. And three months before Italia 90, he'd been in the Cameroon side edged 1-0 by Zambia on Webby Chikabala's 58th-minute goal at the Africa Cup of Nations in Algeria – a tournament both Kalusha and Charles Musonda missed. At Italia 90, they would go on to beat the coruscating Gheorghe Hagi's Romania 2-1, with a late brace by the oldest man to score at a World Cup, a 38-year-old substitute named Roger Milla. With that win, Cameroon went on to top a group that included the Soviet Union.

Then the world would watch in awe as Milla, an erstwhile veteran of the French league, came off the bench again in the Indomitable Lions' last-16 clash with Colombia at what's now the Stadio Diego Armando Maradona in Naples. He'd been a clinical finisher for clubs such as

Bastia, Saint-Étienne and Montpellier in his 17 years in France. Against Colombia and their eccentric goalie René Higuita, he was Maradonesque. Two goals in a two-minute span in extra time – the second one after dispossessing Higuita halfway in the Colombian half – scripted a 2-1 victory while confirming Milla as one of the stars of the tournament. He'd powered the Lions to the World Cup quarter-finals, the first African nation to do so, and would inspire them to a near-upset of England in an epic encounter before succumbing 3-2 in extra time to a Gary Lineker penalty.

Zambia, who'd lost only one of four meetings with the Lions between 1985 and June 1990, could only watch in admiration. A side whose core they'd demolished 5-2 on aggregate in the 1986 World Cup qualifiers had elevated African football to unprecedented heights before a global TV audience in the billions. Its own Olympic core – including goalkeeper Efford Chabala, midfielders Derby Makinka, Charles Musonda and the inspirational Kalusha still intact – Zambia's attention quickly turned to USA 94. It would be the first World Cup in North America and Zambia intended to be there.

FIFA had allotted Africa a third berth at USA 94 – just rewards for the continent's strong showing at Italia 90. It wasn't just Cameroon's heroics. In Group F, Egypt had held European champions the Netherlands and their formidable trio of Ruud Gullit, Marco van Basten and Frank Rijkaard 1-1. They'd also held the Republic of Ireland to a goalless draw before slipping 1-0 to eventual semi-finalists England, captained by Peter Shilton and including all-time greats Paul Gascoigne, John Barnes and Gary Lineker. Consistently one of Africa's top teams, Zambia's odds of finally punching a ticket to the World Cup never looked brighter with the continent guaranteed a third spot in 1994.

* * *

In the intervening years before Zambia's anticipated qualification for USA 94, significant political changes in the southern African nation occurred. They had a tremendous socio-economic impact on the country of then 8.2 million people. Zambia's command control economy, heavy reliance on a depressed mining industry dominated by copper and dissatisfaction with the one-party political system spelled doom for the country's founding president and football aficionado, Kenneth Kaunda.

In 1991, after 27 years in power and the reintroduction of a multiparty system, Kaunda was voted out of office. He was replaced by trade union leader Frederick Chiluba. Listed at just 5ft, the diminutive Chiluba, who'd long donned the mantle of de facto opposition leader during the single-party era, initiated an economic liberalisation programme. It meant the privatisation of many industries including the mines that had been nationalised during the Kaunda era, and that had long been the bedrock of Zambian football. Zambians were overjoyed but the loss of state subsidies was painful. There were lay-offs and retrenchments and with the HIV/AIDs pandemic a growing public health issue in southern Africa, Zambia entered a bleak period.

Yet, aside from the politically necessitated discontinuation of the national football team's 'KK XI' moniker following Kenneth Kaunda's departure, Zambian football remained relatively immune from these seismic changes in the country. Ironically, football seemed to grow from strength to strength, enhancing its role as the nation's panacea or primary source of joy amid the increasing hardship. There were successes both at club and national level.

A year after Nkana had become the first Zambian club to reach the African Cup of Champion Clubs Final, where they'd lose on penalties to JS Kabylie of Algeria, crosstown rivals Power Dynamos went one better. Under the tutelage of Freddie Mwila and former Scottish international striker Jimmy Bone – Alex Ferguson's last signing at St Mirren – Power would bag the 1991 African Cup Winners' Cup. On 1 December, the Kitwe-based club developed by Welshman Arthur Davies completed a 5-4 aggregate victory over cup holders BCC Lions of Nigeria to earn Zambia its first continental club silverware.

A week later, Zambian fans had more to cheer about. On 7 December, Samuel 'Zoom' Ndhlovu sent out a team of home-based players against Kenya in the Confederation of East and Central African Football Association Final in Kampala, Uganda. Zambia had participated in the annual CECAFA tournament since 1973. They'd won the competition – incepted in 1926 as the Gossage Cup – for the first time in 1984 with goalkeeper Efford Chabala the hero in a 3-0 penalty shoot-out victory over Malawi. Chabala kept another clean sheet once again as Kenya's Harambee Stars were beaten 2-0. It would be Zoom's only silverware in five years as national coach.

Zoom's Zambia had morphed since the Italia 90 qualifying cycle. In a nutshell, the team had gelled into a tight unit – solid between the posts, in defence and midfield, and just lacking in one critical position – a consistent, goalscoring striker.

Former free-scoring attacking midfielder Ashols Melu – nicknamed 'Hot-shot' by this writer for what was arguably the hardest shot in Zambian football – had been replaced as defensive pillar by another erstwhile midfielder turned defensive anchor. At the age of 31, Melu had been the oldest member of the Zambian squad at the 1988 Seoul Olympics. His replacement, the steely Nkana defender Eston Mulenga, was ten years younger.

Nicknamed 'Yellowman' for his light complexion, Mulenga was not your archetypical centre-back. He stood no more than 5ft 9in. But he read the game well, was a tenacious man-marker, an uncompromising tackler and had an amazing vertical leap. He was also comfortable on the ball, thanks to his previous incarnation as a link man. Mulenga was capable of making surging runs into midfield. Until April 1993, the Zambian back line tasked with protecting the incomparable Efford Chabala between the posts would be built around 'Yellowman'.

Zoom, post-Seoul Olympics, had also capped two industrious full-backs. John Soko, slender, quick, 5ft 9in and more valued for his defensive skills than his overlapping abilities, slotted into the right-back position. Whiteson Changwe, from Godfrey Chitalu's Kabwe Warriors, made the left his domain. Both were no-nonsense tacklers who would remain automatic picks until 27 April 1993.

Before earning his first cap, Changwe was better known as the player who had ended the career of one of Zambia's greatest players ever and – as it transpired – his future national team coach. The left-back was 23 when Alex Chola, then 31 and the rookie coach of Power Dynamos decided to suit up against Warriors in the Independence Cup Final at Lusaka's Independence Stadium in 1987.

This writer, then a senior reporter for the *Zambia Daily Mail*, recalls meeting Chola at the Ridgeway Hotel reception desk and taking down the Dynamos line-up from him a couple of hours before the final. Clearly visible underneath Chola's thin white T-shirt was a yellow Dynamos' jersey with '9' – for a long time his number – emblazoned on it.

Chola, indeed, started the final. And moments after kick-off he displayed a lot of his old ball wizardry, including an audacious chest pass to Pearson Mwanza for Dynamos' opening goal. Not long after that, Chola, with a free role on the pitch, drifted to the right wing where a pass was threaded to him. Before he could make contact with the ball, Warriors' left-back came sliding in, making contact with Chola.

The vision that remained for those in attendance was that of a football icon – who'd made a career bamboozling defenders and skilfully evading tackles in his prime – being hurled in the air, his right ankle at a grotesque angle. He rolled twice before Dynamos' medics sprinted on to the pitch. The fractured ankle was the first and last major injury of Chola's illustrious playing career. It ended there and then. His stats from the two clubs he played for – Mufulira Blackpool and Power Dynamos – are non-existent. But the ball-juggling attacking midfielder nicknamed 'Computer' retired with 100 international caps and 43 goals – second only to Godfrey Chitalu's documented 76 goals from 108 Zambia appearances.

At any rate, Zambia's midfield and attack were also in transition post-Seoul. In the engine room, Alex Chola's successor as playmaker extraordinaire, Charles Musonda – who was just 19 when his three assists helped sink Italy 4-0 at the Olympics – had by 1990 began to experience flare-ups in his right knee. It was, sadly, the beginning of the end of his precocious career. In a 2022 interview, Musonda would tell this writer, 'People misunderstood my career. The only period I played consistently was 1987 to 1990. Once 1990 started, I started having problems with my knee.'

This was in response to criticism by some fans because of his unavailability for Zambia after the Gabon tragedy. Still, Musonda – whose three Belgian-born sons, Lamisha, Tika and Charly Musonda Jr., would later briefly ignite hopes of another generation of footballing geniuses – would make one more cameo for Zambia after the Gabon crash.

And one that, incredibly, would almost qualify a grieving nation to the World Cup.

With Musonda's frequent absences from 1990 onwards, Zoom's midfield would be heavily reliant on Derby Makinka. He was a multi-talented dynamo with both silky and steely qualities on the ball and a ferocious left-footed shot. Arguably the best home-based link man, he did his job well, but still, the loss of Musonda's vision in the final third would seriously impact Zambia's often explosive forward line. The national side would proceed to struggle especially in the absence of their European-based professionals. In the early 90s, the Belgium-based pair of Stone Nyirenda and Lucky Msiska and the Swiss-domiciled Johnson Bwalya would be on the periphery of the team for injury or other reasons. That left Kalusha as Zambia's primary scoring hope. In the absence of another quality striker, the PSV midfielder would be the difference for the Zambians – especially in the big games, as highlighted in the 1-0 win over Egypt at the 1992 Africa Cup of Nations in Senegal. Inevitably during that period, victory would always hinge on the scoring boots of Kalusha.

10

Enter Malaza

ZAMBIA'S WORLD Cup qualifying prospects had never seemed as bright as they did that brief shining moment in early 1993. Along with Nigeria's Super Eagles and the Black Stars of Ghana, they were then one of the three best African teams never to have played at a World Cup. But this moment seemed different. The Zambians were favourites, in the minds of many, to top one of the three final Africa zone qualifying groups and clinch a berth at the 1994 finals in the United States. Standing between them and a ticket Stateside were Senegal, then an unknown quantity internationally, and an old foe, probably at its weakest, Morocco.

This enviable position was – despite a brief scare in the first-round qualifiers – well deserved. Built around two enormously gifted midfielders in PSV Eindhoven's Kalusha Bwalya and Charles Musonda of Anderlecht, Zambia had fought their way back to among the top footballing nations in Africa. They'd been on that trajectory since that headline-grabbing performance at the Seoul Olympics in 1988. Five years later, Zambia were a tight unit infused with young blood. It was the proverbial mix of youth and experience.

Among the new blood was a young, precocious striker named Kelvin Mutale. Dual-footed, pacy, a dribbler and strong in the air, he was the total package. But his biggest attribute – and the one that really mattered to his fans, coaches and fellow players – was his knack for goals. Mutale had scored goals for fun at every level he'd played at. He'd carry that ability with him in a meteoric nine-month transition from second-tier football to the national side. After Gabon, his cruelly short but sparkling career would leave sweet albeit melancholic memories with fans. Zambia had yearned for a forward of his pedigree in the more than a decade since Godfrey 'Ucar' Chitalu's retirement. Yet Mutale would come and go in a flash.

Kalusha had been a teenage prodigy on the left wing when he broke into the squad just over a decade earlier. In addition to wearing the captain's armband, he'd been -- as previously – Zambia's primary scoring hope in the absence of a consistent striker. In Mutale, Zambia now finally had the regular goalscoring forward they'd long yearned for since the Godfrey Chitalu and Bernard Chanda days.

'He was the same height, almost the same build as me,' said the 6ft Kalusha. 'Kelvin could shoot; he could shoot with the left, he could shoot with the right, he could head the ball, he could dribble, he was quick, so his finishing was incredible. The complete player.'

Lofty props from an outstanding player himself who, in the Brazilian Romário, had partnered one of the greatest all-time strikers in world football during their PSV days.

The noun outlier best describes the talent that was Kelvin Mutale. He grew up in the football backwaters of Kafue, on the banks of a river that shared its name. Then a small industrial town 45km south of the capital Lusaka, Kafue's three major industries were a textile factory, a Bata shoe factory and the Nitrogen Chemicals of Zambia plant.

Mutale's father worked for the latter, which sponsored a football club in the national league's de facto second division.

Noel Kawanu, a Soviet-trained mechanical engineer at Nitrogen Chemicals, was a co-worker of Mutale's father, Edmond. He was also technical manager of the factory team Nitrogen Stars. As gifted as the then 21-year-old was, it was Kawanu who would help set in motion Mutale's meteoric ascension from Zambia's second tier to international star in a matter of months. 'I knew the boy and his capability,' Kawanu said. 'So, immediately I saw him, I knew the best for him was to go to a better team, where he'd get in the national team and then go abroad – I talked to the boy and he agreed.'

Kawanu had a team in mind, football agents being non-existent in the local game then. It was 1991 and the Zambian league – then running from March to November – was on the home stretch. The previous year, Nkana FC had won their seventh championship in nine seasons. They'd also been runners-up in the 1990 African Cup of Champions Clubs, the first Zambian club to reach the two-legged final of what was the continent's version of the Champions League.

The scarlet-clad, Kitwe-based club had risen to dominance under the tutelage of Englishman Jeff Butler and Moses Simwala. Butler was one of five British technical advisers engaged by the government-owned conglomerate, Zambia Consolidated Copper Mines, in 1981 for some of its clubs. Butler and Bill McGarry would be the most successful of the five hires. While McGarry and local coach Freddie Mwila would lead Power Dynamos to the final of the African Cup Winners' Cup in 1982, Butler and Moses Simwala at Nkana would bag the club's first title that year and repeat in 1983. Only Dynamos in 1984 and Kabwe

Warriors in 1987 would interrupt the Nkana dynasty before the 1990s.

There was another reason why Nkana was Kawanu's preferred destination for the exceptional Mutale – one closer to the heart: Kawanu's fraternal twin brother, Chris, an electrical engineer, was an Nkana fanatic, so there was a family affinity for the club. The acquisition of the prolific young goalscorer would be a major coup for a side that, despite its long domestic reign, was renowned more for its defensive prowess than any pulverising attack. Nkana's game was based on the 4-4-2 system. Tight, compact and choking, it would spawn the club's nickname, 'Kalampa', vernacular for 'the clamp.'

The expectation was that Mutale's signing would add a new and incisive cutting edge to the Nkana front line. But there was a problem. Mutale's father, Edmond, wasn't for the idea. He had another club in mind.

'The boy [Mutale] agreed but the father was resisting,' said Noel Kawanu. Still, Kawanu contacted Nkana, and Beston Chambeshi, a member of Zambia's 1988 Seoul Olympic squad as a player and later an Nkana and Zambia coach, was tasked with picking up Mutale from Kafue.

The mission would have elements of a spy thriller and end like an abduction.

Nkana had travelled the almost 380km from Kitwe to Lusaka for a league match and would spend the night at the five-star Pamodzi Hotel in the capital. At some point, Noel's twin brother and Nkana fanatic Chris and Chambeshi drove to Kafue to pick up Mutale. The trip was in vain.

'When they came here, they found the boy was gone – he was nowhere to be seen,' recalled Noel Kawanu.

What happened next was purely fortuitous. But it would help launch Kelvin Mutale's tragically short, brilliant career. Hours after his brother and Chambeshi had struck out in Kafue, Noel drove his young sons to a movie theatre in the bowels of the 23-storey Findeco House, Zambia's tallest building, on the south end of Lusaka's mile-long commercial strip, Cairo Road. As he walked back to his car, he was startled to see an Nchanga Rangers FC vehicle parked nearby. A furtive figure inside attempted to avoid detection. From Chingola, another copper-mining town 47km north-west of Kitwe, Nchanga Rangers were one of the top clubs in the Zambian league and one of Nkana's rivals. The acquisition of a scoring threat like Mutale would have been a major coup for a side from a town famous for the world's second-largest opencast mine – one covering nearly 30 square kilometres.

His curiosity piqued, Kawanu approached the vehicle. Inside was Kelvin Mutale. Kawanu had few options at that point.

'I had to use force,' he recalled. 'I pulled the boy from the car and then asked him which vehicle he wanted to get in – the [Nchanga] car or mine. He chose mine. So, I told him to get his bag and to get in.'

Having earlier given his word to Kawanu, Mutale had no option but to defy his father. But weeks later, Papa Edmond, like the rest of football-mad Zambia, would rejoice in his son's sudden fame at Nkana. 'He was the happiest man around. He was just being difficult,' said Kawanu.

Unknown nationally until then, Mutale lit up Zambian football in Nkana's red strip. His uncanny skills and amazing finishing thrilled fans. Michael Chanda, Mutale's older brother, recalled an unbelievable goal Kelvin scored at Nkana Stadium: 'It was a low and hard shot when it came in and [Kelvin] was quite far away. But then he dived in, literally sliding on the lawn to head the ball into the net – it's very rare that somebody will head the ball which is a grass [daisy] cutter. Kelvin was skilful all round, even when it came to heading the ball.'

The old cliche about a star being born could not have more aptly described Mutale's arrival on Zambian football's biggest stage. In no time, international suitors would come a-calling. Mutale would be capped by Zambia, and two months later he signed with Al Ettifaq FC in the Saudi Professional League. This, in his mind, was only the stepping stone to a career in Europe for the Manchester United fan.

Kelvin Mutale's stunning breakthrough with Zambia's most successful club marked a glorious return to his Copperbelt family roots. Kitwe was less than 20km from Kalulushi, a small mining town that was his birthplace and early football breeding ground. It was there that Kelvin and older brother Michael joined neighbourhood kids, often barefoot, in spirited games using rough-hewn balls.

'The biggest part of our life was in Kafue, but it all started in Kalulushi,' recalled Michael Chanda. 'I was born in Kalulushi, just like Kelvin, in the mine hospital. Our father worked for RCM [Roan Copper Mines].'

Fifteen months separated the brothers, who were both less than ten in 1977 when their father moved the family to Kafue. There the two boys, the oldest of what would be a brood of ten, would continue to excel in football.

'Primarily, we were a sporting family,' said Michael. 'I played football. My father was a footballer and boxer. My mother was a netball player who represented the Copperbelt. Basically, you introduce any one of us to any sport and before you know it, we're better than you.'

Close since toddlers, Kelvin followed big brother Michael into football. 'Yeah, except that he had an advantage; he was dual-footed. For me, I had the strength in my right leg, but he used both legs.'

At any rate, any other footballing comparisons between the two brothers would soon become academic. Upon acing his mandatory ninth-grade exam, with high marks in science and mathematics, Michael was placed in a pure physics and chemistry class in the tenth grade. This required considerably more time in the classroom than on the football pitch. 'That put pressure on me,' he said. Wisely, football was put on the back burner by the future physics teacher and headmaster.

Kelvin, on the other hand, found solving defences and goalies more to his liking than solving physics equations like his big brother.

'Kelvin, for a lack of a better illustration, I'd say, he was made [for] football. He did certain things with the ball that sometimes, even when we were young, you'd find quite amazing,' remembered Michael. 'He had a passion for the sport to an extent that he never allowed his feet to rest.'

In Mutale was the spirit of an outlier. 'He could socialise but the first thing in the morning, he'd go for a road run before he was picked up to train with the rest of the other guys. So, he was already warmed up before they even started training. He was always a step ahead of the other players. That's how serious he was.'

Among the things that separated Mutale from most players of his generation – particularly the forwards – was his phenomenal technique. It was remarkable for somebody who'd spent most of his formative years playing for modest clubs. It surely wasn't luck. He worked at his craft in Kafue, pushing himself hard before and after each team training session. The uncanny ball control, the outrageous headers, the exquisite volleys – like the one he'd score against Mauritius two days before his death – were all the result of extra hours of work on rugged fields.

'There are people early in his career who really helped him to live up to that passion,' recalled Michael. 'One was Sampa Mwanakaoma – he used to be a coach for Bata Bullets in Kafue and they were in the amateur league. That coach identified the potential in Kelvin and decided to work with him.'

So, on many a weekday on a patchy, dusty field in Kafue – after the rest of the team had packed their bags and departed – Sampa and Mutale would stay back at the end of a Bata Bullets training session and go to work again. Sampa would line up balls near the corner flag while Mutale darted about in the goal area waiting for the deliveries. The coach would float in ball after ball while Mutale worked on his finishing, heading or volleying into the net. It would be this kind of functional training that would hone his deadly finishing.

'That's the man, according to me, that really shaped the football destiny of Kelvin,' Michael lauded Sampa. Unfortunately, the amateur trainer would not live to see his protégé play for Zambia. He died before the Gabon Disaster cast a pall on world football.

Sampa had first gotten a glimpse of Mutale when the future star turned out for Kafue's Naboye Secondary School. Remarkably, Mutale had not played competitive football before then, his nascent but still coruscating skills hitherto confined to recreational games.

'Kelvin did not play for his school at primary level. He went to secondary school at Naboye, there he messed up Kamwala, Munali, Kafue Boys, Libala. They knew him,' said Michael, talking about some of the top footballing schools in Lusaka province then. 'He'd score five goals against all of them. He didn't even have a chance to play for the provincial team because [by then] he'd already broken into the [FAZ] division one. He got picked by Kafue Textiles and then went to Nitrogen Chemicals.'

Mutale's prolific finishing for the Kafue teams delighted fans, who were so thrilled by his penchant for scoring late goals that they coined his famous moniker.

'Putting the ball in the back of the net was something he treasured so much to the extent that he'd save a little energy for late goals,' said Michael. 'Just when everybody thought the game was over and he was done scoring, he'd strike again all of a sudden. It earned him the nickname Malaza.'

In the ChiNyanja vernacular widely spoken in Lusaka and Kafue, *malaza*, according to Michael, means *kuma-last*, whose literal English translation is 'at the end'.

Growing up, Kelvin was a big fan of his future national coach, and Zambia's last prolific goalscorer before him – Godfrey 'Ucar' Chitalu. He was also a Manchester United fan. 'I was Arsenal – so you know there was a battle,' big brother laughed. Michael, for one, had heard of the Munich air disaster that had claimed eight United players on 6 February 1958.

The legend of the free-scoring Malaza would spread far and wide during his brief and tragic career.

11

Shooting Star

ON 16 August 1992, in the Netherlands, Kalusha Bwalya celebrated his 29th birthday. It marked just over a decade since the now attacking midfielder and his older brother Benjamin had first lit up Zambian football with their dribbling skills. With each passing year, the younger Bwalya had become his nation's talisman, an erstwhile left-winger whose finishing could decide whether Zambia won or not. In Lusaka, a day earlier, there'd been a certain buzz at Independence Stadium. It was the international debut of Kelvin Mutale, aged 22 and the presumptive heir to Kalusha as Zambia's match-winner.

Mutale had lit up the league with Nkana, scoring one spectacular goal after another for the perennial champions in his rookie season in the Super League. It was punctuated by an emphatic hat-trick against Mufulira Wanderers' Efford Chabala – Africa's top goalkeeper – with Nkana down 2-0 in the 1992 Independence Cup Final. Chabala, who'd returned to his hometown club after a stint with Argentinos Juniors, was subsequently substituted as Wanderers succumbed 3-2.

Having uncannily adapted to the top flight after his jump from the second tier, Mutale's Zambia coronation would just be a matter of time. It came in the national side's first match after the Africa Cup of Nations that January, where they'd bowed out in the quarter-finals with just one goal in three matches. That solitary strike – by Kalusha – was the winner over Egypt.

Jerry Muchimba, Zambian football historian and author of the book *Godfrey 'Ucar' Chitalu*, recalled Mutale's debut against Mauritius, whose status as one of Africa's modest sides meant that even with Charles Musonda injured, Kalusha was not needed, '[Mutale] didn't score and didn't have a particularly good game, and he and [fellow striker] Nicholas Bwalya would sometimes get in each other's way.' Still, Zambia recovered from the shock of conceding a record second-minute goal – the earliest they'd capitulated at home – to prevail 2-1 after second-half strikes by Stone Nyirenda and Derby Makinka.

In retrospect – as evident from his performance in ensuing matches – Mutale's surprisingly tepid international debut against unheralded opposition was less a case of stage fright than the Zambians' inability to click collectively. It was their first match under interim coach Boniface Simutowe. The former international midfielder had replaced long-time boss Samuel 'Zoom' Ndhlovu, who'd been sidelined after Zambia's anticlimactic outing to the 1992 AFCON in Senegal.

Two weeks after the Mauritius game, Mutale was on the bench at Soccer City in Johannesburg, for a historic match – from the South African perspective. It was the hosts' first competitive international match, post-Apartheid. Still, Zambia felt no need to call Kalusha from Europe – although Swiss-based Johnson Bwalya would make his international comeback after four years out. The gambit worked, Timothy Mwitwa connecting late in a 1-0 win.

Ndhlovu was back at the helm, but Kalusha and Musonda were still absent on 11 October, when Mutale was tapped to lead the line in Lusaka as Zambia kicked off their 1994 World Cup qualifying campaign against Tanzania. The two neighbours had been drawn in an intriguing Group H with Madagascar and Burkina Faso. The latter, however, withdrew before kicking a ball and were replaced by Namibia, on their maiden World Cup quest after gaining independence two years earlier. With a tricky West African foe out of the way, Zambia's odds of winning the group at a canter and advancing to the play-offs for one of three African berths at USA 94 couldn't have been brighter.

Thirty minutes into his second cap, the brief and brilliant international legend of Kelvin 'Malaza' Mutale would begin. The young forward, who'd recently turned 23, opened his Zambia account in a 2-0 decision over the Tanzanians at Independence Stadium. He'd follow that performance with a flood of goals in subsequent matches. There was a first-half brace a fortnight later, in a 4-0 rout of Namibia in Windhoek, as Mutale kept Zambia's World Cup campaign flying. The precocious striker then took his scoring boots to Africa's oldest football tournament that November. It was hosted by Tanzania.

Zambia had participated in the annual Confederation of East and Central African Football Association (CECAFA) since 1973. They'd won the competition – which began in 1926 as the Gossage Cup – twice, both times with home-based players. Unbeknownst to everyone, 1992 would be Zambia's last trip to the event and Mutale's only appearance in a tournament. Predictably, Malaza put on a scoring clinic. Still on Nkana's books, he shot Zambia to the semi-finals, netting a hat-trick in an 8-0 drubbing of Zanzibar, and both goals as Tanzania were edged 2-1. There'd be another brace in a 4-0 romp over Malawi in the third-place match on 27

November, consolation for a 4-2 penalty loss to Uganda in the last four.

Mutale's seven goals in the CECAFA tournament brought his Zambia tally to ten from nine matches between August and November 1992. A year earlier, the International Federation of Football History and Statistics (IFFHS) had begun keeping stats on football's ace marksmen. Only goals scored in full international matches and intercontinental club competitions between 1 January and 31 December in a calendar year counted, with the most prolific striker receiving IFFHS' world's top scorer honour.

Erroneously credited for just nine goals by IFFHS, Mutale's 1992 tally – accrued in just four months – would see him tie with French star Jean-Pierre Papin for tenth place on the 1992 chart. Papin, then with Olympique Marseille, had claimed the inaugural award in 1991 with 16 goals.

Mutale's international scoring spree late in the season after emerging from lowly Nitrogen Stars further burnished his reputation as a goal machine. He'd made a relatively seamless transition from Zambia's de facto second tier to the African level in less than a year. Inevitably, international suitors would come a-calling.

In March 1992, Tenant Chilumba, young, wiry and not unlike Mutale in stature, had signed for Saudi professional club Al-Taawoun in Bruidah. Already capped by Zambia, the 19-year-old striker with burgeoning skills became the first Zambian to play in the Middle East. He made a quick impression, so much so that when Al-Taawoun's Brazilian manager offered to help a compatriot coaching in Dammam find a good striker, he turned to his new Zambian acquisition for suggestions.

'Kelvin Mutale!' Chilumba responded unhesitatingly, even though the two had never played together.

Al Ettifaq, the Dammam club, snapped at a chance to have a look at Malaza.

Buoyed by his scoring blitz in the CECAFA tournament, Mutale left for trials in Dammam early in December 1992. According to Simataa Simataa, who would later briefly serve as the brilliant striker's financial adviser, the Saudis paid Nkana $35,000 for Mutale's signature. Another bargain by any account.

Al Ettifaq had thrown in a request for a midfielder. So, Derby Makinka, Zambia's most experienced link man, accompanied him on the flight to the Persian Gulf port. Makinka had debuted for the Zambia under-20 side as a left-back in 1983, and graduated to the senior squad in 1984 aged 19. Pushed into midfield, he morphed into a consistent performer over the years and never missed a game for Zambia while with nondescript Profund Warriors in the local league. At the age of 27, he was already approaching a century of international caps.

By December 1992, Makinka, with more than 90 appearances, was Zambia's second-most capped player after goalie Efford Chabala. Strong in the tackle, solid in possession and with good close control, he'd also been his country's most influential infield player whenever the European-based Kalusha and Charles Musonda were not available. That was before the emergence of Kelvin Mutale. Al Ettifaq would be Makinka's third overseas club after brief stints in 1989 with Pamir Dushanbe in Tajikistan and crack Polish Ekstraklasa side Lech Poznań in 1991. For the 23-year-old Mutale, the Saudi Professional League was expected to be the first stop on his superstar trajectory.

New professional league, new defenders, no problem for the scoring machine from Kafue via Nkana. According to data provided by Khaled Al-Nasser, Al Ettifaq's former manager of media and communications, and sports journalist Dawood Al Mousa, Malaza was just as prolific in the Saudi league during his and Makinka's tragically short period there.

'Kelvin scored eight goals [for] Ettifaq,' said Al-Nasser.

All eight came in a six-week period between 25 January 1993 – when Malaza opened his account with a brace against Al-Najmah – and 11 March, when he hit a hat-trick in a 3-1 decision over Al-Qadsia. The latter would be both his and Makinka's last game with Ettifaq before their fateful return to Zambia on international duty.

Mutale's other goals would be against Al-Riyadh, a 4-1 rout of Al-Nassr and against Al-Ta'ee. Makinka, always pushing forward from his defensive midfield lair, would connect twice during that same six-week period. He contributed to the Nassr drubbing with a bit of skilful play from a stupendous Mutale assist for Ettifaq's third goal. Malaza, playing wide on the left almost like a winger, had picked the ball up near the halfway line and darted forward.

Showing that he had the vision to go with his outrageous scoring abilities, the centre-forward looked up and spotted Makinka overlapping on the far side. Mutale's next play was reminiscent of the Brazilians of old with their incredible and unorthodox technique: with his right foot, he toe-poked a high ball – at least 30 yards – across to the right where it landed outside the penalty box. Makinka skinned an advancing defender, and the goalie who'd rushed out, before shooting into the empty net with his trusty left foot. His other Ettifaq goal came against Al-Ta'ee.

Khaled Al-Nasser recalled that when the two Zambians left on international duty in mid-March, following the 3-1 romp over Al-Qadsia, Ettifaq were second to Al-Ittihad on goal difference in the Saudi First Division. Both had 23 points, albeit Ettifaq, with 18 played, had two games in hand. At the end of the Saudi regular season that July,

Ettifaq, without its fallen Zambian aces, would slip to fourth place and clinch that final play-off berth. They'd finish third overall after the play-offs. Mutale and Makinka would be sorely missed in Saudi Arabia too.

Thirty years after Mutale and Makinka's brief and wistful period with Ettifaq, Steven Gerrard, the former Liverpool and England midfield maestro, was appointed coach of the Dammam-based club. His first signing was England and Liverpool midfielder Jordan Henderson. They were among the several football luminaries – including French stars Karim Benzema and N'Golo Kanté, Brazilians Neymar and Roberto Firmino, and the Senegalese Sadio Mané – to join Cristiano Ronaldo in the now lucrative Saudi Professional League.

Makinka and Mutale's obligations in Dammam in December 1992 meant that they'd miss Zambia's next World Cup qualifier – the team's third in as many months and their most difficult on paper. It would also involve another flight on a ZAF Buffalo plane.

This Buffalo's destination was Madagascar, just over 1,000 miles south-east in the Indian Ocean. Despite its reputation as an exotic landmass of unrivalled biodiversity, the world's fourth-largest island had on previous visits proven inhospitable, football-wise, for Zambia. They'd returned from Madagascar with a 2-1 loss in 1973 and a goalless draw in 1990, both in Africa Cup of Nations qualifiers. Scheduled for 20 December 1992, this World Cup tie offered the battle-tested Zambians a chance to finally get a result on the vast island and cement their lead atop Group H. Zambia would travel to Antananarivo after two qualifying victories in the group against Madagascar's one win and a draw.

Despite the absence of their new scoring sensation and a seasoned link man, Zoom Ndhlovu and his squad boarded their Buffalo transport at the ZAF base adjacent to the International Airport a confident bunch. And that's because two other players worth their weight in gold – Kalusha and Johnson Bwalya – would be on the Buffalo.

The Buffalo took off in a north-easterly direction before gently winging right. At the controls were two of the Zambia Air Force's most experienced pilots on the Canadian-built plane: Victor Mubanga and James Sachika, both lieutenant colonels. Mubanga was a 21-year ZAF veteran and no stranger to high-profile assignments. That included flying a Dakota plane full of Zambian supporters to Cairo in March 1974 for the Africa Cup of Nations Final, and the remains of Simon Kapwepwe, a founding father of Zambia, to his hometown for burial in January 1980. Mubanga had also served as club secretary of Red Arrows, the ZAF-sponsored top-flight club.

But flying with some of the ZAF's best pilots hardly made the Buffalo experience any easier for the generations of players who had been on the plane. Kalusha's first bad experience had come way before boarding the Buffalo to Madagascar. That was in November 1985, en route from Kinshasa, Zaire, where Zambia had participated in a tournament, shortly before his move to Cercle Brugge.

'We landed in Lubumbashi [in southern Zaire] and we were told that we couldn't fly [on] because they said we had no papers and everything,' he remembered. 'Nobody was allowed to come out of the plane, we had to sleep on the plane until we left early in the morning at six o'clock, and there was only one toilet. We had landed there around 6–7pm.'

The flight to Madagascar would be unsettling too. It started with a delay of more than four hours before departure. According to Kalusha, they were told that the pilots had gone to the Bank of Zambia to get traveller's cheques for the trip. Two of the three ZAF pilots were the aforementioned Victor Mubanga and James Sachika. When they finally returned, Kalusha, dressed casually in shorts and a T-shirt, boarded the Buffalo and took a window seat at the back next to Efford Chabala. It had been seven years since the Lubumbashi incident when he'd last been on a Buffalo. He'd forgotten that the seats didn't recline, minimising comfort on the aircraft.

'And an officer stood up and said, "Welcome gentlemen … this flight, it will take us from here [Lusaka] to Maputo where we'll refuel. From Maputo *nga twaima* [when we take off], we'll be over the Indian Ocean for four hours before we reach Antananarivo." So, the plane takes off … very steady, very steady … not too low, not too high. He'd said we'd go over the airspace of Malawi. We're easterly bound. We should pass Malawi, and go to Maputo and the plane suddenly starts to go down, so me, I have the window on the left I can see [outside] … but it says Kamuzu Banda Airport … this is Kamuzu Banda Airport [in Malawi] and we land.'

If landing in Malawi, instead of Mozambique as announced, was worrying, what followed next was beyond disconcerting if not outright ominous. Kalusha recalled the Buffalo refuelling and taking off again – headed across the Indian Ocean for what they'd been told would be a four-hour period.

'Then the [ZAF officer] stands up again and says, "Gentlemen, we'll be giving out life vests. If this thing falls down in the water, it can float for up to four hours." So, they give us *ama* life vests. "No, you have to blow here," we are told … and I think the first one was faulty, so they changed mine … and that is the picture that Johnson [Bwalya] – Johnson had come with a camera from Switzerland – took of me wearing a life vest with Efford … we were taking pictures,' said Kalusha.

Fortunately, neither the quality of the life vests nor the Buffalo's ability to stay afloat on water were tested this time. Kalusha and Co. made it safely to Madagascar. But the Zambia captain remained incredulous, 'In retrospect, when I think about it, why did the first officer say that we'd land in Maputo but then landed in Malawi? *Mebbe* they were told, "You guys are flying over our airspace [without permission], land now." That's what I think now, because there's absolutely no way when you have the [flight path] that you can be able to do that.'

After the scare experienced by the Olympic-bound squad in April 1976 over Uganda, and the ordeals of 1985 and 1988 when Buffalo craft ferrying the national side were detained in Zaire, this was yet another red flag before the awful nightmare that lay ahead.

'The sad part is that if you ask anybody – even before my time – the boys used to say "ichi ichindeke chikatwipaisha" [this plane will get us killed]. That's what the players before us used to say – and that's exactly what happened,' said Kalusha.

Also aboard the Buffalo to Madagascar was *Times of Zambia* sports reporter Chris Kachingwe. He covered the game at the picturesque Mahamasina Municipal Stadium next to Lake Anosy in central Antananarivo. The 40,000-capacity ground was slightly more than half full for the encounter five days before the last Christmas most of the Zambian players would celebrate.

'It was an exciting game' was Kachingwe's immediate recollection 26 years later. 'But I think [Madagascar] had done their homework, they were prepared for Zambia and I think the referee also played some part.'

The latter was an inference to Ethiopian referee Bekele Kidane's first-half dismissal of Johnson Bwalya, which made him the first Zambian ejected in an international game since Simon 'Kaodi' Kaushi in 1974. 'It was a straight red,' recalled Kachingwe. '[Bwalya's] job was to man the midfield, he was a striker, though his job was to make sure he cuts the supply; to fortify the midfield, I think Zoom decided he plays a three-man midfield. So, at some point [Bwalya] was irritated. His job is to score, but I think he was given a wrong role, so he got frustrated.'

In retrospect, Zoom's decision to pull Johnson Bwalya, a hard-running right-winger with a powerful shot, into the middle of the park was likely out of desperation. Bereft of Zambia's two best midfielders in Derby Makinka and the injured Charles Musonda, Zoom opted to sacrifice a potent scoring threat who'd netted a rocket against Italy at the Seoul Olympics to shore up his engine room. At any rate, Madagascar struck twice in the second half against ten-man Zambia, dealing the visitors another loss on the island and a sudden blow to their 1994 World Cup qualifying hopes.

The 2-0 defeat would ultimately cost Ndhlovu his job – but likely saved his life. During his five-year tenure, Ndhlovu had taken Zambia to the Olympic quarter-finals in 1988 and won the CECAFA Cup in 1991, the latter with a squad of local players. He remains the most successful and longest-serving indigenous national coach.

The next day, 21 December 1992, the Buffalo carrying the home-based Zambian players from Madagascar landed safely at Lusaka International Airport and taxied to the adjacent Zambia Air Force base. That same day another Buffalo, one of five remaining in the ZAF inventory of the seven purchased from Canada's De Havilland in 1976, had parked at the base. That DHC-5D, registration number AF-319 from the VVIP squadron, was given 'AOG', or aircraft on the ground, status. The term refers to an aircraft grounded for serious technical reasons.

It was four days before Christmas. AF-319 would remain on the ground, exposed to the elements during Zambia's hot and wet season, whose daily mean temperatures averaged 25 to 30°C, for the next four months.

In the meantime, the Zambia national team would play five competitive games during those 16 weeks in an attempt to undo the damage wrought in Madagascar to their World Cup chances. They'd also resume an AFCON qualifying campaign that would include a reunion with the flamboyant Liverpool and Zimbabwe goalkeeper Bruce Grobbelaar.

12

Moses Simwala

TO GET Zambia back on track after the setback in Antananarivo, FAZ turned to the country's best club coach. In January 1993, Moses Simwala, 43, was approaching his 13th year at the helm of defending champions Nkana, the club from Kitwe's sprawling Wusakile mine township that he'd played for his entire life, earning the nickname 'Chairman'. He'd starred for Nkana as a lightning-fast right-winger with pinpoint crossing ability from the precocious age of 16. Capped for Zambia pre-Ante Bušelić, he was one of the former schoolboy internationals embraced by the Croat when appointed Zambia's first expatriate coach in 1971.

In an age when players were assigned shirt numbers from one as the goalkeeper to 11 as the left-winger, Simwala, when healthy, would have first claim to the number seven for the next nine years. Ditto at club level when Nkana, in their previous incarnation as Rhokana United, boasted the league's best forward line. They had a potent triad comprising young Brighton Sinyangwe on the left wing, the incomparable Bernard 'Bomber' Chanda at centre-forward and Simwala on the right – all key members of Bušelić's crack Zambia squad.

Nkana's midfield and defence were, in contrast, on par with others in the Zambian top flight until, ironically, Simwala hung up his boots aged 31 and was appointed coach in 1980. In tandem with Englishman Jeff Butler who joined the club as technical adviser in 1981, Simwala rejuvenated and retooled a Nkana side dotted with talent into a tight 4-4-2 unit. Tactically disciplined, run by thinking midfielders Jericho Shinde and Dominic Mutale, and with the explosive one-two attacking punch of Michael Chabala – a burly, hard-running target man reminiscent of an old-fashioned English forward – and Jack Chanda, a bandy-legged inside-right with a low centre of gravity, blistering pace and a fierce shot, Nkana became a force. They won the 1982 league title, the club's first, unbeaten in 22 matches. Nkana retained the title the next season. There were five more championships between 1985 and 1990. That included three straight titles after Butler's departure, dispelling any notions that Simwala and Nkana had merely been beneficiaries of the Englishman's tactical nous. While Butler had helped hone Nkana's 4-4-2 system, long in vogue in Zambian football from the national team downwards, Simwala fine-tuned it. That included perfecting the club's defensive, choking game that would spawn its 'Kalampa' moniker – a corruption of the word clamp.

The apex of Simwala's lengthy tenure as Nkana boss would come at the end of 1990. That's when he led his side to the two-legged final of the African Cup of Champions Clubs, precursor of the current CAF Champions League. No Zambian side had gone that far before. Nkana reached the final with a 100 per cent record. They won every game, home and away, over four rounds, dispatching Cameroonian and Nigerian champions RC Bafoussam and Iwuanyanwu Nationale respectively along the way, and conceding just three goals in eight games.

Nkana would carry their defensive prowess into the final against former champions JS Kabylie of Algeria. There'd be no goals from open play in both legs, just Mourad Rahmouni's 47th-minute penalty in Algiers that would inflict the first defeat on Nkana in the competition, and a dramatic Amos Bwalya spot kick ten minutes from time in Lusaka that levelled the aggregate score for the Zambians. The final went to a shoot-out that lasted until big defender Mordon Malitoli missed Nkana's fourth penalty. Hakim Medane's conversion saw Kabylie crowned 1990 African club champions 5-3 on penalties.

The next year, crosstown rivals Power Dynamos ended Nkana's stranglehold on the league. But Simwala's disappointment aside, Zambian football was at its strongest, as results would show. Under the tutelage of Freddie Mwila and former Scottish international Jimmy Bone – Dynamos would one-up Nkana's continental exploits of the previous season by bagging the 1991 African Cup Winners' Cup. A third member of the Dynamos coaching staff was assistant Alex Chola.

Simwala steered Kalampa back to the top in 1992, as they clinched an eighth title in 11 seasons. Deep and talented, Nkana had added the scoring machine known as Kelvin Mutale to their powerful squad. He joined Zambia international defenders John Soko and Eston Mulenga, wingers Timothy Mwitwa and Numba Mwila, and striker Kenani Simambe, providing a cutting edge previously unseen in the red strip of the serial title winners. Signed from second-tier Nitrogen Stars, Mutale's transition to the top flight was seamless, his impact immediate. His goals – like the diving header a few inches from the turf at Nkana Stadium, and a scissor kick against Efford Chabala – were spectacular as the club marched to a domestic league and cup double. The future looked dazzlingly bright.

By 1992, Moses Simwala was in his 13th year as Nkana boss. He was also ailing. Simataa Simataa remembered Simwala travelling by road from Kitwe to Lusaka with Nkana for away fixtures and, exhausted, remaining at the team's hotel while they played. A banker and football aficionado, Simataa would act as Simwala's ears and eyes, providing the coach with detailed post-match analyses and player assessments.

Still, in the wake of the setback in Madagascar, it was perhaps only logical that the FAZ turned to the country's winningest coach to replace a long-serving gaffer who'd done the most to raise Zambia's profile since Ante Bušelić. It was two weeks before the next World Cup qualifier, away to Tanzania on 16 January 1993. A must-win game. As backup for Simwala, FAZ appointed two of his former international team-mates as assistants – Godfrey 'Ucar' Chitalu and Alex 'Computer' Chola. Widely recognised as Zambia's greatest player for his all-time scoring record – 79 goals in 111 internationals – Chitalu had been making his mark coaching his old club Kabwe Warriors. Ditto Chola, Zambia's second-top scorer with 43 goals in 102 appearances, at Power Dynamos. On paper, Simwala, Ucar and Chola made a powerful troika. But Simwala, his health steadily deteriorating, would never sit in the Zambian dugout. He was hospitalised when the squad camped for the Tanzania match. Chitalu and Chola took charge.

Simwala wasn't the only notable absentee when Zambia flew to Mwanza, Tanzania's lush and exotic northern port city, on the shores of Lake Victoria. Kelvin Mutale and Derby Makinka, sorely missed in the Madagascar defeat, would also be absent again as they settled in Saudi Arabia after being signed by Al Ettifaq. But Kalusha and his namesake forward Albert Bwalya – the latter long forgotten after he became one of the first Zambians in the 1980s to play in Apartheid-era South Africa – made the trip. They both scored in a 3-1 victory with Kalusha drawing first blood in the fifth minute. Numba Mwila, a fast, pint-sized right-winger, was the other scorer. But it would be all in vain.

With no hope of advancing to the final qualifying round after the defeat in Mwanza, Tanzania threw the proverbial spanner in the works further complicating Zambia's own qualification hopes.

In a letter to this writer in March 1993, Kalusha Bwalya recounted how things unfolded: 'After we had played against Tanzania, the game which put us back into the race, they pulled out and the points didn't count anymore so we had to play and win by at least four goals against Namibia. FAZ thought it wise to [call] me and Charles [Musonda] at the last minute. So, we arrived on the day of the match [and] all efforts paid off as we beat Namibia. Wisdom [Chansa], Charley [Musonda], me and Kenani Simambe got the goals. And then the all-important game against Madagascar. Unbelievable crowd. So many people, even the Humanism Hill was packed.'

Independence Stadium had seen many epic World Cup ties in the two decades since Zambia's emergence as an African power under Ante Bušelić in 1973, such as the titanic encounters with Morocco, Zaire, Algeria and Tunisia. But the clash with Madagascar on 27 February 1993 would, in retrospect, be memorable beyond its importance as the Group H decider that the Zambians needed to win to advance to the final three-nation qualifying round.

It would be the first time new scoring phenom Kelvin Mutale would play together with Zambia's best players, Kalusha Bwalya and Charles Musonda. Already essential members of the Al Ettifaq squad a couple of months after moving to the Saudi Professional League, Mutale and

Derby Makinka had missed all of Zambia's matches since November 1992. They'd return to international duty for the crucial Madagascar game, FAZ pulling all the stops for another must-win tie.

Kalusha's first impression of his new young striking partner was glowing, as the Zambia captain noted in his March 1993 letter to this writer, 'We led the first half [against Madagascar] by 1-0 thanks to Kelvin Mutale, in my opinion our best centre-forward for a long time. I got the second, a header after 68 minutes, and three minutes later, Timothy Mwitwa got the third, which killed the Islanders, but they got a penalty ten minutes from time and scored. So, in a nutshell, everybody in Zambia is very happy about us reaching the decisive [phase] in which we meet Morocco and Senegal. It's now or never as Dennis Liwewe puts it. Godfrey Chitalu and Alex Chola are doing very well. I always have my own ideas about how the team should play and there is a lot of understanding between the coaches, and we the players, more importantly, are happy both [with] the training and the results.'

The advent of Kelvin Mutale made Zambia complete. The striker, lauded as the country's best in that position in a long time by none other than Kalusha, was the final piece in a side boasting the best goalkeeper on the continent in Efford Chabala; a solid and seasoned defence built around the tough-tackling Eston Mulenga, and the midfield fulcrum of PSV Eindhoven's Kalusha and Anderlecht's Charles Musonda that was as close to world class as any in Africa. Charles Musonda and Kalusha had lost just three games while both playing 90 minutes together for Zambia since 1986. But like a shooting star, Mutale would play only once more with Kalusha, and never again with Musonda. 'He [Kelvin] was bound to be a legend – you could see [a] phenomenal talent,' Kalusha, the great

Romário's striking partner at PSV for four seasons, lauded the tragic Malaza.

Meanwhile, his troublesome right knee steadily deteriorating, Charles Musonda would sit out Zambia's next match, an Africa Cup of Nations qualifier with Zimbabwe on 10 April 1993. This was the top billing in a group also comprising Mauritius and debutants South Africa. It could have been billed as Kalusha Bwalya and Kelvin Mutale vs. Bruce Grobbelaar and Peter Ndlovu. Grobbelaar was Zimbabwe's celebrated goalie – a winner of six league championships and the European Cup, among a bushel of honours, with Liverpool FC – and generally considered one of the finest goalkeepers of his generation. Ndlovu was a Coventry City fan favourite and the second African player in the English Premier League after Grobbelaar.

It was Grobbelaar's first encounter with Zambia since another AFCON qualifying series 12 years earlier. Zambia had won that two-legged affair 3-0 on aggregate, with Fanny Hangunyu, of Zambia Air Force club Red Arrows, netting a memorable brace against the soon-to-be-famous keeper at Independence Stadium. Grobbelaar had just signed a £250,000 contract with Liverpool as Ray Clemence's backup.

In addition to Peter Ndlovu, Grobbelaar had a stronger supporting cast on his return to Lusaka in April 1993. Zimbabwe had assembled a talented squad dubbed the 'Dream Team', in homage to the American NBA All-Star side that had swept basketball gold at the 1992 Barcelona Olympics. It included Peter Ndlovu's older sibling Adam, who'd forge a career with Swiss clubs SC Kriens, SR Delémont and FC Zürich.

Described at times as acrobatic and often labelled 'eccentric' by the UK press during his lengthy career with Liverpool, Grobbelaar kept a clean sheet on this visit. There were few clear chances on either side, neither for Kalusha nor for Kelvin Mutale. And none for the Ndlovu brothers. It ended goalless – with a swarm of bees and a tear gas incident probably factors.

It had been an absorbing affair even before the Zambians stepped it up, like they always did, in the second half at home. It was only the second time Kalusha and Mutale had played together and a goal seemed imminent. Then a bizarre thing occurred. Kalusha recalled a swarm of bees descending on the pitch followed by the suffocating waft of tear gas. This forced a temporary halt to the game. Apparently, police battling rowdy fans outside the Independence Stadium had fired tear gas to disperse them. The conjecture is that the gas might have disturbed a hive in or around the ground, forcing its inhabitants to buzz the open pitch. In Kalusha's mind, this was the turning point of the game.

'The bees killed the momentum of the game,' he remembered. 'The game was disrupted for about ten minutes. It was 0-0, so we couldn't pick up the rhythm.'

A good result for the visitors but disappointing for the home fans. What the reported 12,000 fans at Independence Stadium didn't know that Saturday afternoon is that this was the last time they'd see all but two members of the Zambian side – Kalusha and Johnson Bwalya – again. Coming up on 25 April was another AFCON qualifier, on the Indian Ocean island of Mauritius. And then two days later, a flight to West Africa for what would be a first-time meeting with Senegal in the final qualifying round for the 1994 World Cup.

13

Dark Clouds

BEAUTY LUPIYA was the last reporter to travel with the doomed team. She was also one of a handful of individuals to escape the crash. For that, she owed her life to her *Times of Zambia* sports editor Davey Sakala. Now known as Chanda Kristensen and long settled in Denmark, Lupiya had been at the *Times* for two years when she got her first international assignment with the national team, covering the team's 25 April AFCON qualifier in Mauritius. Her only other foreign trip as a sports reporter had been with a volleyball side that had driven the almost 1,000 miles south to Botswana for a tournament. The journey to Mauritius, just shy of 2,000 miles east across the Indian Ocean, would be a harrowing preamble to the horror that would soon unfold.

The first shock for the young reporter – just a year older than the gifted player who sat next to her on the flights to and from Mauritius – was the din made by their ZAF transport. It was her first flight on a Buffalo.

'We took off from Lusaka in the afternoon and landed in Blantyre, Malawi. We were not in a normal plane – it was noisy and really shaking and we had to talk on top of our voices' was her first recollection.

Some 450 miles east of Lusaka, Blantyre – Malawi's commercial and financial capital – was supposed to be the Buffalo's first pit stop en route to Mauritius. But like many critical events in the last week of their collectively short lives, little went right for the Zambian team.

'We were supposed to refuel there and get something to eat, but I don't think we ate anything,' remembered Lupiya. 'We got off the plane, but just on the runway – we were not allowed to go inside [the airport terminal]. And then we refuelled and took off.'

At the controls of the Buffalo, colonel Fenton Mhone maintained the aircraft's eastward heading from Blantyre. His co-pilots were the two lieutenant colonels, Victor Mubanga and James Sachika, who'd flown the squad four months earlier to their next scheduled stop: Antananarivo, 854 miles away on the world's fourth-largest island, famed for its unmatched biodiversity.

In a window seat at the rear of the loud, throbbing Buffalo as it lumbered over the Indian Ocean, Lupiya stared outside the unpressurised plane with a maximum ceiling of 13,000 feet. 'We were flying very, very low – it wasn't very high like in a commercial plane when you fly high in the clouds – you could see the water all the time and the land all the time. We were flying at a very low altitude. You could see all the way. We never disappeared into the clouds,' she said.

Sitting next to her was Kelvin Mutale, also on his maiden Buffalo flight. The din, the violent vibration and the plane's low altitude on the way to Madagascar may have all appeared surreal for Mutale, by then accustomed to travelling on comfortable commercial airliners on football duty.

He turned to Lupiya and nonchalantly but loudly said in the Bemba language they both spoke, 'Ba Lupiya, imagine if the plane crashed and we died.'

Lupiya was aghast. 'I told him don't talk like that!'

Mutale's voice must have carried above the din of the DHC-5D's turboprop engines, the most improved in the Buffalo series. Several team-mates sitting nearby heard him and, also alarmed, hushed him. 'There was some kind of brief talk about it,' recalled Lupiya. 'The other players said "tefyakulanda ifyo naimwe" [you shouldn't be talking like that] – or something like that,' recalled Lupiya. 'I also told him "not uku landa ifya so" [not to talk like that] – what if it happens?'

After Libreville, Lupiya came up with a premise on what might have prompted Mutale's ominous remark. 'He couldn't avoid talking about it because of the circumstances,' she concluded, alluding to the player's first experience in a noisy and uncomfortable Buffalo on an ill-planned flight.

Yet as the Buffalo began its final approach to Antananarivo – then a city of more than a million, smack in the middle of Madagascar at an elevation of more than a kilometre – Mutale's seemingly light-hearted albeit portentous remark may have raised legitimate fears among those that heard it.

If neglecting to obtain clearance in Malawi for the players to enter the airport terminal was bad enough, their next experience could have spelt tragedy before Gabon. Once again, due to another astonishing bureaucratic oversight, a Zambian military plane was approaching a foreign airport in the dark of night without prior clearance – at least based on the reaction of the Madagascan authorities.

'The funny thing is that when we got to Madagascar, we didn't even land,' said Lupiya. 'The pilot was communicating with the control tower or whoever it is, and we were told to go back to Blantyre – we didn't have the rights to land – we were already there and we were told to get back to Malawi because we didn't have the rights to land in Madagascar. The route was supposed to be Blantyre and then Madagascar and then Mauritius. I don't know why we couldn't just go direct – it seems that wasn't the route the pilot got, so we had to go back to Malawi.'

After circling over Antananarivo – the brightly lit Madagascan capital – several times, the Buffalo disappeared back into the dark westward sky. It landed in Blantyre in the dead of night. Sadly, Malawi, with president for life Kamuzu Banda on his last political legs, would – for the second time in a few hours – be no less welcoming to the Zambians. It was then, according to Lupiya, that the players' morale finally flagged.

'We stayed there on the runway. We weren't allowed to go inside [the terminal] and I think the pilot was still negotiating for the rights to land in Madagascar,' said Lupiya. 'And so that's when the morale really went down with the players. We were talking and they really weren't happy and I talked a lot with Kelvin because I sat next to him. What I remember exactly, because ... you know ... I remember that [the players] surrounded me because they knew that I was a journalist. I remember that the team was split. Some of them didn't want me to write about their displeasure, some of them wanted me to write about it. But Kelvin, for example, he wanted me to write about it, but others like Timothy [Mwitwa] didn't want me to write about it.

'And then Efford ... Efford was the captain and he told me that because they had jobs to keep, he's not going to complain. "It's happened, we are not happy about it," he said.'

Then Lupiya recalled the veteran goalie saying something that would later prove prescient, 'He added that I should just do my job as a journalist and write about the event [game], 'But if anything happens to us and then somehow you survive then you can write about our displeasures but not now. "Twalikwata abana nabakashi kumayanda, tulefwaya ukusunga amachito [We have families. We want to keep our jobs]," Chabala said in Bemba.

'We never ate. We were hungry and thirsty. We were supposed to eat in Madagascar – and then after sometime, one of the officials disappeared inside and then came back with some quick foods [sic] but it took a long, long time – I think it was sandwiches – it wasn't much.'

At some point in that long nightmarish night, the cream of Zambian football, with something in their bellies, resumed their journey once landing rights in Madagascar had been secured.

'We continued and then finally landed in Madagascar – we flew in the night but when we landed, I remember it was morning,' said Lupiya. 'There were small boys playing outside and I said, oh, is this the airport? OK.'

She recollects the team spending several hours at the airport in Antananarivo, and having a meal, before they took off on the last leg. The Buffalo's destination was the village of Belle Vue Harel, nearly 700 miles east across the Indian Ocean, in northern Mauritius.

'We arrived safely, despite everything,' said Lupiya. 'We got there in the afternoon – I think three days before the game.'

The end of their ordeal getting to Mauritius lifted the Zambians. 'Despite everything, the morale was quite high when we arrived – the spirits were high,' recalled Lupiya. 'I had to write previews and I was talking to them and then I talked to Mr Ucar – Godfrey. I used to call him "Mr Ucar" – he always laughed.'

The invigorated spirits showed on that overcast Sunday afternoon of 25 April 1993 at the Sir Anerood Jugnauth Stadium (later rechristened Anjalay). Kelvin

Mutale, in particular, was on fire. He did all the scoring in a 3-0 romp. The first goal came when he outsprinted the Mauritian defence to a long ball. For the second, Malaza held off a defender to smash home from close range. And the coup de grâce was a perfectly executed volley into the net after chesting a corner – skills honed with amateur coach Sampa Mwanakaoma, who was deceased by then, on the dusty fields of Kafue. It was the second hat-trick of Mutale's short but brilliant career with Zambia. The goals came in the 23-year-old's 13th and final international match.

Mutale was mobbed by reporters at the final whistle, including Beauty Lupiya. 'I asked him what the trick was and he said, "Well, I didn't plan it, it just happened,"' she recalled.

Next, in an era before mixed zone interview areas, the reporters followed the match hero and his victorious team-mates to the Zambian dressing room where interviews continued. All but Lupiya. 'I was just waiting outside because I was the only [female] journalist. All the other journalists were in the dressing room because they were men – so I was there getting impatient, I wanted to talk to Kelvin some more,' she said.

Her patience exhausted, Lupiya decided to enter the dressing room. She opened the door. 'When I got in, all the players were naked! And then I quickly rushed out,' she laughed.

The victorious Zambians left Mauritius the next morning – Monday. No one fathomed that – they'd all, with the exception of Beauty Lupiya, be dead.

The return journey was uneventful. 'Going back again, Madagascar, then Blantyre and then Zambia … no problem at all,' said Lupiya. 'We arrived in Zambia the same day. It was really loud [on the plane], you couldn't whisper. I'd have to talk on the top of my voice because it was really noisy inside. And then also on landing, it was quite uncomfortable – it was rough – I don't think even the best of pilots would give you a smooth landing in a Buffalo.

'It would go, boom! Boom! And he'd land and the players would clap. It was really a good feeling whenever they landed. It was late afternoon when we arrived in Lusaka and the next day I was at work.'

Appreciated by the players and their coaches, Lupiya was eager to continue with her Zambia assignment. They were scheduled to depart less than 24 hours later the next day, Tuesday, 27 April for their first 1994 World Cup play-off tie against Senegal in Dakar – one of the closest African cities to the tournament's next host, the United States. 'I'd have loved to continue,' she said.

But Davey Sakala, the *Times of Zambia* sports editor, had other plans, which saved Lupiya's life.

'He said Chris Kachingwe would go instead of me,' remembered Lupiya. 'The players thought I was doing a good job – of course they are not editors, who are they to say? We had a nice rapport – there was some chemistry between the players, the coaches and me. When Dave said I shouldn't go, I said OK. I didn't argue.'

Lupiya's withdrawal left Joseph Salimu of the Zambia News Agency (ZANA) as the only reporter who'd been in Mauritius to continue on the next leg to West Africa. When Lupiya left the airport, it would be the last time she'd see the national team. She was at the Lusaka club on Wednesday, 28 April, covering Davis Cup tennis when she heard about the crash. 'I didn't believe it, of course,' she said.

What followed was a deluge of calls to the *Times of Zambia* from family, friends and acquaintances enquiring if she'd been on the plane.

On the morning of 22 April 1993, as the national side acclimatised in Belle Vue Harel, northern Mauritius, ahead of their AFCON qualifier with the host nation on 25 April, Ronald (Ronnie) Shikapwasha climbed into the cockpit of the Buffalo DHC-5D that had been parked at the ZAF base in Lusaka since 21 December. Born on Christmas Day 1947, Shikapwasha, aged 46, held the rank of lieutenant general and was a commander of the Zambia Air Force. He'd been trained by Britain's Royal Air Force and was certified to fly numerous aircraft. These included De Havilland's Chipmunk, Beaver, Caribou and Buffalo, the Hawker Siddeley HS 748 and the Soviet-built Yak 40, a commuter trijet. Shikapwasha had also spent time at the controls of fighter planes and helicopters. Basically, if it had wings, he could fly it.

Long retired in 2020 and in a new calling as a pastor, he summed up his extraordinary flying skills thus: 'It was important as a pilot who must train others, and as an examiner, to have a wider and specialised experience in order to answer the greater and demanding standards required in the Zambia Air Force.'

Shikapwasha was not only a ZAF commander but one of its leading flight instructors and examiners. The skilled aviator had served as presidential pilot for 14 years, flying Zambia's first head of state, Kenneth Kaunda, and other VIPs when required. But that 22 April morning, Shikapwasha would wear another hat: as a test pilot. He was all too familiar with the Buffalo DHC-5D, registration number AF-319, that he was about to take into the air. It belonged to ZAF's elite presidential and VVIP squadron. The young lieutenant general's test flight went smoothly. He flew AF-319 to Livingstone, Zambia's tourist capital and the site of the famous Victoria Falls, 235 miles or 378km south of Lusaka as the crow flies. After a couple of hours on the ground at the ZAF base there, Shikapwasha flew AF-319 back to Lusaka. The Buffalo had passed its first test after four months on the ground.

AF-319 had rolled off the assembly line in Calgary in 1975 – a year before it was flown to Zambia – part of the ZAF purchase of seven De Havilland Buffalo DHC-5Ds from the Canadian manufacturer. Eighteen years later, AF-319 was designated to fly the Zambia national team to its furthest destination ever by ZAF transport. The squad would return on Monday, 26 April from Mauritius on another Buffalo and depart for Dakar, Senegal the next day on AF-319. It would be an odyssey of close to 4,000 miles, or more than 6,000km, in a turboprop craft whose cruising speed was 261mph. That meant a haul of close to 24 hours for the players with refuelling stops in Congo-Brazzaville, Libreville in Gabon and Abidjan in the Ivory Coast before the final stretch to Dakar – one of Africa's closest points to the Americas. It was precisely for this reason that AF-319 was taken off AOG status and put back into service.

Almost three decades later, Shikapwasha explained why to this writer, '[It] was a presidential plane, a more comfortable plane for the long trip to Senegal. And besides, the Buffalo with the team in Mauritius had to undergo scheduled servicing. All planes in the ZAF are meticulously serviced to very high standards including those that fly the president of Zambia and so the alleged ill-fated plane was serviced likewise.'

For AF-319, that included what in aviation parlance is termed a 'C' check. This is the second-most extensive maintenance check of a plane on the A to D scale used. According to Wikipedia, a 'C' check requires an inspection of a majority of an aircraft's components. Only a 'D' check – that entails disassembling the entire airplane for inspection and overhaul – is more extensive. Both 'C' and 'D' checks are done at the aircraft manufacturer's maintenance site. For AF-319, that meant a marathon flight of over 9,200 miles, or more than 14,800km, from Lusaka to Calgary in September 1991.

A six-man crew of four pilots and two engineers ferried AF-319 to Canada. Flying at a snail-like 260mph and – as it was not pressurised – maintaining a relatively low altitude of 10,000 feet (3,000m), the Buffalo droned north-westerly over Africa from Lusaka. It made refuelling stops in Kinshasa, Libreville, Abidjan and Dakar. With a ferry range (zero payload) of 2,040 miles, the Buffalo then crossed the Atlantic with further refuelling stops on the Canary Islands and the Azores, before touching down in Newfoundland, Canada's easternmost province. The final leg took the ZAF crew more than 3,500 miles west across three quarters of Canada's vast landmass – over the St Lawrence Lowlands, the Great Lakes, Great Prairies and the foothills of the Rockies to Calgary, where the maintenance site was. There were refuelling stops in Montreal and Winnipeg on the way.

Still, just over a year after undergoing that major overhaul in Calgary, AF-319 was grounded for four months. Its AOG status officially ended when Zambia Air Force commander Lt Gen Ronnie Shikapwasha climbed into the cockpit on the morning of 22 April 1993 for a test flight after work on the Buffalo. It went well.

'I flew the plane from Lusaka to Livingstone and back to Lusaka, it was in perfect condition,' he told this writer.

There was a second reported flight test on 26 April – as the national team made its way back from Mauritius on the other Buffalo. A different crew took AF-319 airborne. The results were far from perfect this time, according to an excerpt posted on aviation-safety.net for many years: 'The DHC-5 Buffalo, AF-319, had not been flying from 21

December 1992 to 21 April 1993 so test flights were carried out on 22 April and 26 April. On 26 April both the "A" and "B" checks were carried out revealing certain defects such as carbon particles in the engine and in speed decreased gearbox oil filters, disconnected or unbridled cables and trace of heating.'

From all evidence, little or no action was taken in response to these findings that should have raised a huge red flag 24 hours before such an important flight carrying the cream of Zambian football to West Africa. Power Dynamos' Martin Mwamba (no relation to this writer) had travelled to Mauritius as Zambia's third-choice goalkeeper. He recalled the team landing in Lusaka in the late afternoon on 26 April and AF-319 being pointed out to them, 'When we arrived at the international airport, we found it was being fuelled – and we were told that it would be the plane we'd be flying with to Senegal. It was green.'

14

Eve of Disaster

MARTIN MWAMBA slept soundly at Masiye Executive Lodge on the eve of the Senegal trip. 'I didn't have any bad dreams,' the squad's third-choice goalie said.

But at least one player was unsettled or may have had a premonition.

Said Mwamba, 'I remember the late [Godfrey] Kangwa … saying "uku tuleya uku nakubipishya" … he was saying like that … "uku tuleya nakubipishya" [where we are going, it is very bad]. Monday evening [26 April], that's when he was saying that … "uku tuleya nakubipishya" … Then the late Derby [Makinka] was saying "enemy territory", something like that.'

Mwamba woke up early at Masiye on Tuesday, 27 April feeling good. He sat down for breakfast with his team-mates at 7.30am. On each plate were two fried eggs, a sausage, and two slices of bread and butter. It was washed down with tea. It would be the team's last meal in Zambia. Departure for Senegal was scheduled for 11am. Immediately after breakfast, Mwamba and Andrew Tembo, the latter a promising 21-year-old right-winger from Lusaka club Zamsure, were summoned by coaches Godfrey Chitalu and Alex Chola. What the two fringe players didn't know is that their lives were about to be spared. They were told that they'd be left behind to make room in the squad for Charles Musonda and Kalusha Bwalya, who would join the team in Dakar (while Kalusha had indeed made plans to depart Eindhoven for Dakar via Paris on Wednesday, 28 April, unbeknownst to FAZ, Musonda was sidelined by injury yet again).

'So, I went to my room, I packed my things, then went to the roadside in Emmasdale and caught a cab to the bus station,' said Mwamba.

Mwamba booked a seat on the 1pm bus to Kitwe from the Lusaka city-centre terminus. Then he walked half a kilometre to the Football Association of Zambia office in Anchor House, off Cairo Road, to pick up K150 in travel allowances. He also had in his wallet US$500 in allowances from the Mauritius assignment. At Anchor House, Mwamba encountered some of his team-mates he'd left an hour earlier at Masiye. They were leaving the FAZ offices on the ninth floor after picking up the team's kit for the Senegal match. It would be the last time he'd see his compatriots.

As it turned out, the goalkeeper missed the 1pm bus to the Copperbelt, so he caught the 2pm departure. Mwamba arrived at his council home in Kitwe's Ndeke Changachanga township after midnight safe and sound. Around that same time some 1,574 flying miles away in Libreville, Gabon, elements of the fire service, presidential guard and nautical brigade of the National Gendarmerie were launching a rescue operation after a plane had plunged into the Atlantic Ocean shortly after take-off from Léon-Mba International Airport.

Sometime after 2pm on 27 April, Sonstone Kashiba drove into the Zambia Air Force base adjacent to Lusaka International Airport. A civil servant for more than two decades, he had a seat reserved on the Buffalo carrying the national team to Senegal. As acting director of sport in Zambia's Ministry of Sport, Kashiba and the ministry's permanent secretary, Sipho Mudenda, were designated to travel with the team to Senegal as government representatives.

After parking his government car, Kashiba walked to the tarmac where the green-camouflaged Buffalo DHC-5D, registration number AF-319, was parked. There he was enthusiastically greeted by assistant coach Alex Chola. The former midfield maestro and Kashiba shared a special kinship.

He said, 'We'd joke every time that we came from Congo – Zaire at that time. I'd say, "You and me, we are from Kola – Zaire."'

Chola and Kashiba's private joke was based on their common Luapula heritage in northern Zambia. Whereas Chola had been born in the Belgian Congo where his father had sought employment, Kashiba had stayed behind in Luapula, when his father had crossed over the border to become Chief Kashiba on the Congo side of the sprawling Mwata Kazembe empire that predated the European partition of Africa. Their banter also included Chola's amazing abilities as a player. Kashiba would joke about the latter's skills. He would tease the outrageously talented former player that his ball skills were the result of 'the juju [witchcraft] we have in our land, the Luba Kingdom'.

Chola laughed as he led Kashiba toward the Buffalo. 'He said, "Come inside – come and see where you are supposed to sit. You are supposed to sit in front of me." So, I entered the plane. It was very comfortable – it was not bad.' AF-319 was after all part of the air force's VVIP squadron.

Chola showed Kashiba his seat – in a row right in front of the seats reserved for the coaches. 'It was in the middle of the plane. The officials and the coaches were to sit parallel to the wings. Alex and Godfrey sat next to each other,' Kashiba said. Structurally, the section of a plane where the wings attach to the fuselage is considered its sturdiest part.

To the two coaches' disappointment, Kashiba told them that he and the permanent secretary wouldn't be travelling with the team. The appointment of Dipak Patel as minister of youth and sport two days earlier by President Frederick Chiluba meant that the acting director of sport and his permanent secretary would have to stay behind to oversee Patel's transition to office.

The ZAF crew was already on board. After a rest of less than 24 hours following their return from Mauritius, Col Fenton Mhone, and his two co-pilots, Lt Cols Victor Mubanga and James Sachika, would fly this Buffalo to West Africa and back. Warrant officer Edward Nambote, an engineer, and Corporal Tomson Sakala, a steward, completed the five-man crew. FAZ chairman Michael Mwape, team doctor Wilson Mtonga, Nelson Zimba, a government official authorised by Cabinet Office to travel with the squad to all their World Cup qualifiers, Zambia News Agency reporter Joseph Salimu, and Wilson Sakala, a FAZ functionary, rounded off the 30 people on the Buffalo.

Kashiba disembarked from the ZAF transport and watched as the team boarded. There were 18 players clad in turquoise and black tracksuits. With the exception of the European-based Kalusha, Charles Musonda and Johnson Bwalya, they constituted Zambia's best footballers. One by one, they climbed into the Buffalo, in high spirits despite another delayed departure: stand-in skipper Efford Chabala, at 33, Zambia's starting goalie for a decade and considered the best African-based shot-stopper; tough as nails defender Eston Mulenga, a crunching tackler and relentless man-marker; Derby Makinka, a midfield workhorse with silky skills, a powerful long-range shot and aged 27, just two international caps short of a century. Then there was the new blood epitomised by the free-scoring Kelvin Mutale. Malaza to his growing fanbase, the 23-year-old Mutale, a Manchester United fan, was the future of Zambian football. His hat-trick against Mauritius two days earlier had brought his international tally to 14 goals in just 13 matches. Even more exciting for Zambian fans was the prospect of a lethal partnership with Kalusha that promised many more international goals and triumphs.

That was the expectation as this collection of talent stepped into the Buffalo. Destination: Dakar, Senegal. They were in a jovial mood,' Kashiba recalled. 'Then I saw the plane take off.' It was well past 2pm local time. What he didn't know as he watched the aircraft disappear into the northern sky was that he'd just been the last Zambian to board and disembark alive from AF-319 that day.

On the night of Sunday, 17 August 1980, Profund Warriors, a second division club sponsored by what was then Zambia's largest pension fund, were travelling back to Lusaka after a league fixture in Chililabombwe, then a small mining town abutting the Zaire border. It's likely that most of the team was either asleep or dozing as their minibus approached the final stretch of a 260-mile (422km) road trip following a 2-0 win over Lubengele FC earlier that day. However, some 60km north of the capital, disaster struck on the Great North Road that late night. In what from all signs appeared to be a single-vehicle accident, the team bus careered off the road and slammed into a tree. Eight players and the team manager died. Twelve other passengers survived with serious injuries. The dead players were Chris Chikwanda, Gilbert Chola, Joseph Daka,

Anthony Mulenga, Sydney Mfune, Philip Sakala, Geoffrey Chileshe and Phidelis Ntanganyika; manager Abraham Chibumbwa was the only official to lose his life.

Eerily, the crash occurred 11 years to the day of Zambia's first football-related fatality. That was in August 1969 when the Ndola United team bus overturned, also at night, also on the Great North Road (approaching Kapiri Mposhi). Three players – Paul Mulenga, Joseph Chintu and Winnie Chama – perished. United were returning to Ndola after defeating Lusaka Tigers in the quarter-finals of the BP Challenge Cup at the Matero Stadium.

The Football Association of Zambia's response to the Profund Warriors tragedy was to ban all affiliated clubs from travelling at night after fixtures. Profund would recover from the disaster to earn promotion to the top flight by the mid-80s. In Derby Makinka, they'd nurtured a player who by 1986 was the best young midfielder in the league. He spent six years at the club before leaving in 1989 for stints with CSKA Pamir Dushanbe in present-day Tajikistan, Zimbabwe's Darryn Textiles, top Polish side Lech Poznań and, finally, Al Ettifaq in Saudi Arabia.

Profund, then coached by former international midfielder and both past and future Zambia assistant boss Boniface Simutowe would also briefly claim the hottest player in the domestic game during the 1992 pre-season: Kelvin Mutale. From a nondescript club in small-town Kafue, Malaza raised eyebrows with his prodigious skills that included dribbling past and leaving veteran international defenders on their haunches. He scored numerous times in a few pre-season friendlies, then suddenly disappeared one evening from the four-bedroom Emmasdale house he shared with several other Profund players. Chingola-based Nchanga Rangers had poached the scoring phenom only to lose him to Nkana the next day.

On the afternoon of 27 April 1993, Profund's latest star, a 19-year-old dual-footed forward named Patrick 'Bomber' Banda, was among the 18 Zambian aces who acting director of sport Sonstone Kashiba saw board the Buffalo at the ZAF base in Lusaka. First capped aged 17 in 1991, Banda was 18 when he emerged as Zambia's second best player at the 1992 Confederation of East and Central African Football Association tournament in Tanzania. He twice notched braces in what was Zambia's last appearance in Africa's oldest football competition, dating back to 1926. The four goals by the versatile striker raised hopes of a deadly future partnership with Kelvin Mutale who finished as the tournament's top scorer with seven goals – including a hat-trick. Banda was the second-youngest person aboard Buffalo AF-319 after Kenani Simambe, the 18-year-old Power Dynamos forward.

As it carried the Zambia squad to Dakar for the first match of a three-team play-off to decide one of Africa's three envoys at the 1994 FIFA World Cup in the United States, AF-319 pretty much retraced its flight path of 17 months earlier when it was ferried to Calgary for a 'C' check. It had made refuelling stops in Kinshasa, Libreville and Abidjan then. This time Brazzaville, capital of Congo-Brazzaville a few miles across the mighty Congo River, would be the first stop. The flying distance from Lusaka was 1,172 miles (1,886km). Libreville and Abidjan were to follow.

15

Disaster

IT'S GENERALLY acknowledged in the aviation industry that most plane disasters – in the absence of a terrorist act or severe weather conditions – can be attributed to a series of errors that lead to doom. A 1998 study commissioned by the Federal Aviation Administration in the United States added credence to this school of thought. 'Aviation safety experts have realised for sometime that aircraft incidents and accidents almost always result from a series of events, each of which is associated with one or more cause factors. Thus, the cause of an accident or incident has many aspects,' concluded the National Research Council in its report, *Improving the Continued Airworthiness of Civil Aircraft: A strategy for the FAA's Aircraft Certification service*, published by the National Academies Press.

Canadian journalist and best-selling author Malcolm Gladwell weighed in on the subject in his intensely researched book *Outliers: The Story of Success*. Gladwell noted that plane crashes are much more likely to be the result of an accumulation of minor difficulties and seemingly trivial malfunctions. He even postulated the number of errors associated with the typical accident – seven in his estimation.

At approximately 10.45pm GMT off the coast of Libreville, Gabon, on the night of 27 April 1993, two Zambia Air Force pilots reacted to a sudden explosion in the port (left) engine of their plane by switching off the right engine that was their only remaining source of power. The De Havilland Canada DHC-5D Buffalo transport plunged into the Atlantic Ocean, taking with it the lives of arguably the finest collection of footballers produced by Zambia. It was one of the darkest moments in world sport.

Nobody can accuse the ZAF crew of a litany of errors on that ill-fated flight. Maybe two. But evidently, the flight path – figuratively – to that tragic night in Libreville was strewn with a frightening sequence of poor judgement, on several levels, and astonishingly fatalistic bravado at the end that would have made many an experienced flier shudder: an aircraft parked for four months (for some still-undisclosed reason) under the hot sun at the ZAF base adjacent to the International Airport in Lusaka; then it being repaired and taken on two test flights, the last one raising a red flag; then it being cleared to ferry the national football team on a 7,496-mile (12,062km) round trip to Dakar, Senegal.

In its third edition dated June–August 1993, the magazine *African Soccer*, published in London by Emmanuel Maradas from 1992 to 2004, offered some insight into the Buffalo's fateful last hours after leaving Lusaka.

It reported how AF-319 landed in Brazzaville five hours later. There the first signs of trouble were detected in the plane's port side engine, said *African Soccer*, citing 'unofficial sources'. Still, the Buffalo was refuelled and airborne again, en route to Libreville, more than 500 miles north-west. It landed in the Gabonese capital some two hours later – well after 8pm local time – for what was supposed to be a 30-minute pit stop to top up its 2,108 US gallon-capacity (7,980-litre) capacity fuel tanks. Instead, AF-319 would spend two hours on the ground in Libreville after making its final landing.

In an article entitled 'The View from Libreville', *African Soccer* then pieced together an unofficial account of those final moments. The magazine's sources – according to Ponga Liwewe, son of the renowned Zambian commentator Dennis Liwewe and an *African Soccer* contributor himself – included eyewitnesses and local papers.

Those who saw them say the 30 passengers and crew on board the Zambian Air Force Buffalo were tired by the time the plane finally took off from Léon Mba International Airport, just before 11pm GMT. Already late leaving Lusaka earlier in the day, they had spent two hours instead of the scheduled 30 minutes on the ground in the Gabonese capital. They were told that there was something wrong with the port engine; nobody seemed to know what, but none of the passengers seemed to think it was serious. They had flown with Col Fenton Mhone before, most recently to their victorious Africa Cup of Nations encounter with Mauritius, and seemed confident of arriving at their next destination, Abidjan, later that night. Witnesses say Kelvin Mutale, who scored a hat-trick in that match, was in particularly buoyant spirits as he and the players stretched their legs on the tarmac.

What the players certainly had not seen was the small crowd which had gathered round the Buffalo aircraft's troublesome left-hand engine. The Libreville ground crew were trying to dissuade the Zambian crew from leaving. The breakdown was too serious, they said, to try and patch up at night. Was it stubbornness, or justifiable confidence that the plane would fly? The flight commander said that two hours' repairs had already been carried out at Brazzaville and that they had reached Libreville without problems. As he spoke, the faulty engine sprang into life. The passengers were rounded up, ready for the last leg but one in the long flight to Dakar. As the passengers and crew climbed back on board, the mechanic went to pay the landing charges and settle up for the 2,331 litres of fuel taken on. A final check with the control tower confirmed light cloud over Libreville and a gentle breeze from the west-north-west; perfect conditions in short. Col Mhone launched the plane down the runway.

It was 10.44pm. From the tarmac, one of the ground crew noticed something odd about the take-off. The plane seemed to be flying with one wing pointing downward. He thought, wrongly, that the pilot was making a manoeuvre. In fact, the pilot was limping towards catastrophe. Minutes after take-off, it started its plunge into the sea, just 2km from the coast. It did not take long for the alarm to be sounded in Libreville. Within minutes, the control tower realised something was wrong and launched a rescue operation. The Libreville fire service, presidential guard and Nautical Brigade of the National Gendarmerie were all mobilised in the search for possible survivors. Hope quickly died, however, as eyewitness accounts began to come through. Everything suggested that the aircraft had exploded, either on impact with the sea, or while it was still in flight. People spoke of a noise followed by a huge red light in the sky. But it was not until the next morning that Libreville awoke to the full horror of the first pictures broadcast on television.

Despite an investigation carried out jointly by both ZAF and Gabonese authorities, it would be an acrimonious and frustrating decade later before any official report was released. It came from the Gabonese Ministry of Defence and it corroborated certain aspects of the *African Soccer* piece. Most significantly, that the 'noise followed by a huge red light in the sky', heard and seen by eyewitnesses, was the Buffalo's faulty port side engine exploding and illuminating the night sky. If that didn't doom the stricken plane instantly, what happened in the next terrifying moments surely did.

In the cockpit, the crew rapidly reacted as it was trained to do when an engine catches fire: shut it down. But in the panic, a catastrophic error occurred. The Gabonese report would attribute this to Col Mhone and fatigue on his part after flying the team to Mauritius and back days earlier. Never mind that there were two other pilots on board and that a ZAF source – and circumstantial evidence – would point to these two, and not Mhone, as being at the controls. At any rate, instead of switching off the flaming port engine, it was the starboard (right) engine – still running and the plane's only source of thrust – that was cut off, totally crippling the aircraft.

Still in flames, the Buffalo hit the dark waters approximately half a kilometre from the shore. Lasting just a few unimaginably horrific seconds, its fiery descent into the Atlantic would wipe out the cream of Zambian football. The Gabonese report put the time of the accident at 10.45 GMT – 11.45pm Zambian time. But it would be at least another seven hours before anyone in Zambia had an inkling of the tragedy.

* * *

The fatal pilot error that ultimately doomed the Buffalo was not unprecedented in aviation. Four years earlier, on the night of 8 January 1989, a British Midland Boeing 737-400 from Heathrow to Belfast lost power in its left engine when a fan blade fractured 13 minutes into the flight. According to the Aviation Safety Network, the two pilots 'did not assimilate the indications on the engine instrument display before they throttled back the number two [right] engine'. They misread which engine was losing power and shut down their only remaining source of thrust. Without power, the plane went down just short of East Midlands Airport. Forty-seven of the 126 people on board died in what became known as the Kegworth air disaster.

A similar error by a vastly experienced pilot would claim the lives of 43 of the 58 people on board a TransAsia Airways ATR 72-600 moments after take-off from Taipei's downtown Songshan airport on the morning of 4 February 2015. The commuter plane, almost brand new, had lost thrust in the number two engine when captain Liao Jian-zong, with close to 5,000 hours on ATR 72 planes, powered down the good – left – engine. Its dramatic plunge – tilted port side, left wing clipping a bridge and a passing taxi – into a shallow river would be chillingly captured on the dashcam of a passing car, producing a viral clip. 'Wow, pulled back the wrong side throttle!' were Liao's last recorded words before the crash. He perished along with his entire crew. There were 15 survivors.

* * *

Five years after helping Zambia qualify for the 1988 Seoul Olympics, defender Manfred Chabinga woke up in the wee hours of 28 April 1993 after a disturbing dream. He'd dreamed that he was at a funeral, but didn't know whose. 'I cried bitterly in the dream and woke up grief-stricken,' he remembered. Chabinga told his wife about the nightmare but couldn't fathom whose death would cause him such wrenching sorrow – not until several hours later when, like most Zambians, he'd hear about the crash of the Buffalo. Chabinga's ominous dream, that he estimated between 5am and 5.30am local time, occurred approximately five and a half hours after the Buffalo's fiery plunge into the darkened

Atlantic. Way before it was publicly reported in Zambia. There was no official notification of the accident from the Gabonese authorities.

'The Gabonese government never informed us, that I know of,' said Ronnie Shikapwasha, the ZAF commander then who'd flown the doomed Buffalo five days before it went down in the Atlantic. The numbing news was broken to him by his deputy commander Major General Zaza after a French radio broadcast at 6.30am Zambian time. Subsequent broadcasts by German radio and the BBC, the latter at 8am, verified the calamity.

'The French radio reported to the world that a Zambian military plane had been shot down by Gabon. The German radio reported that a Zambian military plane had crashed [in] the Atlantic Ocean a few miles off the coast of Gabon. We tried to contact the Gabonese military to help us with more information and [provide] the latest reports but they refused. Gabon never informed Zambia,' said Shikapwasha.

The French radio report would be the grist for conspiracy theories that persist in certain quarters to this day – that the Buffalo had indeed been downed as it flew over a French base near the airport.

Shikapwasha was paralysed by news of the crash. 'I was shocked beyond belief. Because the crew was the cream of Zambia Air Force pilots. I didn't believe the plane had crashed. I still do not agree that the plane had crashed,' he said in February 2021. He went to his own grave, aged 76 in January 2024, still believing that.

The catastrophic news was confined to officialdom for several hours after Shikapwasha had briefed Zambian president Frederick Chiluba, then on a state visit in Uganda, early that Wednesday morning. But elsewhere, word was slowly getting out.

16

Grief

AT THE *Times of Zambia* offices in Farmers House – located near the halfway point on the mile-long Cairo Road, Lusaka's main business and commercial thoroughfare – the main phone line had been ringing off the hook since the wee hours of Wednesday, 28 April. When Chris Kachingwe, a sports reporter on the daily paper with a 50,000 circulation, reported for work at 7.30am, he was told by the switchboard operator that the BBC had called several times. They wanted to know what had happened to the plane carrying the Zambian team. Kachingwe felt a chill.

The previous day, Kachingwe had covered the squad's late afternoon arrival from Mauritius. And when *Times* sports editor Davey Sakala asked for a volunteer to relieve reporter Beauty Lupiya – who'd covered the Mauritius game – for the Senegal assignment, Kachingwe's hand shot up. He'd never been to West Africa and was eager to visit that part of the continent. That was less than 24 hours before the squad's departure for Dakar. So, the race was on for Kachingwe, a six-year veteran on the *Times* sports desk, to prepare for the trip. He'd have a free seat on the Buffalo – which was able to carry up to 40 passengers – and all he needed were allowances. In an era before credit cards in

Zambia, that essentially meant getting traveller's cheques issued before departure the next morning.

That evening, Kachingwe and two associates paid the Zambian team a visit at Masiye Executive Lodge – a modest establishment in a light-industrial area north of the Lusaka city centre. 'We sat with the players, trying to find out the travelling modalities. We were told the team was leaving very early the following day,' he recalled.

That raised the ante precipitously for Kachingwe if he was to make the trip. The *Times of Zambia*'s main office – accounts department and all – was in Ndola, more than 200 miles north on the Copperbelt.

'Basically, I couldn't travel because the money was not ready,' recalled Kachingwe. 'So, we didn't go to the airport [next morning] and we realised, I think around 10am, that the team had not left. So, this machinery to raise money and get to the airport starts running. For us it was traveller's cheques. The accounts department was in Ndola, so you had to fax these documents back and forth and somebody at some point must give you authority to get cash from sales, so that was my option – get cash from sales and get to the airport. Then suddenly, I think at 11am, we were told the team is leaving, "You are late, you can't get to the airport." And I was devastated, I was looking forward to this.'

Having missed the Buffalo's departure on Tuesday afternoon, Kachingwe arrived at the *Times* office early Wednesday morning only to be told by the switchboard operator that the BBC had been calling for the sports desk. They were enquiring about the fate of the plane he should have been on. Davey Sakala, the sports editor, got to the office before 8am and was told about the BBC calls by Kachingwe. Sakala said he'd talk to them when they called next. They did, moments later. It was surreal.

'The BBC guy tells Davey that they had a report of a plane crash in Libreville and that the team had perished. No one believed him,' Kachingwe recalled. 'Then suddenly there was a telex – some newsflash – from the Bank of Zambia to the effect that the plane carrying the Zambian team had crashed. So, there was confusion in the office.'

Because of its need to monitor the fluctuation of global currencies in real time, Zambia's central bank in 1993 had the most advanced communication equipment and network in the country. Far beyond anything possessed by the local media, largely state-owned then. So, Bank of Zambia had taken it upon itself to send out a newsflash on the reportedly crashed Buffalo to certain clients. Government, meanwhile, remained silent.

It was shortly after 8am when shell-shocked *Times* reporters walked out of the newsroom and gathered outside Farmers House, trying to make sense of this unprecedented and cruel tragedy. The busy early morning rush-hour traffic flowing past on both sides of the four-lane Cairo Road was still oblivious of the catastrophe that would soon paralyse the nation – all but one vehicle, which was parked on the northbound lane. The crestfallen driver stepped out, crossed the thoroughfare and burst into tears when he saw the reporters.

Simataa Simataa, a banker and avid football fan was, like Kachingwe, supposed to have been on the Buffalo. He'd had a chance encounter with the team on the Great East Road in Northmead as he was driving home two days earlier. It was around 5pm, Monday, 26 April, and the national side was headed to Masiye Lodge on the team bus after arriving from Mauritius. Recognising his late-model white Volvo 740 GL, some of the players had craned their necks out of the minibus and beseeched him to follow them to the lodge.

'Isa mudala! Isa!' – come, old man, come! – they shouted.

Simataa heeded their call and followed the team bus. He was a popular figure among players and was one of the fans who had travelled to Senegal the previous year for the 1992 Africa Cup of Nations. There, Zambia had recorded their first competitive win over Egypt with Kalusha's solitary goal, and narrowly succumbed 1-0 to Abedi Pele's superb individual effort for Ghana – but only after defender Anthony Baffoe had cleared Kalusha's goal-bound shot off the line. The run had ended in the quarter-finals where eventual winners Ivory Coast had eked out a 1-0 result in extra time. That was the pre-Kelvin Mutale period when Kalusha was Zambia's primary scoring hope.

At Masiye Lodge, Simataa sat with star defender Eston Mulenga and some of the senior players in a large dorm-like room with six beds. They reminisced over the 1992 Senegal outing as Eston, who'd bought a CD player in Mauritius, set up the device. Simataa asked if they'd be flying to Dakar on another Buffalo craft and the players replied in the affirmative. He suggested that they stay up late so that they could sleep on the plane. The nearly 3,800 miles or slightly more than 6,000km distance would make for a long flight on the relatively snail-like Buffalo.

'No, come, *mudala*!' one player insisted.

Simataa recalled his response. 'I said, ah! I don't think it will be possible – I think your plane is full.'

The player said no and revealed that there were empty seats on the Buffalo. Simataa's interest was piqued. When he woke up the next morning, Tuesday, 27 April, he'd decided to travel with the team. He drove 27km south of Lusaka to the town of Chilanga, where Michael Mwape lived. A former Bank of Zambia general manager, Mwape was FAZ chairman and would lead the team to Senegal.

Simataa wanted to find out if he could tag along. He missed the FAZ boss by a life-saving whisker.

'I found his wife, and I said I'm looking for Uncle Mike. She says, ah! You just missed him. I said where? She said he's just driven off, sonny. You didn't meet him along the road?'

Simataa hadn't and that saved his life. It was around 9am. Mwape, who'd led the team to Mauritius, had driven to the Zambia Air Force base, adjacent to the International Airport, to catch the Buffalo to Senegal. 'That's how I missed the trip,' recalled Simataa. 'So, when I got back home, I just forgot about it.'

Early next morning at Finance Bank's main Lusaka branch, where he was a corporate director, Simataa was suddenly aware of an eerie silence as he sat at his desk. 'Customers were walking in and there didn't seem to be that talking mood. Everybody was quiet, and every time I looked up from my desk, it's like everybody's eyes were on me,' Simataa remembered.

Then a colleague summoned the courage to approach him. She was considered the office gossip.

'I still remember her walking up to my desk and saying, "Ba Simataa, bushe na mumfya (have you heard)?" And I asked, "Heard what?" And she said, "The national team has died." I used to think that she was a gossip … so I told her to get lost. And she said no! No! No! I know, I've got reliable sources.'

Simataa was intrigued and decided to find out for himself. Anchor House, the ten-storey skyscraper that housed the FAZ office, was a few blocks away on a side street east of Cairo Road. Simataa walked there. He found FAZ general secretary Geoffrey Phiri in his ninth-floor office and asked him what was happening. Phiri, sitting at his desk, didn't say a word.

'He just threw a telegram at me. So, I picked it up, and for some reason I couldn't read. I couldn't. I looked at it and asked, so what is it saying? He just shrugged. Then I realised, there was something terribly wrong. So, I walked out.'

Despite neither official confirmation nor details of the tragedy, Simataa was an emotional wreck when he returned to the bank. 'I must've been crying. When my boss saw me, he suggested I go home,' he recalled.

He got in his car and as he drove along Cairo Road, he decided to stop when he approached the *Times of Zambia* office. If anybody knew anything, it would be the sports desk. He parked opposite the newspaper and, tears falling, walked towards the group of scribes standing forlornly outside the paper. 'What's this I hear?' he asked.

Like the FAZ general secretary less than an hour earlier, sports editor Davey Sakala pulled out a piece of paper. 'Some telex from Reuters,' recalled Simataa.

'This is all we've received,' mumbled Sakala.

Devastated, Simataa got in his car but had no recollection of the more than 10km drive to his Chelstone home east of Lusaka. 'I don't remember how I got home. I don't. It was the worst day of my life. I think I cried all day, all night.'

At the *Times*, it was almost 9am when Davey Sakala decided that it was time to put aside the grief. They had the biggest story in Zambia's history, and probably the most shattering news globally that week to report. 'He kept saying, "This is no time to mourn, this is the time to do our work,"' Kachingwe recalled.

* * *

A little over 18 hours after seeing the Zambia Air Force Buffalo plane carrying the national team to Senegal take off, Sonstone Kashiba, acting director of sport in Zambia's Ministry of Sport, sat in the anteroom of his boss's office. He'd boarded the Buffalo and was shown his seat by assistant coach Alex Chola. But he'd disappointed Chola by telling him that an urgent briefing with the new minister of sport, Dipak Patel, the next day meant that he couldn't travel with the squad. When he disembarked from the plane and the squad boarded, Kashiba was the only government official to see them off. Now here he was in the anteroom, sitting opposite the administrative assistant, waiting for the meeting that had prevented him from flying on the Buffalo to start.

Around 8.30am, the phone rang. The secretary answered. It was for Kashiba, from the Zambian High Commission in Lagos, Nigeria. Kashiba got up to take the call. The conversation was brief but shattering.

'Mr Kashiba, have you heard?'

'No, I haven't heard.'

'*Ati* there's a crash, our players have all perished!'

'Yey! Sure!?'

'Yes!'

The last government official to see the national team, Kashiba was now the first Ministry of Sport official to be informed of the crash. He barged into his boss Sipho Mudenda's office. 'I told him, sir, the plane had crashed!'

As permanent secretary, Mudenda was the most senior civil servant in the Ministry, reporting only to the minister. Mudenda was also supposed to fly on the Buffalo with Kashiba, if not for the scheduled briefing with the new minister that had now saved their lives. The two dashed to Dipak Patel's office. Patel was predictably stunned.

'He came out – it was like he was dreaming,' Kashiba said of Patel. 'He drove himself to State House [the Zambian president's office and residence].'

Frederick Chiluba, a diminutive, 5ft tall, former trade union leader elected to office in 1991 as Zambia's second president, had woken up in Kampala on the morning of 28 April. He was on the second day of a three-day state visit to Uganda when he was told of the crash by his aides. The visit was immediately cut short and within a couple of hours, Chiluba, aboard a chartered Zambia Airways Boeing 737-200, was back in Lusaka.

17

Survivor's Guilt

IN KITWE'S Changachanga township, Martin Mwamba had woken up late after arriving from Lusaka past midnight. Mwamba and young striker Andrew Tembo had been released from the squad hours before its departure to Dakar. They were told by coaches Godfrey Chitalu and Alex Chola that they'd have to make way for Kalusha Bwalya and Charles Musonda who would join the team in Senegal.

It was early afternoon when Mwamba finished bathing and heard sobbing. It was his wife. 'What is it?' he asked in Bemba. She was visiting a neighbour and had just heard that the national team had perished in a crash over water.

'I was very shocked,' said Mwamba. 'I switched on the radio and it was news everywhere. I was very shocked, I even failed to rub vaseline on my body after my bath. So, I went and sat down in the sitting room.

The powerful mix of grief and survivor's guilt, at once intense and confusing, instantly rendered him powerless. He'd spent the last week with his team-mates, experienced a nightmarish trip to Mauritius, had breakfast with them the previous morning and had seen some of them just over 24 hours earlier at the FAZ office when he went to collect his allowances. Now they were all dead. The loss was incomprehensible.

Unbeknownst to Mwamba, his family and friends – unaware of his late omission from the squad and unexpected return to Kitwe – were counting him among the dead as news of the tragedy spread on the radio.

In the neighbouring Copperbelt town of Luanshya, 27 miles away, Mwamba's parents had opened their Mikomfwa township home to mourners. They thought that they'd lost their goalkeeper son, last reported to be on national team duty in Mauritius and headed for Senegal. This was before mobile phones in Zambia, when instant communication was non-existent for those without landlines. Soon, other mourners headed for the player's Kitwe home for the expected wake. There'd be a joyous, Lazarus-like moment when they found Mwamba alive but in mourning himself. They celebrated by throwing corn flour on him.

Within hours of his arrival from Uganda, President Chiluba went on live radio and television. He announced a week-long period of national mourning, a state funeral for the heroes who'd died on national duty, and the establishment of a national trust fund.

In a press briefing once the news of the crash had been publicly announced, air force commander Lt Gen Ronnie Shikapwasha shed the first light on the doomed plane and some of the crew: '[The] aircraft had undergone a major overhaul in Canada, it came back last year, 1992, from Canada after a major overhaul. Prior to its fateful flight, I had undertaken to fly that particular aircraft from Livingstone to Lusaka and it had a mechanical sound [sic] for it to undertake the task as given by the country to take the national team to Senegal. The crew composition, the fateful crew on the aircraft were composed of Colonel Mhone; Colonel Mhone is the commanding officer of the

Zambia Air Force base at the International Airport, he's a qualified instructor, having been trained in the UK and passed through the staff and command college in India. Col Mhone joined the Zambia Air Force in 1970 – he has since been in several appointments and he has flown this aircraft for the past 15 years. The second crew member was Lt Col V.K. Mubanga.

'Lt Col Mubanga, too, has been flying the Buffalo aircraft for the past 12 years. He, too, has been in the service for the past 21 years and was a very experienced crew member. This crew was qualified and capable of undertaking this task. We, however, have to undertake and carry out [an] investigation along with the civil authorities in Zambia and, like the vice president has said, with the French government authority [sic) to determine what might have happened to the aircraft.'

* * *

On the afternoon of Thursday, 29 April 1993, a Douglas DC-8-71 jet in the green and white livery of Zambia Airways landed at Libreville's Léon-Mba International Airport after a three-hour flight from Lusaka. It carried three Zambian government ministers – including Vernon Mwaanga, in charge of foreign affairs and the delegation leader, and Dipak Patel in his first week on the job in charge of sports. There were also air force personnel; both state and military intelligence officers; journalists; an FAZ official; a medical team; and 30 caskets. Economy-class seats in the four-engine 259-passenger craft had been removed to make way for the caskets. The delegation's grim mission immediately hit home the moment it disembarked. Gabonese officials led the weary arrivals to the military section of the airport where what they saw cast a pall on an already sombre lot.

'It was part of the Buffalo wreckage,' said Goliath Mungonge, a sports reporter with the *Zambia Daily Mail*. 'They showed us a wheel and a wing. They were quite a number of things that [they'd] already picked up.'

Staring at pieces of the shattered Buffalo at the airport, Mungonge was pensive. Like Chris Kachingwe of the *Times of Zambia*, he, too, should have been on that plane whose remains he was staring at. And like Kachingwe, faulty logistics – the inability to get travel allowances so late, to be precise – had saved his life. Mungonge had been looking forward to returning with the squad to Senegal. He'd spent nearly two weeks there at the 1992 Africa Cup of Nations covering the Zambian squad, 11 of whom had perished less than 48 hours earlier a few kilometres from where he stood.

Mungonge and Davey Sakala, sports editor of the rival *Times of Zambia*, would, with their communication skills, play a key role in Libreville as liaisons between the Zambian delegation and the Gabonese officials directly involved in the recovery effort. Assigned a press car that they shared with another reporter and a Zambia national broadcasting corporation cameraman, they spent many hours between arrival on 29 April and Saturday, 1 May on the beach that was the primary landing site for the recovery crews bringing up remains and other parts from the Buffalo. At one time when the Zambian reporters were on the beach, a part of the Buffalo fuselage that Mungonge couldn't recall washed ashore.

The Buffalo's fiery plunge had ended approximately half a kilometre from the shore. Part of the fuselage ended up submerged in mud tens of metres below the Atlantic Ocean.

'You could see … there was even a search boat anchored there,' said Mungonge. 'It was near the coast. The problem was it was a muddy place. There were two layers, one was the clear water and then the other was muddish [sic].'

It was also close to a French military installation that would later fuel the conspiracy theories in Zambia that the Buffalo had been shot down as it flew over the base shortly after take-off. Mungonge recalled seeing French troops on the beach, but they were not involved in the recovery effort. The work itself was as grim as can be expected from an air crash scene.

Thirty years after the crash, Patrick Kangwa was, as secretary to the cabinet, Zambia's top civil servant. In April 1993, the former player and coach had been vice-chairman of the Football Association of Zambia's technical committee. He was also, rather curiously, the only FAZ official on the mission to retrieve the remains of its fallen squad. He'd been an economics major at the University of Zambia while playing centre-back for lower-league Lusaka Dynamos in the early 1980s with the club's founder Hanif Adams. That, however, would be no preparation for the highly traumatic and grisly assignment he was handed in Libreville.

He recalled: 'My task was to go and identify the members of the team, [since] I was on the technical committee, a member of the Football Coaches Association, and had dealt with almost everyone who was on board apart from, maybe, some of the other [non-FAZ] officials. So, I was given the task to identify the bodies. On arrival in Gabon, the team leaders put us in various committees. There was the press, there was protocol, there was a team looking at our logistics and I was put together with Professor [Lupando] Munkonge, and we had a nurse from the casualty [emergency room] at the University Teaching Hospital. And … I can't remember the fourth one – from the air force, another doctor – and our task was to identify the bodies. So, we spent our entire duration in Gabon in the mortuary, actually receiving the body parts as they were coming in; and then going through each and every fridge looking at each and everybody and pieces and identifying them. So, I had the responsibility to look at each and everybody in whatever state it was in and do the best that I could to identify, and then label them, put them away and then prepare them for bringing them back home.'

The mortuary itself, located in the city centre, was not the largest, Kangwa remembered, 'The space was not much.' Still, it held all 30 bodies recovered from the Buffalo. They were embalmed, placed in body bags and then in caskets.

Amid the denial in Zambia over the sudden and incomprehensible loss of their heroes was a debate on the state of the remains recovered from the crash. How many were intact, Kangwa was asked by this author.

'There were a number,' he replied. 'I recall there were a number of intact bodies and there were others in pieces and others in two pieces. They were in different [conditions] and later on we were able to understand what had happened in terms of the [seating]; where they sat in the plane, and how that led to their [mutilation] as a result of the [disintegration] of the plane.'

One of the intact bodies was Godfrey Chitalu's, a powerful ball-dribbling striker in his playing days and scorer of those 107 goals in 1972. He'd be laid face down in his casket to hide his missing visage which, according to medical team leader Professor Lupando Munkonge, was eaten away by fish in the long hours he was underwater. Other Buffalo victims suffered a similar fate, said Munkonge, who died in March 2002 aged 85.

Alex Chola, Chitalu's assistant and former national team-mate, was horrifically torn in half at the waist. The result – it was again surmised – of his seat belt cutting into him when the Buffalo either lurched and dropped violently out of the sky or when it impacted the water.

Chitalu and Chola had sat next to each other in the middle of the Buffalo – parallel to where the wings attach to the fuselage, the section of any plane considered the sturdiest.

Also fairly undamaged were the remains of the two pilots in the cockpit, ZAF officer Lloyd Kalima told this author two years after the crash. The pilots' harness seat belts were reportedly a factor in keeping them intact. What Kalima did not say, and what this writer did not ask then, was who was flying the Buffalo at the time of the crash. Kalima would later rise to the rank of colonel and was ZAF Lusaka base commander when he died of a heart attack in June 2011. Years later, another former ZAF flier would answer the question on who was at the controls of AF-319 that fatal moment. It was not Fenton Mhone.

And for the families of the lost players and officials, any concerns over the identity of the remains they were handed to bury outside Independence Stadium on 3 May 1993 were put to rest by Patrick Kangwa, the one person dispatched to Libreville specifically to identify them based on his long interaction with them as a player himself, coach and administrator. In addition to Chitalu, one of the other easily identifiable victims was Eston Mulenga. The hard-tackling defensive kingpin was unmistakable because of his fair complexion that had earned him the moniker 'Yellowman' after the albino Jamaican reggae and dancehall star of the 1980s.

'We did a thorough job,' said Kangwa. 'And am sure you could see each coffin came with a name. We also had the body parts in them. All the [coffins] we brought contained the people whose names were on them. I think we did a thorough, detailed job.'

Still, it was an extremely harrowing experience for Kangwa – the only member of his forensic unit in Libreville with no medical experience – sent to identify the national football team killed in the crash of the Buffalo.

'It was very traumatic because when they said you are going to identify the team, that's not what I had in mind. What I had in mind was identifying them the way I knew them, the way I lived with them. Now to go and find them, some of them in pieces, some of them cut in two – I didn't think about it from that angle. It was a lifetime experience. After you experience something like that, I don't think that you can experience anything much more difficult or worse.'

* * *

By the weekend, the recovery effort had reached its apex. The remains – or parts – of the 30 passengers and crew on the Buffalo had been removed and, according to Mungonge, there were signs that the Zambian delegation had worn out its welcome. The mortuary handling the Zambian remains – not the largest – had been dedicated to the Buffalo victims for four days, limiting service to Libreville residents. 'They could only sympathise with us for a certain period,' he remembered. 'At one point it looked like it would be a problem because we had kept the bodies in their mortuary for too long and there were too many.'

On the morning of Sunday, 2 May, a cavalcade of Gabonese troop carriers with a police motorcycle escort made its way to Léon-Mba International Airport from the private Libreville mortuary where the Zambian remains had been kept. It carried 30 specially made hermetically and water-sealed caskets containing Zambia's fallen football heroes. A news report put the cost of the caskets at $40,000. They replaced the wooden coffins brought by the Zambian delegation on the DC 8-71. Those were deemed inadequate to carry remains recovered after days in sea water and later embalmed. Libreville residents stood solemnly along the winding route to the airport in homage to the team, some of whom they'd watched eliminate Gabon in the 1990 AFCON qualifiers in what was the first encounter between the two nations. Derby Makinka and Wisdom Chansa, both killed on the Buffalo, were among the scorers then in a 4-2 Zambian aggregate win. At the airport, Efford Chabala's casket would draw an enthusiastic crowd. He was revered even in death by the Gabonese for his goalkeeping exploits in that two-legged affair almost four years earlier.

A military brass band played as the 30 caskets were borne into the Zambia Airways DC 8-71. The huge gleaming aircraft was a big contrast to the heroes' small, green-camouflaged turboprop military transport that had cost them their lives, some noted. What few knew then was that that same DC 8-71 taking Zambia's finest players back home in caskets could have been their transport to Senegal. According to George Makulu, then Zambia Airways' chief public relations manager, when the Buffalo took off from Lusaka International Airport on the afternoon of 27 April, a quotation prepared by the airline's marketing department for the charter of the four-engine jet with a cruise speed of 556mph (895km/h) lay on a government official's desk. Like the Buffalo AF-319, the DC 8-71 was a presidential aircraft purchased discreetly a few years earlier for use by then Zambian state president Kenneth Kaunda, but crewed and managed by Zambia Airways. The national carrier, however, had the leeway to schedule the plane in its operations when it was not needed for VVIP use.

Winston Gumboh, then FAZ vice-chairman, had been at Lusaka International Airport on 27 April to see his boss Michael Mwape and the team off to Senegal. Contacted by this author in June 2021 on how much FAZ usually paid to use the Buffalo for the national team back then,

Gumboh, a FIFA referee from 1971 to 1983, texted back from his Malawi home, 'What I knew was that it was for free, offered by gvt. [sic].' It was a fatal free ride.

When President Kaunda's successor, Frederick Chiluba, liquidated Zambia Airways in 1995, the airline went out of business with a 100 per cent safety record after more than three decades of service. Established in 1964, there'd been no fatalities involving passengers or crew during its 31-year existence. Its routes included Johannesburg, London, Rome, Mumbai and New York.

18

'It's Finished'

CHRIS KACHINGWE, the *Times of Zambia* sports reporter who'd missed catching the doomed Buffalo only because he couldn't get traveller's cheques on time, covered the fallen squad's return that early Sunday afternoon on 2 May. There were thousands of others – fans, players, club officials from around the country, members of the bereaved families, government officials – all grief-stricken, on the Lusaka International Airport apron. From the time he'd heard that the plane he should have been on had crashed, Kachingwe had gone through a gamut of emotions.

He said, 'Initially it was relief, and then pain. And it didn't hit me until the day the bodies came back. I kept thinking it was a dream. Then this Zambia Airways plane touches down and instead of seeing the players come out – 'coz I thought one day they will come back – you see all these government officials all dressed in black and suddenly the whole airport starts wailing. And President Chiluba didn't make things easier. He went and sat with the families, so it was difficult. So, you sit there and watch these ZAF, these military people, lifting coffin after coffin, and putting them on military Land Rovers. And you're thinking, one of those could have been me. And what do you do? Do you consider yourself a survivor? People say there were no survivors on that Gabon plane crash, but there were several others [like me] who could have been there. It was a free ride.'

For the second time that Sunday – this time on home soil – a long and winding cavalcade of vehicles, including more than two dozen open-back army Land Rovers carrying the caskets, would form. It would draw tens of thousands along the 20-mile route from the airport to Independence Stadium. That's where the Buffalo victims would lie in state overnight ahead of the largest funeral gathering in Zambian history.

Kalusha Bwalya stood solemnly on the vast Independence Stadium pitch, amid the caskets bearing his comrades. They'd won many a battle there – thrilled countless fans over the years. But that Sunday evening as the sun faded in the west, desolation, tears and pain were all that remained. Offered anonymity by the encroaching darkness, the Zambia skipper surveyed the sad scene, unrecognised by other mourners milling around or keeping vigil next to the caskets of their loved ones.

Three short weeks earlier, Kalusha had led his now dead compatriots on to that same Independence turf for that eventful Africa Cup of Nations qualifier with the Bruce Grobbelaar-led Zimbabwe.

Kalusha had bade farewell to his team-mates the next day, apologising to them that he'd miss the next AFCON qualifier in Mauritius in a fortnight's time because he didn't have permission from PSV to stay back so long. But he'd be available for the World Cup qualifier in Dakar the weekend after the Mauritius game. 'So, we shall meet in Senegal,' he told them.

Wednesday, 28 April 1993, was a day off for PSV Eindhoven and Kalusha Bwalya was home, mulling going for a run when he received a call from Zambia that would redefine his life. It came in sometime between nine and ten in the morning, local time. It was from an FAZ official. He asked how Kalusha was feeling, then he broke the bad news. The plane carrying the national team to Senegal had crashed, he said. Kalusha was shell-shocked. He was scheduled to fly to Dakar later that day via Paris to join the squad. The official initially mentioned survivors, Kalusha recalled, but promised to call back when he received more details. About an hour later, Kalusha watched a BBC report announcing that everyone aboard the plane had perished.

Now, as he viewed the caskets of his team-mates laid on catafalques on the pitch, the enormity of the tragedy, painfully accentuated by the sorrowful scene at the stadium, sunk in. Kalusha was overwhelmed by tremendous grief and despondency. 'And I thought to myself, I don't think that we'll ever play football here again. There were no goalposts … everything was dark … *ati* Zambia to play again? Ah, it's finished now. We'll never play again.'

There would be more grief for Zambian fans after laying their heroes to rest on 3 May. On 16 May, Bernard Chanda, easily Zambia's top striker through the 70s, alongside Godfrey Chitalu, died of natural causes aged 41. His school coach, the Irishman Ronnie Hollywood, recalled Chanda walking around Luanshya's Roan Antelope Secondary School calling himself Pelé. But to his legion of fans, he was simply the 'Bomber'. Hollywood remembers his star striker as a solid 5ft 10in 'built like a well-honed super middleweight prizefighter'. Chanda was also considered more technically gifted than his on-and-off striking partner Chitalu.

Chanda had burnished his reputation as one of the best strikers on the continent by shooting Zambia into the 1974 Africa Cup of Nations Final. His three goals in a 4-2 extra-time upset of defending champions Congo-Brazzaville in the semi-finals was the only hat-trick of the tournament. He was credited with 29 goals from 68 internationals, a tally good enough for fourth place on Zambia's all-time scorer's chart, albeit with significantly less games than the top three – Chitalu, Alex Chola and Kalusha Bwalya, in that order. An astounding dribbler, clinical with either foot and strong in the air – not until the emergence of the tragic Kelvin Mutale would Zambia see such a technically accomplished striker as the 'Bomber'.

19

Roald Poulsen

THE GABON Disaster, as it became known, sucked the air out of Zambia. The loss of its national team off the coast of Libreville was a horrific calamity on a scale unprecedented in world football. Footballers and other athletes had perished in air disasters before: Torino, Manchester United, Chilean sides CD Green Cross and Antonio Varas, The Strongest, FC Pakhtakor Tashkent, Alianza Lima and Suriname's Colourful 11 were among the football clubs involved in tragic plane crashes before 1993. But no country had ever lost its national team in an accident before. Zambia wept. Gone in a flash was the bulk of its best players – the cream of a generation, and two of its best ever; shattering the hopes and dreams of millions of fans in an impoverished country with precious little source of joy during a difficult time socially and economically. Collectively, it was the worst tragedy imaginable. There seemed no immediate relief or solace for the grief-stricken nation.

'No psychiatrists … no grief counsellors to help with pain,' award-winning columnist Leigh Montville would write in *Sports Illustrated* on 18 October 1993.

But catharsis and a measure of solace – at least for fans – would come perhaps unexpectedly. Just when the nation – and most of the world for that matter – had written Zambian football's epitaph, a new fairy tale was about to be scripted.

Even before the DC 8-71 carrying the 30 caskets of the Buffalo victims landed at Lusaka International Airport on 2 May, to be engulfed by a sea of wailing mourners, a decision had already been made by higher-ups to keep the Zambian flag flying in the World Cup. The decision, according to *Zambia Daily Mail* reporter Goliath Mungonge, was effectively made aboard the DC 8-71 as it roared thousands of feet above the rain forests of Zaire towards Libreville.

While Mungonge and other non-VIP members of the delegation sat in what was remaining of the economy class after it was gutted to make room for the 30 Zambian-made coffins they hoped to bring the remains back in, the VIPs huddled in business class. 'They were making decisions already on the plane – there were meetings going on,' recalled Mungonge.

The sports reporter and his fellow economy passengers had no inkling of what was being discussed in the mid-air conference until new minister of sport Dipak Patel, just days on the job, ambled in from business class to sound out the media. 'Dipak Patel came to get our opinion on whether Zambia should continue or not to participate in the [World Cup] competition – I think from there that's when the decision was made' was Mungonge's recollection.

Putting grief aside, the media was unanimous in supporting Zambia's continued participation in the World Cup. 'Yes, we were in agreement, we should continue,' confirmed Mungonge.

In Mungonge's estimation, Patel presumably relayed this to his fellow VIPs in business class. And that sealed it. 'It was done in the plane and I think they communicated it to the head of state [Chiluba].'

Zambia captain Kalusha Bwalya had, initially, been of the same opinion. He was bullish, on arrival in Lusaka from Europe on 3 May, on the need for Zambia to continue with both World Cup and AFCON campaigns. But after witnessing and taking in the massive, collective grief of a nation, and viewing the caskets of his comrades, the captain had succumbed to despondency and thrown in the towel. *How could they go on without his team-mates – the cream of Zambian football – who were now lying in hermetically sealed caskets and awaiting interment outside the national stadium where their reputations had been forged?* It was over, he conceded. Zambian football had died with its heroes.

But unbeknownst to Kalusha, his despondency would last for less than 24 hours. Little did the left-footed genius – whose first name translated into fighter, or *ka lwisha*, a person who doesn't give up, in the Bemba language – was about to live up to his appellation spectacularly. His world-class skills and leadership would carry a rebuilt Zambian side post-Gabon on a fairy-tale quest for glory while helping wipe away the tears of millions of fans.

The day after his moving, tear-jerking prayer at the team's burial, President Chiluba summoned Kalusha to State House. 'Skipper,' Chiluba said to Kalusha. 'We have to play for the fallen heroes because if we don't play, then their deaths will be in vain.'

That resonated with Kalusha. He acquiesced. 'I said to myself, "Yes!" Because I'd thought [until then] Zambia was finished and there was no need to play.'

On 18 May 1993, exactly three weeks after the crash of the Buffalo, Roald Poulsen, a boyish 42-year-old Danish coach, received multiple phone calls in his Odense home from his country's FA and the Scandinavian nation's Ministry of Foreign Affairs. A coach since age 26, he'd left the manager's job at his hometown club Odense Boldklub the previous season after a four-year tenure during which he'd led OB to the Danish league title in 1989 and the domestic cup in 1991. One of the best young coaches around, Poulsen was the perfect pick – from both the Danish FA and foreign office's perspective – to handle an extraordinary request from Africa: help rebuild the Zambia national team over a six-week period in Denmark so that it could continue with its quest to qualify for the World Cup and Africa Cup of Nations.

According to Sonstone Kashiba, then acting director of sport in Zambia's Ministry of Sport, once the decision had been made to rebuild the team and continue with the dual qualifying campaigns, they reached out to foreign governments for assistance. This would be based on technical agreements Zambia had with them. Kashiba was involved in sending out the requests through Zambia's Ministry of Foreign Affairs. The Danes, whose national team had made international news of its own the previous year, were simply the first to respond.

Denmark had failed to qualify for the 1992 UEFA European Championship after finishing a point behind Yugoslavia. But when civil war broke out in Yugoslavia and both FIFA and UEFA suspended the Yugoslav federation from competitive football ten days before the start of Euro 92 in Sweden, the Danes were invited to replace them and given five days to submit a 20-man squad. Denmark's top stars were urgently summoned back from their summer holidays. That included Peter Schmeichel, Manchester United's larger-than-life goalkeeper, Brøndby centre-back Kim Christofte, and forward Brian Laudrup, then on Bayern Munich's books.

The Danes tore up the form book. They upset defending champions the Netherlands, with their vaunted Gullit– Rijkaard–Van Basten triumvirate, 5-4 on penalties in the semi-finals, and then shocked a unified Germany, Jürgen Klinsmann and all, 2-0 in the final. To date, Denmark remain the only team to have won an international tournament they never qualified for.

Two members of that triumphant side had played for Roald Poulsen – the young, sandy blond coach identified by the Danish FA to rebuild the Zambian national team – at club level. Kim Christofte, elegant in all defensive positions, was under Poulsen's wings at Odense Boldklub in 1988. He left the club in 1989. Christofte featured in all of the Danes' five games at Euro 92. Another Poulsen protégé, forward Lars Elstrup, would play a pivotal role in the 'Danish Miracle'. After a goalless draw and a 1-0 loss, to England and Sweden respectively, Denmark needed a win against the French to avoid a quick resumption of their summer vacation. Elstrup came off the bench to snatch a late 2-1 win in Malmö on his Euro 92 debut. Both Christofte and Elstrup scored in the penalty shoot-out over the Dutch in the semis.

Elstrup was at Randers BK when he first appeared on Poulsen's radar in 1986. He had stints with Brøndby IF and Feyenoord, before Poulsen finally lured him to Odense BK in 1988. OB won the Danish league title in 1989 and Elstrup was sold to English club Luton later that year.

In Odense, Denmark's third-largest city, Poulsen, like a lot of people in the sports world, knew about the tragedy that had recently befallen Zambian football. 'April 27, 1993, [a] disaster outside Gabon. I heard about it on radio and TV and paid attention,' he reminisced more than two decades later. 'I was shocked, and at the same time did not realise the scale of the catastrophe. It was far away and in Africa. I remembered Zambia beating Italy at the 1988 Olympics – Kalusha's three goals, etc. After that, he played for PSV in Holland.'

It took Poulsen just a few minutes to mull over the Danish FA and foreign office request. 'I said I would love to help if they wanted me to do so, and if they found me qualified for the task.' He suggested that Emil Bakkendorf from Brøndby be appointed team manager, 'to take care of all the logistics, accommodation, equipment, uniforms, contact with the media, etc. And I should be the head coach for the players and the two [accompanying] Zambian assistant coaches.'

He also asked to take charge of all specific coaching tasks. The new squad would train for three weeks in Brøndby – on the fringes of Copenhagen – and three weeks in Vejle, 147 miles west of the capital in southern Denmark. The Danish and Zambian authorities both acceded.

The rebuilding process actually began in Zambia. Once state president Frederick Chiluba announced that they would continue the World Cup and AFCON qualification campaigns in memory of the fallen heroes, FAZ summoned 60 of the top home-based players for trials to select a new national side. Wilted to 22, the squad sent to Denmark comprised mostly uncapped talent that had been kept out of the squad by the incomparable skills of those killed on the Buffalo.

Of the exceptions, the most experienced was Linos Makwaza, son of former Zambia captain and defensive titan Dickson Makwaza. Aged 27 then, the lanky midfielder was dubbed 'Sócrates' by fans for his similar physical stature to the Brazilian great of the 70s and 80s. Linos had been in several Zambia squads going back to 1985, including those for the 1990 and 1992 AFCON tournaments. Defenders Harrison 'Wawa' Chongo and Evans Sakala, midfielder Emmanuel Munaile and forward Wedson Nyirenda – the young brother of Belgium-based Stone Nyirenda – were the other players called up at one point before the crash.

The selection of a new national team boss was more straightforward for FAZ. They went for a pioneer. Freddie Mwila and compatriot Emment Kapengwe, both midfielders, had become Zambia's first overseas-based professionals in 1967 when they signed for Atlanta Chiefs, then in the USA's National Professional Soccer League. They both starred when Atlanta stunned visiting Manchester City, then newly crowned English champions, 3-2 on 26 May 1968. Mwila, 21, notched a brace while Kapengwe got the other goal. Mwila netted a penalty in a second game, a 2-1 Atlanta victory. The two Zambians would also play in the Chiefs' 6-2 shellacking by Pelé and his Santos FC that summer.

Aston Villa boss Tommy Docherty – with Chelsea already on his CV, and Porto, the Scottish national side, Manchester United and Wolverhampton Wanderers still to come – was sufficiently impressed. He signed Mwila and Kapengwe on two-year contracts in August 1969. Nine months later – after three appearances for Villa by the latter and one by the former – the Zambians returned home. Mwila was Ndola United player-coach when he made Ante Bušelić's 1974 AFCON squad to Egypt as cover for younger midfielders Jani Simulambo, Willie Phiri, Richard Stephenson and Boniface Simutowe.

By May 1993, Mwila's coaching legend spanned 20 years. It was highlighted by success with Power Dynamos – the Kitwe side that until April 1993 had played second fiddle to crosstown rivals Nkana in the league. With former England international and Wolverhampton Wanderers manager Bill McGarry as technical adviser, Mwila took a Power side built around Alex Chola and Peter Kaumba to the 1982 African Cup Winners' Cup Final. They lost 4-0 over two legs to Egypt's Arab Contractors.

Mwila and McGarry went one better the following year. Invited to the Rothmans Cup, a one-off international tournament in the Ivory Coast featuring clubs from the host nation, Gabon, Nigeria and Cameroon, Power went undefeated en route to the final. There they edged Tonnerre Yaoundé 5-4 on penalties after a goalless draw. Then came a second bite of the cherry in the African Cup Winners' Cup. Nine years after losing the 1982 final, Mwila – with Scotsman Jim Bone as technical adviser this time – took Power back. A 5-4 aggregate victory over cup holders Nigeria's BCC Lions bagged Zambia's first continental club silverware.

Despite his vast club coaching experience, Mwila's national team exposure was, as of 1993, limited. He was Zambia co-coach briefly in 1977 with Brightwell Banda, and had a stint as Samuel 'Zoom' Ndhlovu's assistant coach before the Seoul Olympics in 1988. Mwila was Botswana boss in May 1993 when former FAZ vice-chairman Winston Gumboh – elevated to chairman after Michael Mwape's death on the Buffalo – flew to Zambia's southern neighbour to negotiate his release with the Tswana FA. Together with former international midfielder Boniface Simutowe, Mwila would oversee the selection of a new national side. Their next stop would be Denmark where Roald Poulsen would whip the new squad into a formidable unit.

Having signed on for a task few coaches in world football have ever imagined, Poulsen's recollection of this unique and deeply emotional experience would be vivid. It would cover the gamut – and it wasn't all smooth sailing.

Years later, Poulsen would, along with the uplifting memories and special bonding, recount the challenges and political interference that were part of this singular task. And that's not to mention the impact of the grief-stricken Kalusha Bwalya and Johnson Bwalya, both of whom had escaped the Gabon tragedy and made tough emotional decisions to be part of the rebuilt squad in honour of their fallen colleagues.

Poulsen said, 'June 1993. Sixteen players, two coaches [Fred Mwila, Boniface Simutowe] and one physio [William Ngosa] arrived at Copenhagen Airport [a few more players arrived a week later]. I had no clue of their background/history on or off the field, but the football language is fantastic and it can break down any barrier.'

The beginning was archetypical to any fresh training camp, as Poulsen told the *New York Times*' Christopher Clarey in August 1993, 'I have to admit that after I saw them train the first two or three times, I was a bit worried about the future. But I tried to get them to play in a more international way, to share responsibilities defensively. I never touched the way they attacked, though. They love to attack, to touch the ball, to dribble and to make passes.'

To this author, Poulsen reminisced, 'I had to start from scratch in all the different aspects of training, attitude, behaviour, agreements, punctuality, etc., and after a few sessions and days, we were on the same [path]. After a meeting with the staff from Zambia, I made a training programme where the physical aspect had a main priority; aerobic endurance, anaerobic capacity and functional strength – all football-related and all composed to the style of play and the various positions in the system/team. Most days we trained twice, but I was aware of the importance of recovery training, physically and mentally. A few days we were off and we arranged other activities, e.g. sightseeing, cinema, the Tivoli Gardens amusement park and pleasure garden.

'We, the players and the staff, had many small and big challenges on and off the field. The climate was a problem for the players. The daylight for one. In the summertime it is light in Denmark for 18 hours, so it was hard for the

Zambians to sleep. Another new thing was the Danish food, no *nshima* and stew [Zambian staple], and the temptation of [overeating]. Three weeks in Brøndby. Lots of training and more friendly matches against various teams from lower and higher leagues. In Copenhagen, and in the vicinity, we played Frederiksvaerk, BK Frem, Slagelse BK and Brøndby IF. Many losses and few wins, but a lot of progress in [our] style of play, organisation, mutual understanding, physical capacity and self-confidence. In Jutland, we played Arhus Fremad BK and Vejle BK, but the three weeks in Vejle were shortened to one and a half because FIFA demanded the national team fly back to Zambia and play the World Cup qualifier against Morocco in Lusaka the following week [Senegal, Morocco and Zambia were in the same group].

'It was within the original six-week period the Danish Ministry of Foreign Affairs had offered/budgeted to help the national team. So [I] and [team manager] Mr Bakkendorf would travel to Lusaka with the team and [be] in charge until that game [against Morocco on 4 July] was over. Before we left Vejle, Kalusha came from Holland with his family and observed our last match and talked to the players and coaches.

'Personally, I think that experience had a huge impact on his mind and he told me how impressed he was with the progress of the new team. He would be a part of us! It was tough for Kalusha and Johnson to play in the national team after they lost all their team-mates in the crash. Emotionally and mentally, they really had to overcome some psychological barriers before they committed themselves. Personally, I think, when they saw the progress of their new mates and they realised what kind of effort all people had invested in the rebuilding process, Kalu and Johnson wanted to be a proud part, not for their own sake, but for all their former team-mates who [perished] in the tragedy.

Charles Musonda was not involved in that phase, but tried to come back after 1994, but sadly his injury prevented him from playing at the highest level again.

'July 1993. One week in Lusaka polishing up with final training sessions amid internal disagreements and political interference off the field. The two local coaches and some officials wanted to take charge, and Mr Bakkendorf had his fights with the different people [while] I focused on the players and ignored the coaches' disgraceful attitudes and talking behind my back. The few sessions we had were basically the same as we had in Denmark, and all the players, including Kalusha and Johnson who joined us, were comfortable with the intensity and content.

'All kind of media and a lot of fans watched every move we made, and Sunday [4 July] we played the match vs Morocco and the whole nation saw or followed the game.'

The entire football universe, Poulsen could have added. For their fourth visit to Independence Stadium for a World Cup qualifier, the Moroccans were drilled by Abdellah El Ajri. Nicknamed 'Blinda', one of El Ajri's six international caps had been earned in Morocco's 4-0 drubbing by a then unknown Zambian side in October 1973. Blinda's return almost 20 years later came a little over eight weeks after it was the venue for a moving open-air funeral mass for arguably the greatest collection of Zambian footballers. Tens of thousands attended then. The stadium was again packed to the proverbial rafters on 4 July 1993, like it had always been for Morocco's previous visits; five in total if you include a vital Africa Cup of Nations qualifier in 1981. Zambia had won them all, the last being four years earlier when Kalusha's Bwalya's late free kick had secured a 2-1 victory in that qualifier for Italia 90. This latest encounter – the most emotional game in Zambian history – would also be a thriller.

The author [far right] with Frank Taylor in Moscow. Taylor was the only journalist out of nine to survive the 1958 Munich air crash involving Manchester United.
Jay Mwamba

Ronnie Hollywood [far left] and his Roan United team, ca. 1970. Then in the first division, Roan included several alum of Hollywood's Zambia schools squad, among them Bernard "Bomber" Chanda [squatting far left], who'd become one of several international standouts from the Zambia schools programme.
Ronnie Hollywood

Hollywood with childhood friend Pat Jennings, the great Irish goalie. Decades before remote learning, Jennings would send goalkeeping tips to Hollywood for his star shot-stopper Emmanuel Mwape – another future Zambia great. Ronnie Hollywood

Kalusha's stellar Seoul Olympics performance earned him a move to then defending European club champions PSV Eindhoven.
Kalusha Bwalya

Midfielder Charles Musonda wins silverware with Belgian giants Anderlecht.
Charles Musonda

From left: Kalusha, Charles Musonda and Zambian coach Samuel 'Zoom' Ndhlovu at the 1988 Seoul Olympics. They shocked the football world there by demolishing Italy 4-0 and reaching the quarter-finals.
Charles Musonda

From left: Kelvin Mutale, Kalusha Bwalya and Charles Musonda after playing together for the first time in Zambia's 3-1 World Cup qualifying victory over Madagascar in Lusaka on 27 February 1993. The win put the Zambians in the second round, where tragedy awaited. Kalusha Bwalya

Kelvin Mutale [20] and Derby Makinka [10] with Al Effitaq in the Saudi Pro League, February 1993. Al Effitaq

AFRICAN S⊕CCER

Quarterly

No. 3 June – August 1993

Belgium BF 110
CFA zone FCFA 700
Gambia D 15
Germany DM 6.50
Ghana C 700
Kenya KSh 40
Liberia L$ 25
Netherlands HFI 7.00
Nigeria N 30
Sierra Leone Le 500
Switzerland SFr 5.00
Tanzania TSh 250
Uganda USh 1,200
UK £1.50
USA $3.00
Zimbabwe $6.00

On the night of April 27 a Zambian
military plane went down off the coast of
Gabon. On board were 18 members of the
national football squad and 12 other
technical staff and crew, on their way to
Senegal for a World Cup fixture. All
perished. This is their last team picture,
taken in Mauritius just two days earlier.

REST IN PEACE

Also in this issue:
Nations Cup: the final hurdle
Orlando Pirates profiled
World Cup USA 1994

African Soccer *magazine cover featuring the last team photo taken of the
Zambian squad two days before it perished off the Gabonese coast. This is the side
that beat Mauritius 3-0 on 25 April. Standing from left: Efford Chabala, Wisdom
Chansa, Whiteson Changwe, hat-trick hero Kelvin Mutale, Derby Makinka and
Robert Watiyakeni. Front row from left: Eston Mulenga, John Soko, Godfrey
Kangwa, Numba Mwila and Moses Chikwalakwala.* African Soccer

The national team at Zambia Army HQ days before the trip to Mauritius, and a week before the tragic jaunt to Senegal. National Archives

Gabonese recovery unit brings ashore remains from the crashed Buffalo. National Archives

A stretcher with the body of a crash victim is carried past the Zambian delegation sent to retrieve the remains. Far left is Zambian Minister of Foreign Affairs Vernon Mwaanga. The towering figure in the background is ZAF Commander Lt-Gen. Ronnie Shikapwasha. National Archives

AFRICAN SOCCER

30 dead in Gabon air crash

Zambia mourns

African Soccer reports from Lusaka and Libreville on one of the world's worst ever sporting air disasters

The ill-fated Zambian Airforce DHC-5D Buffalo took off from Lusaka Airport approximately six hours late. Originally scheduled to have departed Lusaka on the morning of the April 27, there had been a delay as officials from the Foreign Ministry sought to obtain flight clearance on the scheduled route. As with most military flights, this was proving an obstacle and the pilots were advised to await confirmation from the Ministry before taking off.

With permission duly granted, flight No. AF 319, call-sign AFZ 502, made a perfect lift-off and begun the first leg to Brazzaville, the capital city of Congo.

On board were 18 members of the Zambian national football squad, in good heart after taking the lead in their African Cup of Nations qualifying group by thrashing Mauritius 3-0 in Port Louis two days earlier. They were on their way to Dakar for their first World Cup second-round qualifier against Senegal.

European-based professionals Kalusha and Johnson Bwalya and Charles Musonda were not on board, but the whole of the rest of the squad was there, along with the team coaches and doctor, and top football administrators.

Five hours later the plane arrived in Brazzaville for the first technical and refuelling stop. At this point, unofficial sources say its main engine showed the first signs of trouble.

With its tanks fully replenished, the Buffalo took off again, overflying the towns of Moanz and Kilec on the two-hour stretch to the Gabonese capital, Libreville. The scheduled 30-minute stop there was extended as further technical checks were carried out. But a little before 11.00 pm, local time, the plane left again for Abidjan, Côte d'Ivoire, where the players were due to spend the rest of the night. In the morning, having rested and refuelled the plane, they were to have made the remaining five and a half hour flight to Dakar, for their match against the Senegalese Lions.

Just minutes after Colonel Fenton Mhone took off from Libreville, however, the plane plunged into the Atlantic Ocean with the loss of all 30 passengers and crew on board. The Gabonese authorities almost immediately launched a rescue operation, but within a few hours it had become

Players:
Efford Chabala (31, Mufulira Wanderers), John Soko (23, Nkana Red Devils), Whiteson Changwe (29, Kabwe Warriors), Easton Mulenga (26, Nkana Red Devils), Robert Watiyakeni (24, Dynamos, SA), Derby Makinka (26, El Ettifaq, Saudi Arabia), Moses Chikwalakwala (19, Chambishi), Godfrey Kangwa (26, Olympic Casablanca), Wisdom Chansa (23, Dynamos, SA), Kelvin Mutale (24, El Ettifaq, Saudi Arabia), Numba Mwila (21, Nkana Red Devils), Richard Mwanza (35, Kabwe Warriors), Timothy Mwitwa (25, Nkana Red Devils), Patrick Banda (24, Profound Warriors), Kenan Simambe (19, Nkana Red Devils), Samuel Chomba (29, Dynamos, SA), Moses Masuwa (22, Roan United), Wine der Mambo (23, Power Dynamos)

Technical staff
Godfrey Chitalu (team coach), Alex Chola (assistant coach), Wilson Mtonga (team doctor)

Officials
Michael Mwape (FAZ Chairman), Nelson Zimba (Deputy Permanent Sec), Wilson Sakala (FAZ cttee member), Joseph Bulimu (Zambia News Agency)

Crew:
Col. Fenton Mhone (pilot), Lt Col. Victor Mubanga (pilot), Lt Col. J.M. Sachika (pilot), W/O E.S. Namchote (technician), Corporal T. Sakala (steward)

A military detail carries a casket from the Zambia Airways DC 8-71 on arrival in Lusaka on 2 May 1993. Zambia Airways had reportedly prepared an invoice for FAZ to charter the DC 8 to Senegal. But the football authorities opted for the Buffalo, that, according to then vice chairman Winston Gumboh, was offered for free.
African Soccer/Ponga Liwewe

Roald Poulsen (standing second from left) with the new Zambia squad at Brøndby stadium during the rebuilding period, May–June 1993. On Poulsen's right is team manager Emil Bakkendorf. Roald Poulsen

The Zambia national team, 25 April 1993. African Soccer

20

Resurrection

IN THE fourth grade, students in Zambia are taught in social studies class the meaning of the national flag – that attractive, predominantly green emblem with a tricoloured rectangular block on one side and an orange African fish eagle, wings spread, hovering above the block. The rich green hue of the flag represents Zambia's lush, verdant vegetation, they are told. The three colours running vertically in the rectangular block also have meaning: red for the blood shed in the independence struggle; black for the indigenous people of Zambia; and orange for the nation's enormous copper wealth. Then there's the hovering fish eagle – it symbolises Zambia's ability to overcome its problems.

From the moment news of the plane crash involving Zambia's top footballers started spreading, the assumption was that the nation – its collective heart shattered – would succumb to stifling sorrow and withdraw from both World Cup and Africa Cup of Nations qualifiers. Instead, Zambia opted to close ranks, pick up the fallen standard, and continue with its double quest. An African powerhouse for two decades, Zambia had hastily put together a second unit and handed it to Roald Poulsen. The Dane in turn had spent close to six weeks whipping this disparate collection of players – who'd never played together for any significant time – into a formidable group. The return of captain and long-time talisman Kalusha Bwalya and his one-time Mufulira Wanderers replacement Johnson Bwalya were major boosts.

The real test of rebuilt Zambia's mettle – and the nation's wisdom in returning to international football so soon after that horrific tragedy ten weeks earlier – came at 3pm on 4 July at Lusaka's packed 30,000-capacity Independence Stadium. It started badly.

Minutes in, midfielder Linos Makwaza – the son of 1970s skipper Dickson Makwaza – caught a boot to the face. Bloodied, he was stretchered off. It was an early blow for the new squad. With international experience at a premium, Linos was one of a smattering of players in Poulsen's squad previously capped before the Gabon Disaster. He was replaced by Emmanuel Munaile, who'd earned three caps himself in the four years before 1993.

It got worse in the 11th minute. That's when Moroccan midfielder Rachid Daoudi, with a long-range left punt from 35 metres, scored a stunner. First deprived of an experienced link man and now a goal down with 11 minutes played, despondency began to descend on Independence Stadium. There were reports later of fans atop the eastern stand turning despairingly to the 30 brown mounds laden with wilted wreaths outside the stadium. That's where Efford Chabala, Eston Mulenga, Derby Makinka, Kelvin Mutale and Zambia's other fallen heroes lay, in graves arranged in a horseshoe formation.

In the grandstand, Zambian president Frederick Chiluba – as later narrated to this writer by one of the Zambian defenders on the pitch – decided to take a more practical approach as the new squad sought its rhythm against one of Africa's most accomplished national sides. Chiluba reportedly scribbled a note suggesting that Poulsen make a substitution to improve the team's performance.

According to the source, the note was handed to Poulsen on the bench by one of Chiluba's aides. The young coach proceeded to read and then tear up the missive. This, according to the source, was witnessed by players and officials on the bench who later recounted it to their colleagues in the starting XI after the game.

Asked to comment on the incident 29 years later, Poulsen said in an email to this author, 'Yes, I had some "good" advice, also from the "president's suite" [sic], but also from other "important" persons in FAZ, who wanted to affect my selection of the national team … I stood my ground and principles, and won the battle off the field.' He won the battle on the field, too, that gripping afternoon.

As the match progressed, Zambia found their rhythm. They were attacking the east end in the second half when they won a free kick on the hour. Some 20 metres from the goal and close to a 90-degree angle, it was a putative penalty for Kalusha Bwalya, given his deadly proficiency from set pieces. His last goal against Morocco, four years earlier, had come from another free kick, from a slightly longer distance, against the great goalkeeper Badou Zaki, on the Humanism Hill end. His magical left foot struck the ball flawlessly. Up and under. Kalusha had equalised.

Independence Stadium exploded in thunderous rapture. The Moroccans were left standing akimbo. It was the first mass expression of joy by hitherto grieving Zambians in the ten weeks since the Gabon horror. The despair was lifted totally seven minutes later when the other Bwalya, Johnson, pounced on his own blocked pass. It was from almost the same spot as Kalusha's free kick. As the ball came off a

Moroccan defender, Johnson lashed out with his lethal right foot. He'd beaten Juventus goalie Stefano Tacconi from 30 yards with the same foot five years earlier. Ten yards closer this time, Johnson couldn't miss. The stadium and nation erupted again with a massive cathartic roar that expunged all the pain and grief of the previous ten weeks. Just what the doctor might have ordered. It ended 2-1.

For the euphoric Poulsen, it was mission accomplished, 'We came from 1-0 down and won 2-1, the new team was born in six weeks. The people were ecstatic, everyone was celebrating and proud. The unbelievable happened, and I became a hero in Zambia. It was the most emotional game I ever experienced. Mission impossible accomplished! In the first five weeks of that rebuilding period, you never know where you are at the international scene. How strong the team is [if] it would last or break. We were fit and organised. It was a manhood test. I was confident but I had not seen the team at such a crucial level – World Cup qualifier.

'Millions of people expecting and hoping, [30,000] spectators at the Independence Stadium. Lots of pressure on the players. I knew we had worked very hard but could we stand the mental pressure on home soil? We did, due to a fantastic team effort, a strong fighting mentality, a desire to make the nation proud, an unbelievable faith in each other, a wish to play every second to show respect for the team that perished, and two deciding capacities [sic], Kalusha and Johnson. After that game, I had a lot of confidence in the team and the players and I never doubted we could go further, maybe to the [World Cup] in USA. But we were not allowed to give it a try.'

Any narrative around the horrific disaster that befell the Zambian football team in April 1993 could have ended emphatically with the triumph over Morocco.

Losing practically all your best players – bar three – regrouping and rebuilding in six weeks, and then coming from behind to defeat an African giant such as the Atlas Lions with virtually a new squad was unbelievable. It was unprecedented. An analogy for older fans would be the Netherlands, at their peak, losing most of their stars, then rebuilding around Ruud Gullit and Jan Wouters, and six weeks later defeating Germany in a stirring qualifier. It was the stuff of fairy tales. Honed by Roald Poulsen, driven by a desire to honour their fallen comrades and inspired by two extremely gifted players, the Zambians had lived up to the symbolism denoted by the hovering fish eagle on their flag. Like the eagle, they had – this one time at least – stunningly demonstrated the nation's ability to rise over its problems.

And it was no flash in the pan. Kalusha and his de facto second unit's next exploits would evoke comparisons to another bird of valour – albeit a mythical one this time. Like the phoenix, Zambia – on a foundation laid by Poulsen – would continue to rise from the ashes. The man with sandy blond hair had become a cult hero in the hitherto grief-stricken southern African nation.

Poulsen said, 'After that [Morocco] match, [team manager] Emil Bakkendorff and I [were supposed] to return to Denmark, but our Zambian flight was grounded in London due to financial problems and we had to wait five or six days before we could return to Denmark. In the meantime, the players and the press wanted me to stay and be their coach, but FAZ had already an agreement with English sponsors, that [Ian] Porterfield should be the one. Lots of protests. But he took over my team and [eight] months later they played in the 1994 AFCON final.'

The parting was hard and emotional, as recounted by Joel Bwalya, Kalusha's dual-footed young brother. Then with Belgian club KSV Harelbeke, Joel highlighted the intense bond established between the young coach and the team he'd forged during their short period together – under such extraordinary circumstances – and the success they'd reaped, 'I remember the day Poulsen and the manager were leaving was a Tuesday after the South Africa game. The whole team escorted him to the airport, which didn't look good to Porterfield, Ba Freddie [Mwila] and Simutowe. Such was the relationship with the man. Everyone was so emotional at the airport. He was a good coach, [a] good man, very calm in his coaching and approach.'

Poulsen conceded, 'Joel (was) right, it was a very difficult goodbye at the hotel and at the airport. The farewell situation with the players was very emotional. We were so close after six intensive weeks. They wanted me to stay and I wanted to be by their side, but it was impossible due to other plans by FAZ. There were many phone calls in the following long period – back and forth from players and myself. But as you know, we were united in 1994. It was a long wait. I was struggling for a long time with my emotions and my wishes to be close to the players and "my team".'

On 11 July 1993, a week after the cathartic, come-from-behind World Cup qualifying victory over Morocco had helped wipe away tears from countless sad faces, Zambia returned to Independence Stadium, drawing another sellout crowd. With Roald Poulsen's rebuilding mission complete, local coaches Freddie Mwila and Boniface Simutowe took charge of the new squad. South Africa, a year back from international football exile after the end of Apartheid, were the visitors this time for an AFCON 1994 qualifier. Bafana Bafana had fallen 1-0 to a largely home-based Zambian side in Johannesburg in August 1992, with no Kalusha or Charles Musonda, and with the emergent Kelvin Mutale – on just his second international call-up – on the bench.

This second fixture was a nightmarish experience for South Africa, particularly their Mozambican-born goalie Roger De Sá, who won the sole international cap of his career in those torrid 90 minutes. Zairean referee Ntambidila Wa Wtambidila adjudged De Sá to have caught Zambian left-back Aggrey Chiyangi's cross behind the goal line, seconds after kick-off, awarding the hosts their fastest-ever goal. There was no goal-line technology then.

That was the only goal until the Zambians went into their traditional second-half act. A Kalusha penalty in the 66th minute and Linos Makwaza's strike five minutes later saw off South Africa.

That 3-0 triumph in Zambia's penultimate AFCON qualifier meant that Kalusha and Co. needed just a draw against Bruce Grobbelaar and Peter Ndlovu's Zimbabwean 'Dream Team' in Harare two weeks later to qualify for the 1994 Africa Cup of Nations finals in Tunisia. That would be a truly remarkable achievement for a nation that had practically lost most of its key players weeks earlier.

On 25 July, three months after the Gabon Disaster, Zambia trailed Zimbabwe 1-0 with ten minutes left at the crammed 60,000-capacity Rufaro Stadium – site of reggae icon Bob Marley's last African concert 13 years earlier. Bristol City defender Henry McKop had scored for the hosts in the 28th minute. It looked bleak. But then Johnson Bwalya wiggled past a defender on the left and floated a long ball into the penalty box. Kalusha, all 6ft of him, leapt high and nodded the ball into the net, past the great Grobbelaar. Equaliser! When the final whistle blew nine minutes later, the rebuilt Zambian squad had punched its ticket to the 1994 Africa Cup of Nations.

The first chapter in a football fairy tale had been written.

In mid-February 1993, a little more than eight weeks before the ill-fated ZAF Buffalo DHC-5D's brief final flight in Libreville, Ian Porterfield was dismissed as Chelsea boss. It was one for the history books as the Scotsman became the first manager to be sacked in the Premier League era. Porterfield had made other big news 20 years earlier. While Ante Bušelić's Zambia were announcing their emergence as an African power in 1973, Porterfield starred in May that year in one of the biggest upsets in the FA Cup's storied history. The midfielder struck the only goal in Second Division Sunderland's shock 1-0 upset of a star-studded Leeds United at Wembley Stadium.

Leeds would end the 1972/73 season third in the league and slip 1-0 to AC Milan in the European Cup Winners' Cup Final. As fate would have it, Porterfield's next gig after the Chelsea job would be in Africa. He'd inherit Roald Poulsen's Zambia. And he'd make a big splash in his first game as coach.

Porterfield had been in the grandstand at Independence Stadium on 4 July when Zambia came from behind spectacularly to beat Morocco 2-1. He had watched the 3-0 thrashing of South Africa a week later, also from the stands. His third view of his future side came on 25 July in Harare. Thanks to Kalusha Bwalya – once again Zambia's primary match-winner with Kelvin 'Malaza' Mutale gone – Porterfield would have a major tournament on his to-do list in early 1994.

Next on the horizon was Zambia's holy grail: qualification to the World Cup that had eluded one of Africa's top footballing nations for decades. It had exacted a horrific toll thus far – costing the southern African nation the cream of its players. The 2 May Senegal match that Kelvin Mutale and his companions were headed for when they perished off the Libreville coast had been rescheduled to 7 August. And much to Zambia's advantage, it would be in neutral Abidjan, the Ivorian capital. That was punishment for the Senegalese by FIFA, following crowd trouble in Dakar after their 3-1 loss to Morocco on 17 July. Souleymane Jean Sané, then with German side SG Wattenscheid 09, had the lone goal for the Teranga Lions in that match.

Sané, whose son Leroy would find fame with Manchester City, Bayern Munich and the German national team, would be kept off the scoreboard in a goalless draw with the Zambians at Abidjan's Stade Félix-Houphouët-Boigny. Porterfield was not at the game, helmed by Freddie Mwila and Boniface Simutowe. The draw, before mostly 15,000 pro-Ivorian fans, would end the Teranga Lions' USA 94 quest. To their credit, a Senegalese side captained by the French-reared Aliou Cissé would next be seen in the quarter-finals of the 2002 World Cup in South Korea and Japan.

The paperwork finalised, Ian Porterfield finally took charge of Zambia for the return fixture with Senegal at Independence Stadium on 26 September 1993. It was a happy debut for the erstwhile former Chelsea boss. His charges romped to a 4-0 victory on goals by Gibby Mbasela, an enigmatic right-winger with a mesmerisingly slow dribble, towering centre-back Elijah Litana, Kenneth Malitoli and Kalusha. The victory put Zambia atop the three-team Group B with five points, one above Morocco, with their final match ahead on 10 October. That was in the era when a win earned you only two points, so, in essence, Zambia were 90 minutes away from qualifying for the World Cup, provided they avoided defeat in Casablanca. A draw would see them through at Morocco's expense. It was a remarkable position for Zambian football to find itself in five months after losing its best players in the Gabon Disaster. Miraculously, the nation's USA 94 dream was still alive.

But sorrow would continue to trail Zambia. A week before the 4-0 drubbing of Senegal put Zambia on the cusp of the USA 94, Moses Simwala, the country's most successful club coach, died after a long illness. Capped pre-Ante Bušelić, Simwala had been Zambia's first-choice right-winger for the better part of a decade until his swansong after the 1980 Moscow Olympics. He spent another 13 uninterrupted years as coach of his lifelong club Nkana, leading them to their first title in 1982 – his rookie year as head coach with Englishman Jeff Butler as technical adviser. Nkana went undefeated in all 22 Super Division fixtures that season. Seven more titles would follow, including six between 1985 and 1992, as well as reaching the two-legged final of the African Champions Clubs Cup, the first Zambian team to get to that stage.

That Nkana side assembled by Simwala comprised exceptional players, many with national team experience. Key performers included Eston Mulenga, Mordon Malitoli, Amos Bwalya and John Soko in defence, Kapambwe Mulenga in midfield, with Gibby Mbasela, Beston Chambeshi and Kenneth Malitoli pivotal in attack. Simwala had long developed Nkana into a tight, cohesive unit that lined up in a compact 4-4-2 formation. It had been ruthlessly effective in the domestic league. In the run-up to Christmas 1990, Simwala's lads were now on the verge of conquering Africa. Alas, on 22 December, they'd succumb 5-3 on penalties in Lusaka to Algerian side JS Kabylie in the African Champions Clubs Cup Final, after a 1-1 aggregate draw over two legs.

The success enjoyed by Simwala with Nkana in building successive championship sides and nurturing talent made him the logical choice to lead Zambia's USA 94 revival effort following the loss to Madagascar in December 1992 that finally cost long-time national coach Samuel 'Zoom'

Ndhlovu his job. If the 'Chairman' could replicate his club success with Zambia – five of whose squad members were from Nkana at that time – all would be swell. But Simwala's health was failing. He'd never take up the appointment, leaving Godfrey Chitalu and Alex Chola to take charge. In a cruel irony, illness would spare Simwala's life four months later when the Buffalo plane he should have been on crashed in Gabon. But he'd finally succumb to it on 19 September 1993 in Kitwe. He was 44.

21

'Charlie Cool'

BY HIS own estimation, Charles Musonda's top-flight career lasted a mere four years. He arrived in Belgium – Cercle Brugge's second Zambian signing after Kalusha Bwalya – shortly after his 17th birthday in August 1986. By 1990, his massively promising career was in jeopardy.

In a 2022 interview, Musonda told this writer that he felt people had misunderstood his career. The only period he played consistently was from 1987 to 1990. Once 1990 started, his knee problems began.

The cerebral midfielder, apt successor to Alex Chola as Zambia's playmaker par excellence, was a key member of Anderlecht, traditionally Belgium's best club, when his right knee started flaring up. The pain initially kept him out of three legs in Anderlecht's eye-popping 1990 European Cup Winners' Cup run, but not the big one: their 3-2 second-round upset of Johan Cruyff's fancied Barcelona. There'd be further wins over Austrian club Admira Wacker and Romanians Dinamo Bucureşti as Anderlecht, also comprising Icelandic striker Arnór Guðjohnsen – father of former Chelsea and Barcelona forward Eiður Guðjohnsen – Belgian internationals Marc Degryse and Luc Nilis, and the Nigerian defensive stalwart Stephen Keshi reached the final in Gothenburg, Sweden.

Italian side Sampdoria, approaching their all-time peak, were Anderlecht's opponents in the final at the Nya Ullevi on 9 May 1990. It would be a mini reunion of sorts for the now 20-year-old Musonda. In the Sampdoria starting XI were two familiar faces from Zambia's destruction of Italy at the Seoul Olympics two years earlier, and a third alum of the tournament. Gianluca Pagliuca, the Sampdoria goalkeeper, had been on the Italian bench when Stefano Tacconi shifted four goals against the Zambians in Gwangju – Musonda, then 18, the architect with three assists. Pagliuca would make the Italia 90 squad that summer and play in the next two World Cups as well. Sampdoria also trotted out defender Luca Pellegrini for the final. He'd come on in the 61st minute in Gwangju, in an attempt to shore up an Italian back line rocking at 2-0 by Kalusha's brace. Italy would concede twice more after Pellegrini's introduction.

Midfielder Srečko Katanec was the other 1988 Olympian in the Sampdoria team. He was on VfB Stuttgart's books when he represented Yugoslavia in Seoul, and would later play at Italia 90 too. Pagliuca and Pellegrini, at any rate, might have been surprised at the different side of Musonda's game they saw in Gothenburg that spring evening. A visionary playmaker for Zambia, he was a defensive midfielder for Anderlecht, albeit one with massive ball skills. His specific role in that Cup Winners' Cup Final was to shadow Roberto Mancini, the future Manchester City and Italy coach, who was partnering the pacy Gianluca Vialli in the Sampdoria attack.

The versatile 20-year-old did a good-enough job on Mancini while probing forward whenever the Belgians had possession. Anderlecht played out a goalless draw in regulation time with the 1989 Coppa Italia winners. It took

Vialli's double strike in extra time to snatch a 2-0 victory for Samp. The highlight of Musonda's relatively brief club career had ended in disappointment.

In retrospect, the young Zambian could probably look back with pride on his performance. Five years after his first competitive league game in southern Africa aged 15, he'd once again held his own against some of the top European players of his generation. The next year, Sampdoria went on to win the Supercoppa Italiana, and their only *Scudetto*. In 1992, Ronald Koeman's extra-time free kick denied the Italians the European Cup in the last final before it was rebranded as the Champions League.

Sadly, Musonda's fortunes would not be as good. His career would go into stop-start mode after 1990 – mostly stop, as he was hampered by the debilitating injury to his right knee. Still, Zambians would twice be thrilled by the vintage Charlie Cool during the 1991 European summer break.

On 14 July, Musonda broke the proverbial ice for Zambia – during the southern hemisphere's cold season – against familiar rivals Madagascar. It was his third international goal. Kalusha also connected to complete a 2-1 victory at Independence Stadium in the 1992 AFCON qualifier.

Two weeks later at the same ground, Musonda nodded in a last-gasp Kalusha free kick a minute from full time to dramatically edge Angola 1-0 and seal Zambia's qualification for the 1992 Africa Cup of Nations. Fans wildly celebrated Musonda's winner, his fourth international goal. But their hero would sit out the entire 1992 for both club and country because of his crocked knee.

The year-long break seemed to do Musonda's knee good. He was back in action in early 1993 as Zambia attempted to salvage its World Cup hopes, after the 2-0 defeat in

Madagascar the previous December had left them on the brink of elimination. Following Tanzania's withdrawal, Zambia needed to win their next match – against debutants Namibia in Lusaka – by a four-goal margin just to equal Madagascar's goal difference. Then they simply had to beat the islanders, again in Lusaka, in their final second round qualifier, to top Group H and advance to the third and decisive qualifying round. Musonda came through.

As Kalusha recollected, 'FAZ thought it wise to [call] me and Charles at the last minute. So, we arrived on the day of the match [and] all efforts paid off as we beat Namibia.'

Musonda was among the scorers in a rout by the required 4-0 margin on 20 January that kept Zambia in contention for USA 94. It was his fifth and final international goal. He returned to Lusaka the next month with Kalusha for the must-win group decider on 27 February against Madagascar. He didn't score in a memorable match, but he ran the midfield as the Zambians prevailed 3-1. It was memorable for reasons beyond the outcome.

For one, it was a briefly transformational event that saw both Musonda and Kalusha play with new star Kelvin 'Malaza' Mutale for the first time – providing a sneak preview of a potentially new and more potent Zambia with a front line led by Kalusha and Mutale (both on target against Madagascar), and Musonda the midfield fulcrum behind them.

After the only two games he'd play with Mutale, Kalusha would draft a blueprint for Zambia's future attacking strategy. Kalusha recalled, 'He [Kelvin]was bound to be a legend. He was already campaigning in Saudi Arabia and you could see [a] phenomenal talent. I know that when I was there as captain, I'd draw the attention of defenders because they knew me, but they'd take their eyes off Kelvin, and Kelvin would destroy them.'

It had worked to a tee against Madagascar in that vital must-win World Cup qualifier; Zambia took it 3-1 with Malaza netting the first goal. Sadly, it wasn't to be. It would be Musonda's last game in Zambia and Kalusha would only play once more with Mutale.

Musonda's bad knee would preclude him from participating in Zambia's continued World Cup and AFCON qualifying campaign after the Gabon Disaster. He'd missed the emotionally charged 2-1 win over Morocco in Lusaka, the 1-1 tie with Zimbabwe in Harare and the two USA 94 qualifiers with Senegal, all to the chagrin of Zambian fans oblivious of the severity of his injury. Lack of communication on the midfield genius's part may not have helped.

Still, as World Cup qualification went to the wire with Zambia needing a point in Casablanca on 10 October 1993 to punch a ticket Stateside, there would be renewed clamour for Musonda's inclusion. What the world didn't know is that Musonda hadn't kicked a ball in the six months since the Gabon Disaster, as his latest injury ordeal persisted. Dejected, he mulled retirement. It took Jan Boskamp, Anderlecht's Dutch manager, to convince him to persevere – assuring him that he'd recover and play again. Boskamp okayed Musonda's trip to Casablanca.

'The manager said you can go now,' Musonda recalled. 'He said you don't play so just go so they can see you. I wasn't even training; I wasn't even going for treatment.'

So Musonda joined up with the new Zambian squad for the first time. His first national team duty since the 3-1 defeat of Madagascar the previous February. On the morning of the game at the Mohammed V Stadium, Musonda went down to the team hotel's grassy courtyard with assistant coach Freddie Mwila for a brief workout. Ian Porterfield had now taken over as head coach.

'Then I said to Ba Fred, "I haven't touched the ball for six months, I wasn't training." I was even about to quit [football] but [Boskamp] was still insisting and [saying] that you are going to recover, you are going to recover, so I was training not with the ball, just in the gym working on the knee. I was with Ba Fred, so I started kicking the ball with him, and he said, "Charles, I've got you, but the country is dying for this game." He said, "You are not starting. You'll be on the bench, let's hope things go well." Then I juggled a bit and run a bit.'

When the game started that afternoon at the raucous, bursting-at-the-seams, 90,000-capacity Mohammed V Stadium in the heart of Casablanca, Musonda was praying – almost against hope – that Morocco wouldn't score.

'When the first half ended 0-0, I was thinking these guys always score at home, so they're going to get a goal, whether we like it or not. And they scored, and immediately they scored, Porterfield – he didn't even know who I was – he said warm up, go in.'

Zambia were 28 minutes from qualifying for the 1994 World Cup when Abdeslam Laghrissi scored the most important goal of the 17 he'd net in his 35 caps for Morocco. He'd stoop low in the 62nd minute to head in Abdelkrim Hadrioui's cross from the left following a quick break. James Phiri, Efford Chabala's successor between the Zambian posts, was beaten that one moment. He'd otherwise put on a performance worthy of his legendary predecessor.

Despite his inactivity the previous months, Musonda's introduction sparked Zambia. They went in search of the equaliser that would restore their ticket to USA 94, and they nearly got it.

In the 78th minute, a long ball from Joel Bwalya found Gibby Mbasela on the right. The Nkana striker with the deceptive slow dribble shrugged off his marker outside the penalty box and squared a low ball across the yawning Moroccan goalmouth, with the keeper out of position and no Zambian attackers within a leg's distance. *Times of Zambia* deputy sports editor Gerald Mulwanda recalled the stadium letting out a deep 'WHOOSH!' as Morocco dodged a bullet.

Joel Bwalya was the catalyst again a minute later as Zambia nearly levelled. He swerved past a defender on the right and with the outside of his right foot delivered a searching, diagonal, 25-yard ball to his older brother Kalusha on the left side of the penalty box. Kalusha in turn nodded the ball to the onrushing Charles Musonda on his left. Musonda dived at it with his head, taking a boot to the face from a defender attempting a clearance. He ended up prone on the turf.

'I directed the ball towards the goalkeeper,' he remembered. 'But when I looked up, the ball was outside and I'm asking, what happened here?'

Jean-Fidèle Diramba, who'd officiated the 1990 AFCON Final between Algeria and Nigeria in Algiers, called no foul. Anything else would have meant a penalty. The Gabonese referee would, until his passing on 5 January 2022, be brutally derided by Zambian fans for that and other perceived no-calls throughout the emotionally charged qualifier.

In his *New York Times* match report published on 11 October 1993, Christopher Clarey captured some of the emotions Zambian fans and many neutrals were left with: 'There will be no historic first berth in the final round of the World Cup, no national holiday declared on Monday, no better-than-fiction comeback from the wreckage of the military transport plane that crashed into the sea off Gabon in April and took the lives of 18 Zambian national team players and their two coaches. Instead, the Moroccans will be the ones going to America in 1994. They and their new coach, Abdellah Blinda, earned that right today with a convincing 1-0 victory. They did so with considerable help from a crowd of at least 90,000 that already was in full voice three hours before the match and eventually spilled out of the 80,000 seats into every remotely inhabitable cranny of the imposing Mohammed V sports complex. "I am very sad for Zambia," said Blinda, who was promoted from coaching the national "B" team last month. "But what happened today is the law of football. There must be a winner and a loser." "We felt if we could hold on for the first 20 minutes of the second half, we would be OK," said Ian Porterfield, the Scotsman who began coaching the Zambians after the victory over Morocco. "But it was a good goal.'"

And so, a World Cup campaign marred by unimaginable tragedy came to a painful end. It was also Charles Musonda's last game for Zambia. Arguably his nation's best-ever pure midfielder, the Anderlecht star would never play at the top level again because of his knee injury. A brilliant international career that had started aged 16 in 1985, with a goal against Zambia's first major rival, had ended prematurely eight years later at 24. Although under different circumstances, Zambian football had lost another player of immense talent in that awful year of 1993.

22

Vintage Zambia

ON 20 January 1994, as Zambia were commencing their preparations for the Africa Cup of Nations in Tunisia kicking off on 26 March, Sir Matt Busby died. He was 84. The iconic Manchester United manager had survived the Munich air disaster that claimed eight of his players 36 years earlier on 6 February 1958. He'd rebuild his 'Busby's Babes' around the other survivors, including Bobby Charlton. Ten years after the Munich tragedy, Busby led United to the European Cup with a 4-1 extra-time victory over Eusébio's Benfica at Wembley Stadium.

Busby may have no doubt gone to the grave aware of the Gabon Disaster that occurred nine months before his death. He might even have been proud of how the Zambian squad rebuilt by Roald Poulsen performed in the months afterwards.

Having come within 28 minutes of completing their fallen comrades' mission and qualifying for USA 94, Zambia would continue their country's phoenix-like resurrection with one of the greatest comebacks in any sport. The stage was the 19th Africa Cup of Nations scheduled from 26 March to 10 April in Tunisia. Kalusha Bwalya's late header past Zimbabwean goalie Bruce Grobbelaar had clinched

Zambia's berth. He'd carry the rebuilt squad into the 12-nation tournament.

According to journalist Goliath Mungonge, expectations of success in Tunisia ahead of the tournament were low – even in Zambian quarters. 'Ian Porterfield was satisfied with reaching the quarter-finals, but Kalusha and [assistant coach] Ben Bamfuchile pushed Zambia forward,' said the *Zambia Daily Mail* reporter, who'd been in the delegation sent to Libreville to retrieve the remains of the Buffalo crash victims.

Ironically, Zambia's preparations for this AFCON had been unparalleled. Porterfield had taken the squad to England three weeks before Zambia's first group match with Sierra Leone on 29 March. Like on previous UK outings in 1978 and 1979, under their last full-time British coach, Brian Tiler, Zambia's opposition was modest again.

Birmingham City, a former mainstay in England's top flight between the 1950s and mid-80s, were in the Second Division when Zambia edged them 3-2 at St Andrew's on 18 March 1994. Kalusha notched a brace with Kapambwe Mulenga the other scorer. Five days later, Brentford, also in the Second Division then, were beaten 2-0 at their Griffin Park stadium in London by goals from Johnson Bwalya and Kenneth Malitoli.

Then it was on to Tunisia, where Malitoli played for Tunis-based Espérance and had been the league's top scorer in his rookie season in 1993. Zambia set up camp in the south-eastern coastal city of Sousse, less than 90 miles south of the capital Tunis – in a Group C also including defending African champions Ivory Coast and debutants Sierra Leone.

Although two teams from the group would advance to the quarter-finals, Ivory Coast put early pressure on Zambia with a 4-0 drubbing of Sierra Leone in which Le Havre hitman Joël Tiéhi hit a hat-trick. Zambia thus could not afford defeat in their opening match against the Sierra Leonese.

It was a nervy affair from the beginning, Kalusha recounted, 'I remember Ian Porterfield, the first game that we played against Sierra Leone, he was looking for a blackboard at the stadium.

'And we are all seated, and he's pacing up and down, saying, "Let's have the blackboard, we need to put the squad on the board – on the flipchart." And he was nervous, of course and everybody is nervous. And then they say no, let's do without it so he just announces the team. And then we got the [0-0] draw result. So, yes, belief was minimum. It was not there.'

There'd be a massive surge of confidence – two days later – and a measure of payback. Two years earlier in a titanic quarter-final that went into extra time at AFCON 92, Ivory Coast had edged Zambia 1-0 in Senegal. The Elephants went on to lift the cup. This meeting also seemed headed to a goalless tie at the Stade Olympique de Sousse until a Kalusha through ball sprung substitute Kenneth Malitoli. With his first touch, the 1993 Tunisian league's top scorer connected in the 79th minute.

* * *

Stunning victories over cup holders Congo-Brazzaville (4-2) in Egypt in 1974 and Nigeria (3-0) in Libya in 1982 had seen Zambia create a reputation as the slayer of champions in AFCON tournaments. The 1-0 win over Ivory Coast by rebuilt Zambia further burnished that notoriety. Belief was now growing, as Kalusha pointed out, 'If you talk to the old team, the Malitolis and the guys who were in Sousse, they will tell you that "Mr Kalu used to take us on a run every morning". Then I'd warm the team up and get them ready, but the running was incredible. And slowly, slowly, we started to believe in our capabilities; the singing. I still remember the singing was incredible. So, the team played [beyond normal] because we were able to beat Ivory Coast, then we went to the quarter-finals [where] we played against Senegal, Evans Sakala scored a beautiful, beautiful goal!'

What the talismanic Zambian captain omitted is that he had the assist on the midfielder's world-class strike from close to 40 yards in the 38th minute. Kalusha rolled a pass to the charging Sakala who struck the ball on his second touch, beating the outstretched arms of Cheikh Ahmed Seck as the goalie dived to his right. Senegal, with Souleymane Sané leading the line, had no response. Sakala's goal and excellent form in the tournament would earn him a move to an Al Ettifaq side still missing its departed Zambian stars Kelvin Mutale and Derby Makinka.

It was Kalusha'ʂ first tournament without his old comrades lost in the Gabon crash – 'the best of the best' – he called them. But there were moments, then and before, when it felt like old times.

He recalled, 'In 1993, the [old] team was on a high. We had the best of the best. [But] I always say that sometimes the 1993 replacements – or the substitutes as you might say – at times played for 20 minutes or 30 minutes of a game, like the fallen heroes. It was always a motivation. Then we were supposed to play Mali – but Zambia was confident.'

Mali had had a great tournament, Kalusha noted, 'They were serious contenders for the Africa Cup of Nations. They beat host Tunisia 2-0 in the first game and in the knockout phase they beat Egypt, so the people, they thought now it's Mali's turn. And we went out and beat them 4-0.'

The West Africans had run into vintage Zambia.

'Kenneth [Malitoli] scored his second goal of the tournament, Elijah [Litana] scored, [Zeddy] Saileti scored, and I also scored. It was like a practice match if you think about it because Litana scored after eight minutes and starting with the second half we were already 3-0 up. And when Kenneth scored it was in the last 15 minutes,' said Kalusha.

Exactly 20 years after twice squaring off with the Zaire Leopards in the replayed AFCON 1974 championship match, Zambia were back in the final with a bang – and with a de facto second unit to boot.

'Yeah, it's the belief. And I can agree with what Goliath [Mungonge] said that nobody fancied Zambia to go all the way,' Kalusha said. 'And when we reached the final against Nigeria, I still think – and I am not wrong because I was there myself – I thought that Zambia was the better team on the day. Yes, Nigeria, [Emmanuel] Amunike playing I think probably his first game of the tournament came in and scored two goals after we had gone ahead after three minutes with an Elijah Litana header. They were lucky that they [equalised] immediately after we scored, otherwise it would have been a different game altogether.'

Again, Kalusha didn't mention that it was from his corner that the towering Litana powerfully headed past Nigerian goalie Peter Rufai. The skipper's third straight assist and Litana's second consecutive goal after nodding in another early goal against Mali in the semis.

Going into the final at the Stade El Menzah in Tunis, Kalusha told the broadcaster Eurosport, 'We'll say a prayer for our dead comrades before the match but then we'll be on our own.' They did just that. But in the end, they'd be roared on by the majority of the 25,000 fans in the 45,000-capacity El Menzah, a better-than-decent turnout for a game in which the hosts weren't involved.

Kalusha said, 'I thought Zambia was the better team but we lost, and, of course, Nigeria afterwards went on with their stars – Rashidi Yekini, of course, one of our favourites – to make history. If you have Jay-Jay Okocha, and the Finidi Georges, and [Daniel] Amokachi, and all those players that they had – and they were just starting – that's why they were called the Super Eagles, because of the calibre of players that Nigeria was able to field in 1994, especially in the final.

'But I make no apologies. Zambia was the better team – the better playing team and we [still] lost the final!'

Playing his first AFCON Final on his third try, Kalusha knew what he was talking about. Trailing 2-1, Zambia had the pick of the chances in the second half as they chased the equaliser. Kalusha himself had two of those opportunities. The first was a shot – albeit from his weaker right foot – from outside the six-yard box that was smothered by Rufai in the 58th minute. The second was a bullet left-footer from 25 yards that crashed against the post 19 minutes later.

In between these two Zambian chances, Litana had a header from another Kalusha corner saved by Rufai, before the goalkeeper pulled off a tremendous point-blank stop from Malitoli in the six-yard box. Johnson Bwalya had taken a throw-in deep in the Nigerian half to Kalusha, who swung the ball in from the edge of the penalty box. Malitoli connected but Rufai raised his hands to prevent an equaliser.

The tiring Nigerians' best chance was a Rashidi Yekini shot on the break that hit the post late in the 86th minute.

Eurosport, broadcasting the final globally, provided this narrative in the second half as the green-clad Zambians chased the leveller, '[Nigerian coach Clemens] Westerhof is now like some crazed marionette out on the touchline, gesticulating, trying to get some life out of his team in midfield where they've largely disappeared, ten minutes remaining – Zambia [in] the fight of their lives now. Two-one down and everybody back for Nigeria defending. Oh, this is stunning stuff by Zambia!'

Then after the camera panned to the great Pelé, one of the many celebrities at the final, the commentator said, 'And I am sure Pelé must be admiring the fighting, courageous spirit of this side in green.'

Like he'd done spectacularly since the Gabon Disaster, Kalusha carried Zambia and deservedly earned credit. Eurosport hailed his effort in the final. 'Kalusha's had a marvellous second half,' said the commentator.

Nigerian skipper Stephen Keshi, who'd played in two of the Super Eagles' games in Tunisia, later paid his injured and absent Anderlecht compatriot Charles Musonda the ultimate compliment. 'He said if you were there [at AFCON 1994], you [Zambia] were going to beat us,' Musonda recalled.

Two months after holding off Zambia 2-1, Nigeria were the surprise package in the group stages of the World Cup in the United States. Forward Yekini produced one of USA 94's most iconic moments when he was captured, wide-eyed with excitement and passion, shaking the net in celebration after scoring the Super Eagles' first World Cup goal, in a 3-0 rout of Bulgaria in Dallas.

They'd go on to top a group also comprising Diego Maradona's Argentina, who beat them 2-1, and Greece, who they beat 2-0. Nigeria would then implode spectacularly against ten-man Italy in a 2-1 last-16 extra-time defeat in Foxborough, Massachusetts.

The Zambian squad, meanwhile, would be rewarded by their government on their return with a US$10,000 bonus each. For coach Ian Porterfield – whose third gig as club manager was replacing one Alex Ferguson in November 1986 as Aberdeen boss in the Scottish Premier Division – Zambia would be his first and most high-profile international job. He'd declare that the best was yet to come. But with his stock raised by Zambia's AFCON exploits, he'd soon be on his way, paving the way for the return of the rebuilt squad's original mentor.

Ian Porterfield was 61 and national coach of Armenia when he died of colon cancer on 11 September 2007.

23

The Reggae Boyz

JUST OVER a year after the squad he'd forged had downed Morocco in one of the most emotional games in football, Roald Poulsen returned to Zambia, in October 1994, this time on a three-year contract as national team coach. The Dane's second stint would be as memorable as the first. There'd be an emotional qualification campaign for the next biennial AFCON, consequential tours of Jamaica and South Korea and the discovery of new players. With Zambia's first AFCON 96 qualifier scheduled for 13 November, Poulsen had to hit the ground running. The absence of the talismanic Kalusha Bwalya complicated things early on.

As a result, Zambia would make an inauspicious start to qualifying. They needed a Kenneth Malitoli penalty four minutes from time against South Africa to avert a first home defeat in Lusaka in 11 years. Doctor Khumalo had scored for Bafana Bafana in the 68th minute.

A week later, there'd be a poignant first trip for Poulsen and his lads to the country where the future of Zambian football had been inexorably altered: Gabon. The Group 5 AFCON 96 qualifier in Libreville, on 20 November 1994, marked the first time Zambian footballers had set foot on Gabonese soil since Efford Chabala, Kelvin 'Malaza' Mutale and the ill-fated squad had landed in Libreville on that fateful night of 27 April 1993.

Without Kalusha and Johnson Bwalya, Africa's second-best side were second best that Sunday afternoon at the Stade Omar Bongo. Wedson Nyirenda, young brother of 1988 Olympic squad forward Stone Nyirenda, scored a late goal in a 2-1 defeat to the Gabonese.

AFCON 96 was originally scheduled for Kenya, but when the East Africans pulled out, South Africa stepped in as hosts. Bafana Bafana subsequently withdrew from the qualifiers, and the three games, including the 1-1 draw in Lusaka, were annulled. It apparently didn't matter at that point. Three months into Poulsen's second tenure, Zambia were cranking.

Kalusha and Johnson Bwalya were back when Zambia returned to Mauritius in January 1995 and repeated their fallen compatriots' 3-0 romp over the islanders. Kalusha came a goal short of reprising Kelvin Mutale's hat-trick performance; Johnson was the other scorer.

Kalusha would once again reproduce his big game-winning form in Zambia's second qualifying victory. It came against Group 5 leaders Gabon in Lusaka on 8 April and the visitors, wary of his presence, would park the proverbial bus long before José Mourinho had coined the term. With seven minutes remaining that long, agonising afternoon, Kalusha's solution was to slalom through a forest of green-shirted Gabonese defenders and into the penalty box from where he notched the only goal of the match. Then he returned to Club América, Mexico's most popular club, who he'd joined in July 1994 after five years with PSV. In 1994, Club América had signed the Netherlands' 1990 World Cup coach Leo Beenhakker to capture a long-elusive Liga MX title. The Dutchman in turn made Kalusha and lanky Cameroonian striker François Omam-Biyik his top acquisitions for América. Omam-Biyik, 28 then, had, of course, made history at Italia 90 with his winner against world champions Argentina.

Kalusha and Omam-Biyik had first crossed paths nine years earlier when Cameroon and Zambia had clashed in the first leg of a World Cup qualifier on 7 April 1985 in Lusaka. Kalusha had been mesmerising on the left wing as Zambia led 4-0 after 40 minutes with the Nkana striker nicknamed 'Big Mike' for his burly size, Michael Chabala, hitting a devastating hat-trick. In the second half, like he'd do against the Argentines in Milan five years later, Omam-Biyik, a former goalie turned striker, would nod in a cross past the outstanding Efford Chabala – a former striker turned goalie – for Cameroon's consolation goal.

Kalusha and Omam-Biyik became cult heroes in their four seasons together at the fabulous Estadio Azteca, an expansive 87,500-capacity stadium, sitting 2.2km above sea level in Mexico City, and the largest football ground in Latin America. On Club América's centenary in 2016, the two Africans were voted by fans to an exclusive list of 'Historic Players' during the club's 100-year history then.

With Kalusha back in Mexico after his exhilarating winner over Gabon, Roald Poulsen – reserve goalie Davies Phiri recalled – would lead a mostly under-23 side back to the land of Zambia's greatest victory – South Korea. In addition to Phiri, other under-23 players in the Korea Cup squad would include left-back Hillary Makasa, central defender Elijah Tana, powerful winger Andrew Tembo and a short, explosive forward with superb finishing named Dennis Lota.

Before an 18-year-old Michael Owen momentarily lit up the 1998 World Cup with a blistering solo goal for England against Argentina, Zambia had boasted a player of similar qualities. At 5ft 8in, the same height as Owen, Dennis Lota had bounced around several clubs as a midfielder before landing at Konkola Blades. There, Kalusha's retired older brother Benjamin, the Konkola coach, had converted him into a striker. Lota found his calling with the same pace and clinical finishing Owen would display on the big stage. At 20, he was top scorer in the Zambian league. At 21, he'd give the world a glimpse of his potential at the 1995 Korea Cup.

It started inauspiciously for Lota and Co. Korean fans with wistful memories of the old Zambian squad's 1988 Olympic exploits, and in awe at the country's strong recovery after the Gabon Disaster, may have been a trifle disappointed by the Africans' opening result in a Group B also comprising Belgian club KV Mechelen, Swedes Trelleborgs FF and the Ecuadorian national side. In their second encounter with a South American national side (the first being the 2-1 collapse to Venezuela at the 1980 Moscow Olympics), Zambia were steamrolled 4-1 by the rampaging Eduardo Hurtado, Ecuador's 6ft 3in centre-forward aptly nicknamed 'El Tanque', or 'The Tank'.

Johnson Bwalya, the only survivor of the 1988 Olympic side, had cancelled out Hurtado's opener in Changwon. But El Tanque, one of Major League Soccer's early stars in 1996 with Los Angeles Galaxy, struck three more times in the second half. A goalless draw with Mechelen two days later left Zambia bottom of the group after two matches and seemingly headed out.

Davies Phiri, then aged 19, and at 5ft 7.5in the shortest goalie to play for Zambia, recalled the delegation leader booking the squad's return flight to Zambia – even before its third and final game, against Trelleborgs. It would be a short tournament in the official's mind. According to Phiri, the players had been paid US$1,200 each by the Football Association of Zambia for their participation with nothing more guaranteed unless they reached the final.

'When we got to Korea, we were told that if we won the final, we'd get $6,000 each, and if we were runners-up, we'd get 4,000 US dollars. So, we were calculating that if we were runners-up, we'd make $5,200 total and if we won, it would be $7,200.'

That amounted to a king's ransom for the young players during those harsh economic times in Zambia. For one, Phiri's monthly wages at Kabwe Warriors amounted to K2,500, or equivalent to US$500. Hence defeat against Trelleborgs in that last group game was not an option. Dennis Lota and fellow under-23 forward Sunday Kalunga connected in a 2-0 win which secured second place in Group B, and a semi-final date in Seoul with Group A winners South Korea.

With rousing partisan support, South Korea had emerged undefeated from their group. They'd beaten a Carioca select side from Brazil 2-0, edged Costa Rica 1-0 and routed Scottish club Kilmarnock 5-1. Once again, Zambia's pessimistic delegation leader, anticipating defeat against the high-flying hosts, made plans for the squad to return home after the semi-finals.

'We had the first chance, Lewis Mulenga – from nowhere, keeper beaten, 1-0,' said Phiri. Ten minutes had lapsed at the Dongdaemun Stadium.

The lead held for half an hour before Roh Sang-Rae equalised. However, when midfielder Vincent Mutale restored Zambia's advantage six minutes into the second half, the Koreans responded with a fury.

'It was pressure after pressure,' said Phiri, who was watching from the bench. 'They were hitting the crossbar and missing chance after chance.'

The pressure paid off with Kim Do-Hoon's leveller on the hour.

'Immediately they scored to make it 2-2, Dennis Lota went with the ball, faked a pass, dribbled, and one-on-one with the keeper went with power: 3-2,' said Phiri, as the young Zambians became just the second African team after Egypt to beat Korea at home. They were also in the final and guaranteed a minimum $5,200 per player.

The final would be a rematch with El Tanque and his Ecuadorian mates. They'd edged Costa Rica 2-1 in the other semi-final, with Hurtado netting his fifth goal of the tournament. Yet, while equally towering Zambian centre-back Elijah Litana and his team-mates had done their homework and would keep Hurtado goalless, Energio Díaz would slip in and score the third and final goal of his brief international career in Ecuador's 1-0 victory. They'd fly back to Quito with a $200,000 cheque, according to Phiri. Second-placed Zambia received $100,000 and more respect, no doubt, from Korean fans who fondly remembered the 1988 Olympic squad.

A month after banking his $5,200 bonus from the Korea Cup, Dennis Lota helped secure Zambia's qualification for the 1996 AFCON. He bagged the first goal in a 2-0 win over Mauritius in Lusaka on 15 July, with Johnson Bwalya the other marksman. Roald Poulsen would finally get a chance to lead his young team to the Africa Cup of Nations. This, as Lota, his star home-based striker, was popping up on many a European radar.

But first there would be a historic Jamaican tour in August 1995 – Zambia's first trip to the Caribbean – and one that would spawn one of the most iconic team monikers in world football. It was the result of an impromptu jam session at a Kingston hotel before their first match.

Davies Phiri recalled walking into a dimly lit reception room with his young team-mates and noticing unattended musical instruments on a bandstand. Soon a few individuals picked up the instruments and started playing. The beat was pulsating, throbbing – unmistakably reggae.

'We thought they were band members,' said Phiri. 'They played good. Later, the real band came and that's when we realised that the first group were the Jamaican team members we were going to play against.'

Another young Zambian player whose name Phiri couldn't recall then blurted out a compliment. 'He said something like, "Don't play with the reggae boys!"' said Phiri, who joined in the praise. Then he recalled another Zambian player telling a Jamaican compatriot, 'You are reggae boys – the way you were playing! Like real musicians.'

The Jamaicans acknowledged the props, but from all indications the reggae boys moniker was quickly forgotten, with two friendlies to be played. Going up against a side drilled by Brazilian René Simões, who'd had previous stints with Brazil's Olympic, under-17 and under-20 squads, Poulsen's Zambia played out a 1-1 draw in Kingston on 18 August 1985. They'd succumb 3-1 to the hosts three days later in Montego Bay.

Three months later, Simões took Jamaica on a reciprocal two-match tour of Zambia. They lost both games – 1-0 in Kitwe on 3 November, and 4-2 in Lusaka on 5 November – but would return home rebranded. The 'Reggae Boys' nickname had popped up again on the brief African jaunt. It would stick this time.

Years later, Jerry Muchimba, author of Godfrey 'Ucar' Chitalu's eponymous posthumous biography, came across an article in a Jamaican publication collaborating the Zambian source of the moniker, 'When thinking of Jamaica you think of reggae, the world-famous music that originated on this island, so it is only natural that the national football squad are referred to as the Reggae Boyz. But no one would ever suspect Zambia of having first conjured up this internationally recognised nickname. Earl Bailey explained, "When Jamaica went to Zambia to play a friendly in 1995, the Zambians on their local news christened us the Reggae Boyz. The name was used extensively in the media here when we came back, and during the World Cup it became an international hit used by radio and TV.'"

So first coined in a Kingston hotel by young Zambian players impressed by the musical talents of their opponents, the nickname 'Reggae Boys' resurfaced during Jamaica's Zambian tour. Brilliantly apt for the national squad from the home of one of the world's most popular musical genres, it was tweaked to Reggae Boyz and gained traction.

'We didn't know that the name would catch on,' said Phiri.

It grew legs two years later. When a goalless draw with Mexico in Kingston in 1997 saw Jamaica qualify for France 98, they became the second Caribbean nation, after Haiti in 1974, and the first English-speaking one to compete at the World Cup. The nickname went mega-viral.

Known locally – at least until 1991 when founding president Kenneth Kaunda was voted out of office – as the KK XI – Zambia also got a new nickname in 1995, albeit one not as catchy as The Reggae Boyz. Their 'Chipolopolo' or 'Copper Bullets' moniker was derived from the refrain in a football song this writer first heard from enthusiastic fans of third division Malaiti Rangers back in 1982. The song later made a resurgence at international games after the Gabon Disaster. It had its roots in Zambia's Copperbelt.

Meanwhile, Zambia's AFCON 96 preparations continued under Roald Poulsen. Fresh off the back-to-back victories over the newly christened Reggae Boyz that November, the Dane took Dennis Lota and his other home-based squad to South Africa for the four-nation Simba tournament. Lota, who'd scored in the 4-2 romp over Jamaica in Lusaka, got both goals in an exciting 2-2 draw with South Africa in Pretoria, further raising his stock. Ironically, it would set in motion events that would briefly stall his career.

Zambian football pundit Ponga Liwewe recalled Lota signing a contract with Swiss side Sion prior to the Simba tournament. His form in the competition – also featuring Egypt and Zimbabwe – generated further interest from clubs in the wealthy South African league, including Witbank Aces. Rather naively, noted Liwewe, Lota signed with Aces as well. The move would come to haunt him and Zambia.

There was another emerging Zambian star at the Simba tournament ahead of AFCON 96. Young attacking midfielder Andrew Tembo, having barely escaped the Gabon Disaster, had returned to flourish with Zambia more than two years later. As can be recalled, the then promising 21-year-old had awakened at Masiye Lodge with his national team compatriots on the morning of 27 April 1993, prepared for a long haul to Senegal for a World Cup qualifier aboard a Zambia Air Force transport plane. That changed when Tembo and reserve goalie Martin Mwamba were notified by coaches Godfrey Chitalu and Alex Chola after breakfast that they'd be left behind to accommodate European-based professionals, including skipper Kalusha, who would join the squad in West Africa. That saved their lives.

While Mwamba finally made the squad to AFCON 94 in Tunisia, and even played in the 4-0 semi-final rout of Mali after initially declining a call-up immediately after the crash to recover from the shock, Tembo would not make his return until 1995 under Poulsen. He starred in the Simba tournament with goals in a 1-1 draw with Zimbabwe and in a 3-1 defeat to Egypt. The latter would be a sneak preview to probably the most pulsating competitive clash ever between the two old rivals eight weeks later at AFCON 96.

In a final tune-up three weeks before AFCON, Dennis Lota and veteran defender Mordon Malitoli saw off fellow South Africa-bound Tunisia 2-0 in Lusaka. The result handed Henryk Kasperczak, the former Polish international and then Tunisia coach, his second defeat to a post-Gabon Zambian side. The first was at AFCON 94 when, as Ivorian boss, Kasperczak's defending champions were edged 1-0 by a late goal from Mordon's older brother Kenneth.

Reinforced by Kalusha, Zambia headed off to South Africa on a high. It was arguably the most talented post-Gabon Disaster squad assembled by Poulsen. It had to be as AFCON 96 would boast all the continent's best teams with the exception of Morocco's Atlas Lions and defending champions Nigeria. While the former had surprisingly missed out on their second consecutive biennial AFCON, the Super Eagles, in a fit of pique by then Nigerian dictator Sani Abacha over political tensions with South Africa, had pulled out at the 11th hour.

Then 32 but still coruscating, Kalusha would again give Zambia that extra spark. He'd have the best supporting cast nurtured after the Gabon Disaster as Zambia put on a scoring clinic at Free State Stadium in Bloemfontein. In addition to the 22-year-old Lota, there was Andrew Tembo, Kenneth Malitoli and Johnson Bwalya. Collectively, they'd produce the highest-scoring Zambian performance at any tournament as they topped Group B.

It started rather inauspiciously, a goalless draw with Algeria, African champions in 1990 and World Cup qualifiers in 1982 and 1986. Then Zambia exploded with a 5-1 Kalusha-inspired destruction of Burkina Faso. Kalusha notched a brace while Kenneth Malitoli, Lota and Johnson Bwalya each struck once. A Kalusha hat-trick and Mordon Malitoli goal in the 4-0 rout of a Sierra Leonese side led by Mohamed Kallon followed. It punched Zambia's ticket to the quarters. They'd welcome Egypt to Bloemfontein.

The Pharaohs – under former Dutch defensive stalwart Ruud Krol who'd played in the finals of the 1974 and 1978 World Cups, succeeding Johan Cruyff as captain in the latter – had finished second to South Africa in Group A despite edging the hosts 1-0 in Johannesburg. But eight weeks after besting Roald Poulsen's largely home-based squad 3-1 in the Simba tournament, Krol's charges must've more than fancied their chances of drubbing the Zambians again and advancing to the semi-finals.

Forty-three minutes in at the Free State Stadium, a short Egyptian corner, a cross into the box, a defensive header and a vicious, swerving right-footed blast from the rebound into the top right-hand corner by defender Samir Kamouna put the Pharaohs ahead. One of the best defenders of his generation, Krol sent on an extra defender. Enter veteran Fawzi Gamal, 29, for 22-year-old striker Ali Maher in an attempt to fortify the Egyptian rearguard against Zambia's free-scoring front line. It would be in vain.

Over an 18-minute period – after trailing for a quarter of an hour – Zambia ran rampant. First towering defender Elijah Litana, loitering in the penalty box after a corner, nodded in a powerful header on 58 minutes for the equaliser. Then midfielder Vincent Mutale knocked in a rebound after Egyptian goalie Nader El Sayed had parried a Kalusha header, from Tembo's hanging cross, into his path. Finally, Lota, released by Mordon Malitoli, went one-on-one with

El Sayed and from close range at the near post drilled the ball between El Sayed's legs for Zambia's third goal.

Beaten 3-1 by the Pharaohs in a tune-up tournament two months earlier, Poulsen's side had returned the favour when it really mattered. It was on to the AFCON semis for the second time after the crash of the Buffalo. Nearly three years after the Gabon Disaster, Zambian football still lived.

Lota and Kalusha – the latter on five goals going into the knockout stage – were in good company in the last four. Hosts South Africa, on the big stage for the first time since returning to the international fold, had names such as the Leeds United duo Lucas Radebe and Phil Masinga, midfielders John 'Shoes' Moshoeu and Doctor Khumalo, forward Shaun Bartlett and defender Mark Fish, and were making waves.

Coached by the Durban-born Clive Barker, Bafana Bafana would meet a formidable Ghana side. The Black Stars had two of the continent's all-time greats in Anthony Yeboah – then on Leeds United's books – and the incomparable Abedi Pele, who less than three years earlier had starred in Marseille's 1-0 triumph over AC Milan's Marco van Basten, Frank Rijkaard and Co. in the 1993 UEFA Champions League Final.

Plucked out of the relative sea-level comfort of Port Elizabeth, where they'd played three of their previous four matches including a 1-0 win over Zaire in the semis, Pele and gang from the former Gold Coast would face Bafana well over a mile above sea level in Johannesburg. There they'd be thumped 3-0 before 75,000 fans at FNB Stadium, with Moshoeu striking twice and Bartlett once.

Henryk Kasperczak's Tunisia completed the final four. The Carthage Eagles had finished second in their group behind Ghana and ahead of 1992 AFCON champions Ivory Coast and Mozambique, in that order. They had quality in

Club Africain forward Adel Sellimi, midfielder Zoubeir Baya of Étoile Sportive du Sahel, and two of Kenneth Malitoli's Espérance de Tunis team-mates, defenders Khaled Badra and the ill-fated Hédi Berkhissa. Voted both Tunisian and Arab Footballer of the Year in 1995, Berkhissa would collapse and die during a friendly match between Espérance and visiting French side Olympique Lyon on 4 January 1997.

On 31 January 1996, for the second time in five weeks, Zambia would face Tunisia. It was, yet again, a remarkable achievement for Poulsen's rebuilt side to reach its second consecutive Africa Cup of Nations semi-finals less than three years after the Gabon Disaster. Zambia went into the match the sentimental favourites. And besides, they were in free-scoring form. Aside from the goalless opener with Algeria, Kalusha, Lota and Kenneth Malitoli had torn apart defences – including Egypt's vaunted one – tallying no less than three goals per match.

But once again, there'd be another twist to this tale. Surprisingly, they'd unravel at Kings Park Stadium in Durban. Sluggish early, they'd trail 3-0 after 47 minutes to goals by Adel Sellimi, Zoubeir Baya and Kaies Ghodhbane, before Lota raised hopes of a dramatic late comeback with his third of the tournament. Sellimi's 85th-minute penalty would be answered by a Hillary Makasa strike on the stroke of full time. It would be too little, too late. Tunisia had triumphed 4-2 and denied Poulsen's Zambia a second consecutive AFCON Final appearance.

Poulsen summed up Zambia's second major competition after the Gabon crash thus: 'The AFCON in South Africa was not an easy tournament. Zambia were runners-up in 1994, but we had a pretty good team with a lot of potential, a good mix of experienced and young players, and we did well until the semi-final in Durban. It was the first international football event in SA after the FIFA boycott, due to the Apartheid government.

'It was a big arrangement for the SA football association and CAF and they struggled with some important issues such as travel and transport arrangements, accommodation, training grounds, security, etc. All in all, it was a huge disappointment for us not to play the final, but we got the bronze medal and it was handed over by Mr Nelson Mandela himself. It was a moment I never will forget, and he had a few private words for me, also.'

Musa Kasonka Jr., FAZ delegation leader, would blame poor logistics on the part of the organising committee for Zambia's stunning loss. They'd arrived in Durban in the wee hours, less than 48 hours before the clash with Tunisia and would not be accommodated until hours later. Kasonka said, 'The move was very badly organised by the committee. We arrived in Durban at 2am. We had one rest day – the team that had been eliminated and should have left, Gabon, was still in their hotel rooms which we were going to occupy. By the time we got into our rooms it was [late] so that really contributed to it. So the following day we spent sleeping. We spent a little time at the stadium. The players didn't rest enough and the game was the next day.'

There'd be one more game for Zambia before they left South Africa, the one that would earn Poulsen and his squad the bronze medals presented to them by Mandela. On 3 February at the FNB Stadium, Joel Bwalya's rasping 30-yard drive into the top-right corner snatched a victory over Ghana in the heartbreak match. It was the first senior Zambia goal by Kalusha's kid brother, and it kept Zambia's winning streak in AFCON third-place matches going. It was their third after victories in the third-place match at AFCON 82 and 90.

CRASH OF THE BUFFALO

By August 1996, the sum total of Zambia's results – including a dramatic 3-2 aggregate win over Sudan in World Cup qualifying in June, following a 2-0 loss in Khartoum without Kalusha – had helped Poulsen's side rise to 15th in the world on the FIFA rankings. In Africa, they'd be ranked number one by FIFA. It would be the apex of Poulsen's post-Gabon project, as he recalled, 'From my acting period 1993–96, I [had] a lot of exciting memories on and off the field, many fantastic training sessions and 27 official matches. We were ranked number 15 in the world on the official FIFA list and number one in Africa, so the rebuilding lasted for more than just one or two games. I was also heavily involved in the building of the youth national teams, produced and lectured a lot of coaching courses, and became a life member of the Zambia Football Coaches Association.

'Being in charge of the national team was quite demanding, but I always felt it was a privilege and I enjoyed the challenges and all the training sessions with the players, because they gave me a lot of positive response. Besides that, most of the officials and staff I worked with were loyal and grateful for our working climate and culture of planning and executing.

'But the biggest bonus was the kindness and respect from the Zambian people, they treated me with manners, respect and love. I was welcome wherever I [went]. That is still extremely deep in my heart and I will never forget.'

Then, to his regret, it ended. 'We had some problems with negotiations around a new contract and, looking retrospectively, it was a bad decision for me to leave Zambia. I should have stayed but I lost my patience due to bad communication from the person in charge from the Ministry of Sport, but I take the blame.'

Poulsen returned home to coach, for the second time, top Danish side Odense Boldklub. He wasn't alone: 'I had identified Andrew Tembo and Mwape Miti to be strong enough to play in the Danish Super League, and they had a ten-year-long career at OB. Mwape Miti was the last player I selected for the AFCON 1996 team. He was very young at that time but extremely talented.'

Years later, during Odense Boldklub's 125th anniversary, both Tembo – who escaped the Gabon crash only after being fortuitously dropped from the national team hours before departure – and Miti were voted by fans to OB's All-Star First XI.

Zambia's fortunes, meanwhile, would gradually decline after Poulsen's departure at the end of 1996. It started with the squad's first post-crash World Cup campaign for the 1998 finals in France. After navigating past Sudan in the first round, Zambia were drawn in what on paper appeared a winnable group. There were jaded old foes Zaire (re-named Congo DR in May 1997), South Africa and Congo-Brazzaville. And, for the first time, none of the difficult north African sides that had previously stymied Zambia's World Cup hopes.

It didn't help that Zambia were handicapped from the start of the qualifiers by Dennis Lota's suspension from club football by FIFA. This while the two clubs Lota had naively signed for at the same time – Swiss side Sion and South Africa's Witbank Aces – haggled over who owned him. So, while cleared to train and play for Zambia, the young striker who'd emerged as a competent successor to the late Kelvin Mutale could not play at club level until his contract issue was resolved. Predictably, the lack of club action hurt his form – particularly his timing – consequently impacting Zambia's striking force.

With Lota misfiring, Zambia had played one qualifier, a 1-0 defeat away to Congo-Brazzaville in what was Poulsen's final game in charge, when FAZ once again turned to old hands Freddie Mwila and Samuel 'Zoom' Ndhlovu to lead the squad. But failure to beat Bafana Bafana in Lusaka (0-0) and Zaire in neutral Harare (2-2) in the next two qualifiers made it a short-lived reunion with the two veteran coaches.

On just their second attempt, South Africa, under AFCON-winning coach Clive Barker, qualified for the World Cup ahead of Congo-Brazzaville and Zambia, in that order.

* * *

Postscript: there'd be one more Roald Poulsen stint as Zambia boss as he'd once again respond to an FAZ request for help. Like the first one in 1993, it would be brief. He'd pause his role as technical director of FC Copenhagen's South African academy in Port Elizabeth for three months to prepare and lead Zambia to the 2002 AFCON in Mali after the departure of Dutchman Jan Brouwer, who'd qualified the squad to the tournament.

He recalled, 'I agreed and it was a déjà vu. I [had] four weeks to prepare in December 2001, in Zambia, before travelling to Burkina Faso and play one friendly game and then to Mali for the tournament. We played OK, but were not lucky at all. More players got the flu in Mali before the group matches due to very poor accommodation and climate conditions. The people were extremely helpful and kind in that very, very poor country. We could only manage to provide 12 players for one of the games. We trained in the garden of the hotel, so it was harsh to compete. To show how tight it was in our group after three games: we scored one goal and got one point, Senegal scored two goals and got seven points – success or fiasco on an edge. That was the third and last time I was the national coach of Zambia.'

Zambia, without the retired Kalusha, had once again ended up in the dreaded Group of Death. There was a goalless draw with World Cup-bound Tunisia, a 1-0 slip-up in the 90th minute to the Aliou Cissé-captained Senegalese, who would reach the World Cup quarter-finals that summer, and a 2-1 loss to Egypt, resulting in a quick return home.

It would not be until the arrival of another young, sandy blond-haired coach that Zambia's fortunes would pick up again, and a holy grail attained.

Poulsen died of natural causes on Oct. 16, 2024. He was 73. According to Danish journalist Buster Emil Kirchner, Poulsen requested that he be buried with the bronze medal presented to him by President Nelson Mandela after Zambia's third-place finish at the 1996 AFCON in South Africa.

24

Ghosts of Libreville

NINETEEN YEARS after losing the country's finest collection of players on the shores of the steamy Gabonese capital, Zambia made an emotional return to Libreville in February 2012. The occasion? The national team's biggest match since the 1994 Africa Cup of Nations Final against Nigeria's Super Eagles in Tunis.

More than a few eyebrows had been raised when the Zambians, now under the tutelage of a young, hitherto unknown Frenchman named Hervé Renard, on his second stint with the squad, advanced to the final of the 28th AFCON. Gabon was the co-host nation with its tiny oil-rich northern neighbour Equatorial Guinea. It was a dramatic tournament in more ways than one. Some pointed at the absence of traditional African powers such as Nigeria, Cameroon, Egypt, Algeria and South Africa, who had all failed to qualify.

But a Senegalese side led by the in-form Demba Ba, then shooting the lights out for Newcastle United in the English Premier League, had qualified. And so had Ghana's Black Stars, who'd been so close to a historic World Cup semi-final berth in South Africa 18 months earlier. Then there was, of course, Didier Drogba, Yaya Touré and

Co. with pre-tournament favourites Ivory Coast. Hervé Renard's Zambia would beat them all.

Youthful, well travelled and with long, sandy blond hair, Renard would have back in the 1960s matched the profile of a globetrotting hippie. He was far from that. A teetotaller and, with nary an ounce of fat on his 6ft 1in frame, he was a sculpture of athleticism that validated his first job as a physical trainer. Renard first arrived in Zambia in 2008, hired by then FAZ boss Kalusha who'd relinquished his coaching responsibility after making history as the first person to serve as both president of a football association and national team coach simultaneously. The Zambia job was Renard's first as head coach of a national side. It would be followed by several other successful international gigs.

He'd only heard of Zambia once before the morning of 28 April 1993. That's when he woke up, like the rest of the world, to riveting, breaking news from Gabon – a former French colony – of the crash of a Zambian military plane carrying that country's national football team.

'I was 24 – [which] means I remember, because when you're a football player and you [hear of a] crash and the team completely dies, it's something you think about because it can happen to any team. Unfortunately, that's the second time I heard about Zambia – honestly because at that time [it] was not the focus in Europe to talk about African football,' Renard told this writer.

He'd been a lanky 19-year-old centre-back for Cannes when Zambia made waves at the 1988 Olympics in South Korea with that demolition of Italy. He said, 'The first time I heard about Zambia, because when you get a good result against Italy – you are the focus of the world because, of course, it's a big surprise for everybody. It was a fantastic performance from Zambia.'

In early 2008, 15 years after the Gabon Disaster, Renard was assistant to Claude Le Roy – mentor to several west and central African national teams and then Ghana coach – when Kalusha Bwalya came a-calling. Now Football Association of Zambia chairman, the icon was in the hunt for Zambia's next expatriate coach after Roald Poulsen's third stint on a three-month contract six years earlier.

Earlier, Kalusha, with a UEFA A coaching licence and Mexican Director Technical diploma in his possession, had taken charge of the squad himself, from 2003 to 2006. He'd even make history on 4 September 2004 by coming out of retirement aged 41, subbing himself on and scoring one of his trademark free kicks in a 1-0 stoppage-time win over Liberia in a World Cup qualifier at Lusaka's venerable Independence Stadium. His next act would be helping launch the career of one of international football's most dashing young coaches.

It was never in Renard's wildest dreams, after hearing of Zambia's Kalusha-inspired demolition of Italy, and then the Gabon Disaster, that he'd one day end up in that same southern African nation, helping it regain its reputation as one of the continent's best.

'No, I never imagined that,' he confessed to this writer. 'When I came the first time [to] Ghana, Claude Le Roy told me that he'd met Mr Kalusha Bwalya and he was looking for a young coach and I spoke about you. The first question I asked (Le Roy) is "Is it a good team?" because I didn't know a lot of things about Africa.'

Renard found out the answer himself after a little research: 'After a while, I look at the history of the Zambian football, of course, and I discover it was a good team in Africa with a lot of respect from everybody. I was very happy and [Le Roy] told me, I think for you it's a good [place] to start as head coach. And he was completely right because it was a fantastic start.'

Everything seemed perfect. 'Of course, when I arrived in Zambia in 2008, I met Kalusha Bwalya. Immediately I understood for me it was a good chance because he was a good player, he was coach as well before, and he has a certain philosophy of football that I like and I think it was a good combination.'

Inheriting a squad built by Kalusha during the icon's three-year stint as national coach, Renard qualified Zambia for the 2010 AFCON in neighbouring Angola. There they were drawn in yet another tough Group D with Samuel Eto'o's Cameroon, a Gabonese side featuring a young Pierre-Emerick Aubameyang, and Tunisia. Zambia won the group on goal differential after finishing level on four points with the Indomitable Lions and Gabon.

Jacob Mulenga, gangly, long-striding and on the books of Dutch side FC Utrecht, struck first against Tunisia, in a 1-1 draw at Estádio Nacional da Tundavala in Angola's second city, Lubango. First capped by Kalusha in 2004, Mulenga, then 25, would draw first blood again eight minutes into Zambia's second match – against Cameroon in Lubango four days later.

The Indomitable Lions would roar back through the versatile Geremi of Real Madrid and Chelsea fame, and Eto'o, to lead 2-1 until the 81st minute. That's when Zambia's live wire 5ft 7in forward Christopher Katongo – in a harbinger of what was to come two years later – beat goalie Carlos Kameni from the penalty spot. It was 2-2 until four minutes from time when Mohamadou Idrissou snatched a 3-2 victory for the World Cup-bound Lions.

In their last game, a must-win encounter with Gabon, Zambia triumphed 2-1 to top Group D and book a quarter-final date with a Nigeria squad chock full of some of the continent's best talent. Renard's high-octane pressing game was a perfect mesh with Zambia's traditionally high-tempo game based on the football the southern Africans had learned from their British colonisers. To that the young Frenchman added a compactness and fluidity that made up for Zambia's lack of that one standout player after the retirement of Kalusha. This new approach would make the Zambians competitive against teams with better talent, particularly the physically bigger West African sides.

The first high-profile game of Renard's nascent international coaching career came before 10,000 fans in Lubango on 25 January 2010, with a semi-final berth on the line. That's when he sent out his young Zambian side against another World Cup-bound side and old nemesis, Nigeria.

The Super Eagles had Chelsea's Mikel John Obi, Peter Odemwingie of Lokomotiv Moscow and Everton's Yakubu in their starting line-up. Obafemi Martins – then with VfL Wolfsburg after stints with Inter Milan and Newcastle – and Málaga forward Victor Obinna would come on. The legendary Nwankwo Kanu and Joseph Yobo would remain on the bench. Sixteen years after the two nations' titanic clash in the 1994 AFCON Final, Zambia and Nigeria would battle to a goalless draw after 120 minutes.

And for the first time since that World Cup elimination by Morocco in November 1980, Zambia would lose a penalty shoot-out, succumbing 5-4 to the perfect Eagles. Still, the Zambians, with their best AFCON performance since Roald Poulsen's rebuilt squad reached the semi-finals in South Africa in 1996, had made an impression, much to their young French coach's credit. With his two-year contract winding down, Renard succumbed to overtures from the Angolan FA and left Zambia. FAZ was left to find a new mentor for the squad that its chairman, Kalusha, had built during his stint as national boss. They decided to go Italian.

Big and powerful at 6ft 2in, and twice capped for Italy, Dario Bonetti was a tenacious centre-back during his Serie A career with several clubs including Roma, Sampdoria, AC Milan and Juventus. His biggest accomplishment as a player would be bagging the Coppa Italia and UEFA Cup double with Juventus in 1990. In his first national team coaching job, Bonetti would qualify Zambia for the 2012 AFCON finals, from a group comprising Libya, Mozambique and the Comoros Islands. His only loss in six matches was 1-0 away to Libya in Tripoli. Then he was gone, replaced after 15 months by his predecessor, Hervé Renard. With assistant coach Patrice Beaumelle in tow, Renard would return to remake Zambian football.

Bonetti had, in turn, inherited Renard's squad, whose core – including goalie Kennedy Mweene, skipper Christopher Katongo, his dribbler of a brother Felix, old-school link man Isaac Chansa, tricky playmaker Rainford Kalaba and the battering ram of a forward, James Chamanga – had been blooded by Kalusha during his stint as national coach. Reunited with his charges, second time around would be better for Renard.

He went to AFCON 2012 with just two European-based players in midfielder Chisamba Lungu, a 20-year-old from Russian side Ural Yekaterinburg who was deployed as a left-back, and striker Emmanuel Mayuka, 21, from Swiss club Young Boys. There were two players from Chinese clubs – Christopher Katongo being one of them – with the rest from African sides. Of the latter, just four were Zambian-based. And only one of the domestic players, midfielder Nathan Sinkala, was a starter.

But it didn't matter as the intense, savvy and detailed Renard drilled them into a compact, high-octane and dynamic side with – for *Star Trek* fans – a Borg-like collective consciousness. This was evident from the first game against Senegal in Bata, Equatorial Guinea, on 21 January. Given the two teams' respective fortunes over the past decade, the points were supposedly for the Teranga Lions' taking.

Papa Bouba Diop's goal in the 1-0 defeat of world champions France in the opening match of the 2002 World Cup in Seoul had introduced Senegal and its other standouts, Aliou Cissé, Salif Diao, Khalilou Fadiga and the impressionable El Hadji Diouf, to the world. They went on to reach the quarter-finals Cup while Zambia's delayed post-Gabon Disaster decline continued.

A new Senegalese squad had emerged by 2012, one led by one of the hottest strikers in Europe then, the aforementioned Demba Ba, who'd netted 29 goals in 54 appearances for the Magpies when pried away by Chelsea a year after facing Zambia at AFCON 2012. Kalusha, then FAZ president, would be a factor in the outcome of the Zambia-Senegal clash.

It was 21 January, the opening day, and Equatorial Guinea had kicked off in the opener against Libya, a game they'd win 1-0 with former Real Madrid and Benfica winger Javier Balboa's 87th-minute strike. Zambia and Senegal, on next at the 37,500-capacity Estadio de Bata in the port city of Bata to complete the double-header, had been availed two separate pitches outside the stadium for the customary pre-match warm-ups. This was Kalusha's recollection when he stepped out to observe the two teams warming up, 'I saw there were [no Senegalese] warming up. Everybody was doing his own thing while Zambia was getting ready on the other side. [Senegal] didn't do nothing, they were just like stretching, this one doing his own thing, the other his own … And so when the referee called us to go back in the changing room because we had to get ready, I said to Hervé, because Hervé didn't come out, it was [assistant coach] Patrice [Beaumelle] warming the team, so I said to Hervé, guys, these guys haven't warmed up, I'm telling you! They were just lazing about. So when we start, let us go guns blazing! And I am telling you they are cold, we'll catch them cold and we should take advantage of that. That's how we got the two goals in the early minutes.'

Emmanuel Mayuka, just two and a half years old at the time of the Gabon Disaster, and Rainford Kalaba, a throwback to wiry Zambian attacking midfielders of yore, had connected inside 20 minutes against the perhaps over-confident Teranga Lions. Mayuka, in rich scoring form for Young Boys in Switzerland, would strike again, along with captain Katongo, as Zambia twice came from behind in a 2-2 draw with Libya on a waterlogged turf at Estadio de Bata. Both celebrated with acrobatic backflips; Katongo reprising his four days later in Malabo with the solitary goal in a 1-0 victory over Equatorial Guinea.

There'd be more backflips by the Zambian skipper in the quarter-finals with his third tournament goal. It would come from a penalty this time, in a 3-0 romp over Sudan in the quarter-finals in Bata. It was sandwiched by a near-post header by big centre-back Stophira Sunzu – then 22 and on the books of TP Mazembe in his father's native DRC Congo – and James Chamanga's curling effort from just inside the penalty box. Zambia were back in the semi-finals for the first time since 1996.

Standing between Renard's side and a third AFCON Final appearance were a Ghana side that 19 months earlier had been denied a World Cup semi-final place in 2010 by the width of the crossbar from Asamoah Gyan's late penalty against Uruguay. He'd spurn another penalty seven minutes in against Zambia – Kennedy Mweene beginning his heroics from 12 yards with an outstanding save to the bottom-left corner.

Then 12 minutes from time, Mayuka came off the bench to put Zambia in their third AFCON Final and second since the Gabon Disaster. Holding off a defender, he curled a low right-footed shot from where the penalty arc and box intersect, into Adam Kwarasey's left corner. Zambia were headed to the championship game in Libreville, the Gabonese capital on whose shores the nation's heroes had perished 19 years earlier.

In retrospect, the 2012 AFCON Final was cloaked in some eerie coincidences. It's not just that it was played in Libreville, a few kilometres from where the Zambia Air Force Buffalo had plunged into the Atlantic Ocean, wiping out a golden generation. The Buffalo's next stop upon take-off from Libreville was to be Abidjan, economic capital of the nation Zambia were to face in the final. And picked to referee the final was Diatta Badara from Senegal, the Buffalo's final destination.

The final itself would pull all the emotional chords in the Zambian squad and at home. On arrival in Libreville, ahead of the big game on 12 February against an Ivorian side with some of the best African players in Europe – and a goalie who had not conceded a single goal en route to the final – the Zambians made their way to a beach closest to where the Buffalo had plunged into the ocean half a kilometre away. They laid flowers and sang songs in remembrance of their fallen predecessors. It was a particularly poignant moment for then FAZ boss Kalusha – captain of the 1993 squad who'd escaped death on the Buffalo only because he was to join the team in Dakar from his Dutch base.

The ritual was repeated on the day of the final when two plane-loads of Zambian fans touched down at Léon-Mba International Airport in Libreville. Zambian vice-president Guy Scott led supporters on the first plane.

Aboard the second aircraft was the 87-year-old Kenneth Kaunda, Zambia's founding president and long-time football aficionado. His initials had given the Zambian national team its first moniker – the 'KK XI' – for his patronage during his 27-year tenure. Travelling with Kaunda was one of his successors, Rupiah Bwezani Banda.

Zambia's state president from 2008 to 2011, Banda landed at Léon-Mba with a strong sense of déjà vu. Back in 1974, he'd helped charter two flights to Cairo after Zambia had upset defending champions Congo-Brazzaville 4-2 and reached their first Africa Cup of Nations Final. He'd even sat next to an excited Muhammad Ali as Zambia wrestled the Zaire Leopards for the African title. Now a week before his 75th birthday, Banda had arrived on foreign soil once again, on the second of two planes carrying fans to cheer Zambia on in another African final. It began sombrely.

'Our people, when they arranged [the trip], they arranged it in such a way that when we landed at the airport, we were all taken – each plane which lands – they're all taken to the place where they put the [Gabon crash] memorial. They built one on the nearest point to the sea, so that's where we went to lay the flowers. So we went there and it was very emotional for us,' Banda told this writer in February 2018.

Kaweche Kaunda, accompanying his father, remembered Kenneth Kaunda leading the fans in a moving Bemba rendition of the old hymn 'Rock of Ages' at the site. A couple of hours later, it was on to the stadium hosting the final, seven kilometres north.

As the travelling Zambian fans entered the 40,000-capacity Stade de l'Amitié Sino-Gabonaise and he took his seat in a VIP box, Banda recalled some of the locals' opinion on the final: 'Since Gabon wasn't playing, the majority of the sympathy was with us. They were saying, "We're coming to see the Zambians who died in our sea.'"

But by kick-off, many a Gabonese opinion had changed, Banda recalled: 'We ended up with Ivory Coast. It's a French-speaking country, and they've bigger names in football. So, when they started showing the players on the screen, ours looked very small, and so [the Gabonese] started, "Ah! No! No chance, Zambie! Zambie zero! Ivory Coast four!" … But within minutes, our boys had shown how skilful they were.'

Watching from the VIP box with leaders from Ivory Coast, Banda said it took 15 minutes for the West African dignitaries to realise that the Elephants had a game on their hands, 'They started saying, "I think these boys, what they are doing, there's a plan to this smallness of theirs."'

Aside from towering centre-backs Stophira Sunzu and Hichani Himoonde, both peaking around 6ft 3in, only a couple of other Zambian players could be considered of average European height (5ft 11in according to research by the World Health Organization), with the rest, including 5ft 9in Kennedy Mweene, below that.

It was a mismatch on paper in more ways than one. Tipped before the tournament, Ivory Coast, with their big guns, had kicked off heavy favourites on 12 February. While Zambia had only two European-based players in their squad – and from modest clubs in Ural Yekaterinburg and Young Boys – the Ivorian squad was wholly European-based, many of them from notable clubs. Three of the Ivorians who lined up against Renard's side were among European football's top wage earners.

Chelsea target man Didier Drogba, one of the biggest names in world football then, had made €6.2m in wages alone in 2011, according to Bleacher Report. Arsenal defender Kolo Touré earned €6.5m, while his younger brother Yaya, Manchester City's midfield dynamo, ranked joint third with Fernando Torres among the sport's highest earners in 2011 with €10m each. Only Lionel Messi (€10.5m) and Cristiano Ronaldo (€12m) had earned more than Yaya. Collectively, Drogba and the Touré brothers' 2011 earnings alone exceeded not only the Football Association of Zambia's annual budget, but that of Zambia's Ministry of Sport, by several times.

The Zambians were unfazed.

In their 2022 World Cup opener against Argentina, Saudi Arabia trailed 1-0 to a Lionel Messi penalty after 45 minutes. Their coach's half-time harangue – imploring them either to press Messi and the Argentines, or continue to stand off and take selfies with the then Paris Saint-Germain icon – went viral. It powered them to a 2-1 victory, and one of the World Cup's biggest upsets. That coach was Hervé Renard.

A decade earlier, there were no mobile phone recordings in Libreville when Renard – younger, hair longer but still with his trademark white shirt – rallied his Zambian players before the final with the star-studded Ivorians.

Rupiah Banda recounted what right-back Davies Nkausu told him. Nkausu was one of several internationals nurtured by Lusaka-based Chiparamba Academy, owned by Banda's son, Nenani. Said Banda, 'Renard told them, "I know you are afraid of their size, that they are big, and they are famous, but answer me this question: if you have two people, one is carrying a 50kg bag of mealie meal [corn flour] on his head and he's running and the other one is carrying 10kg, who is likely to win the race?" Of course, the one who is carrying less was the answer … "That's you!" said Renard. "I don't want to hear about their size, just run them and I want the first 15 minutes, I know you Zambians, I've been your coach, you can dribble, you can embarrass somebody, don't bother about trying to score. Dribble them, embarrass them.'"

The master motivator's pitch worked. A minute into the final, Zambia skipper Christopher Katongo won a corner which the tricky Rainford Kalaba took. Midfielder Nathan Sinkala drilled the incoming ball low and hard towards the bottom-right corner. It took a neat save from the alert Ivorian goalie Boubacar Barry to deny Zambia a shockingly early lead. That early warning would set the tempo for the night.

Said British football commentator Peter Drury on the international feed, 'It has the feel, in a sense, of an old-fashioned English cup tie. We've got an outright favourite, we've got an underdog, we've got to half-time, the underdogs are still in it, and there's that sense now that anything can happen, and it would be a huge upset if Zambia were to pull this off.'

There was a scare in the 67th minute when Gervinho, pursued by Nyambe Mulenga and Isaac Chansa, was bowled over by the latter just as he stepped into the box. Referee Badara Diatta pointed to the spot, to fervent protests from the Zambians. 'Gervinho grounded, and poor old Zambia floored – because they do not deserve to go behind here,' said Drury on the international TV broadcast.

Drogba placed the ball on the penalty spot to face Kennedy Mweene, Zambia's 5ft 9in goalie. 'And he's fired it over! It's a dreadful penalty!' Drury screamed, to the roar of the pro-Zambia crowd.

Mweene, a fast-emerging penalty-stopper, had dived the wrong way, but it didn't matter as Drogba, with his powerful right foot, launched the ball into the dark Libreville night – like an NFL punter.

With little between the two sides, the game would end goalless – then go to extra time, and then penalties. 'This is our time!' Drury quoted Zambia coach Renard imploring his side.

Midfielder Cheick Tioté, who would collapse and die while training with his Chinese club five years later, scored the first Ivorian goal in the shoot-out. Zambian captain Christopher Katongo coolly converted his side's first penalty. He was the first player to put the ball past Elephants shot-stopper Boubacar Barry in the entire tournament.

Mweene saved giant Leicester City centre-back Sol Bamba's effort, aimed for the left, but was adjudged to have moved before the shot. The 6ft 4in Bamba blasted his second attempt into the roof. Wilfried Bony, then on the books of Dutch club Vitesse and Max Gradel of Saint-Étienne converted their penalties too.

Emmanuel Mayuka, Isaac Chansa and Christopher Katongo's younger wing wizard of a brother, Felix, all responded in kind. Felix Katongo's conversion tied the shoot-out at 4-4, effectively turning it, as Drury observed, into a sudden-death situation at the point. The next missed penalty would be decisive.

It would go on like that – tit for tat.

Drogba's botched 69th minute spot kick had led to this marathon final. His team's captain, talisman and icon – as summed up by Drury on international television – he now stepped up to take the last of the five penalties initially allotted to each team. Mweene dived in the correct direction this time – to the right – but Drogba kept his hard shot below the crossbar to atone for his earlier miss and keep the Zambians under pressure.

Renard's side had to score their next penalty to stay alive.

Ironically, the burden to score that vital spot kick wouldn't fall on any of Zambia's outfield players.

'And now the Zambian nation holds its collective breath … the goalkeeper is going to take,' Drury announced to millions watching around the world. 'Mweene, who saved critically in the semi-final, is obliged to score in the final or they lose. These fabulous underdogs from Zambia, leaning on their keeper now … Mweene … CALM AS YOU LIKE! Five each!'

Mweene sent Barry the wrong way with a coolly taken low shot. He then shook hands with his Ivorian opposite number and returned between the posts where he conceded a sixth Ivorian penalty to defender Siaka Tiéné. Midfielder Nathan Sinkala – whose father Moffat Mutambo and brother Andrew Sinkala had both been capped by Zambia – cancelled that out with his conversion into the roof of the net. Didier Ya Konan scored next for the Ivorians, only for Chisamba Lungu to equal that too.

At 7-7 in sudden death, it was Kolo Touré's chance to convert a penalty. The Arsenal man had been at the heart of an Ivorian defence that had conceded no goals in the tournament. After a long run-up, Kolo struck low and hard to Mweene's left. But the Zambian goalie was up to the task and blocked the shot. Advantage Zambia.

It fell to the lithe midfielder Rainford Kalaba to win Zambia's first African title. He'd been one of Renard's best players in the tournament with his trickery and technique. A winning penalty from him would be validation of his performance. Alas, he missed, blasting his shot over the bar.

The Ivorians, who'd won their first AFCON 11-10 on penalties over Abedi Pele's Ghana after a goalless draw in 1992, two decades earlier, were back in charge. Another Arsenal man, the dreadlocked forward Gervinho, had been designated to take the next penalty. There was a quick pep talk from Drogba, and then Gervinho proceeded to send

Mweene the wrong way – and the ball too. It went high and wide off Mweene's left post.

'And again, Zambia is on the cusp of continental glory!' exclaimed Drury.

The goal that finally earned Zambia their holy grail would come from the latest of the country's Congolese connection. Previously, Simon 'Kaodi' Kaushi, near-hero of the 1974 final against some of his former domestic club opponents in Zaire, and the Lubumbashi-born and bred Alex Chola, who helped lead the KK XI to the 1982 semi-finals, had been the two notable internationals with links to Zambia's once-dreaded northern neighbour. Since 2008, big centre-back Stophira Sunzu, the son of a Congolese-born goalkeeper, Felix Sunzu Sr., had turned out for Zambia. His older, equally towering, centre-forward brother, Felix Jr., had also been capped in 2008. He'd win 14 caps.

Amid songs of prayers from his team-mates, Stophira (also known as Stoppila) would slam in one of the best penalties of the night, an emphatic effort that violently shook the net after sending Barry the wrong way. Le Stade d'Angondjé erupted.

'Sunzu!! … Champions against all odds!!' screamed Drury on global TV. 'Barely fancied on day one! Still rank outsiders on the day of the final! But somehow Zambia, and their smart coach … have climbed every successive hurdle! Tonight, they climb the highest of them all, and for the first time they are Kings of all Africa. Emotional, poignant of course, that it should occur in the very city where 30 Zambians lost their lives two decades ago. For the team of 93, for all Zambia, for every party-goer in Lusaka, for the Copper Bullets, the gold medal – for the Ivorians, pain! The 14th different champions of Africa are Zambia!'

There were personal honours too. Live wire skipper Christopher Katongo – joint top scorer on three goals with six others including compatriot Emmanuel Mayuka, Didier Drogba and Pierre-Emerick Aubameyang – was named Player of the Tournament.

Katongo was also one of four Zambians who made the CAF team of the tournament. Kennedy Mweene, all 5ft 9in of him, earned, for that moment at least, bragging rights as the best goalkeeper on the continent. Match-winner Sunzu also made the CAF All-Star Team, as did Young Boys hitman Emmanuel Mayuka.

Then there was Hervé Renard, himself making history as the youngest coach ever, aged 43, to win the Africa Cup of Nations. Zambia had swept AFCON 2012.

Three years later, Renard and assistant Patrice Beaumelle would lead Ivory Coast to victory in the 2015 AFCON Final, 9-8 on penalties against Ghana. They'd then qualify Morocco to the 2018 World Cup in Russia. And months after his exploits with Saudi Arabia at the 2022 World Cup, Renard would return home and lead the French women's national team to victory over Brazil, and a quarter-final berth at the World Cup in Australia. They lost on penalties to the hosts in the last eight.

For Rupiah Banda, Zambia's 2012 Africa Cup of Nations triumph completed his personal football odyssey dating back to the Bola Bola days in 1973. His country's fourth state president, he died aged 85 on 11 March 2022. For many others, victory that long, pulsating February night in Libreville had also brought closure to one of the darkest moments in sports history.

25

Missing Report

CLOSURE TO a 19-year-old nightmare was indeed the assumption for many that ecstatic night in Libreville. How could it not be? The trophy that had long eluded them since the Bernard 'Bomber' Chanda-led charge at the 1974 tournament in Egypt was finally Zambia's. And in Libreville of all the places, where the cream of Zambia – whose replacements had gone on to surprise the world – had perished. Tears of sorrow had been replaced by tears of joy. But not for everyone.

The AFCON victory did not expedite the Zambian government's release of the long-awaited Gabon Disaster report – perpetuating the anguish of the families of the victims, and others, who'd been left wondering how exactly their loved ones and heroes had died. There was still no report after a rather low-key observance of the tragedy's 30th anniversary, held on 28 April 2023, at Heroes' Acre, where the victims are interred. And for a good reason, perhaps.

The following conjecture – put forward for the first time – is that no official Zambian report of the crash was ever written or exists. If it does, surely this assertion – three decades and six state presidents later – should finally prod its release. In February 2018, affirmation that no report existed came from Rupiah Banda – Zambia's fourth state president, from 2008 to 2011, and before that vice-president from 2006 to 2008. 'To the best of my knowledge I didn't see any report regarding the Gabon Disaster,' Banda told this writer seven years after leaving office.

If anyone wanted to find out what caused the crash of the Buffalo, it would have been Banda, the erstwhile diplomat, foreign minister, businessman, politician and avid sports fanatic. Banda had co-founded the Bola Bola travelling supporters' club during Zambia's giddy emergence as an African power under coach Ante Bušelić in 1973. He'd sat next to the great Muhammad Ali as they watched Zambia battle Zaire in the 1974 Africa Cup of Nations Final in Cairo. He'd served as Football Association of Zambia vice-chairman and – after being plucked out of retirement on a farm in eastern Zambia in 2006 – was appointed state vice-president. Upon the death of incumbent Levy Mwanawasa in 2008, Banda was sworn in as Zambia's fourth president aged 71.

Banda also had a profound recollection of his last encounter with the doomed squad. Then a private citizen and bearing cases of Fanta, Coca-Cola and Sprite, he'd joined the list of visitors unknowingly bidding farewell to the national team at Masiye Executive Lodge in the final days before the disaster. Wishing them safe travels, Banda left the lodge for his Kabulonga home unaware that he'd never see them again. On the night of 27 April 1993, Banda went to sleep only to be rousted out of bed in the wee hours by state security officials. He was accused of treason in a conspiracy dubbed 'Zero Option'.

Along with other alleged 'Zero Option' co-conspirators, Banda was taken to Emmasdale police station – coincidentally, less than a kilometre from Masiye Lodge where the national team had spent its last night. The detainees were met at the police station by a sceptical officer in charge who privately confessed to Banda the absurdity of the charges. The embarrassed officer declined to confine them to the filthy cells occupied that early Wednesday morning by a motley collection of drunks, delinquents and petty criminals. Instead, he cleared his modest office and let Banda and a couple of his co-accused recline on the furniture there until daybreak.

'We were in court later that day when we heard our team had crashed,' said Banda. The charges were later dropped. Fifteen years later, Banda, by then president of Zambia, would seek out his compassionate jailer and promote him.

Apparently, Banda, who died on 11 March 2022 aged 85, was not the only person who doubted the existence of an official Zambian report.

Kaweche Kaunda, sixth son of Zambia's founding president, had come to the same conclusion. 'How many presidents have there been?' he asked rhetorically. 'This report should have been done when President Chiluba was there. Nothing was heard of it. President Mwanawasa came, nothing was heard of it. President Rupiah Banda came, nothing was heard of it – if anybody was going to release, it would have been him. Then, President Rupiah Banda left, then came President Sata, nothing came of it. Then President Lungu, and now we have President Hichilema and no one talks about it.'

Edgar Lungu – head of state from 2015 to 2021, and before that minister of defence between 2013 and 2015 with authority over the Zambia Air Force – was another with a compelling reason to want to know what caused the crash. He'd served as legal counsel for families of the Buffalo victims before entering politics. In May 2002, Lungu helped the families win an estimated US$4m in compensation from the government.

'Edgar Lungu, one of the family lawyers, said the government now had to stand by the agreement and honour the payments,' reported the BBC, in a piece titled '$4m for Zambian air crash families' posted on Monday, 13 May 2002. The report then continued, tellingly (emphasis added by the author), 'The government may hope the agreement will reduce the pressure on them to release details of the investigation into the disaster. *So far it has refused, claiming the report is incomplete and blaming Gabon for delays in concluding its part of the investigation.* Critics say the government is trying to hide the truth, and there has been speculation that the plane was shot down.'

Casting further doubts on the existence of an official report are the recollections of former *Zambia Daily Mail* reporter Goliath Mungonge. He travelled with the group sent to Libreville to retrieve the bodies of the crash victims. On arrival in the Gabonese capital, the delegation comprising air force personnel, both state and military intelligence officers, journalists, medical professionals and one FAZ official was divided into teams. This included press, protocol and a forensic unit of sorts in which Patrick Kangwa – the lone FAZ official – was co-opted in to identify the victims.

To the best of Mungonge's recollection, most of the work in Libreville was done by the forensic and press teams. While the former spent its entire time at the mortuary receiving the remains recovered from the sea and preparing them for the journey home, the latter was assigned a car and a driver and spent long hours at the recovery site. There they interviewed the locals. The rest of the Zambians would spend their time at their hotel where they'd wait for Mungonge and the press team to return before debriefing them.

Said Mungonge, 'There was [*Times of Zambia* sports editor] Davey [Sakala], me, the cameraman from ZNBC and the other [reporter]. So, we were the only ones who were like [doing the work], so all the intelligence officers … they were all waiting for us at the hotel … including the officials, the leadership, basically they used us as a way of reporting what we found … they were just sitting at the hotel, so we did the running round. We did most [of the work]. They could have done something, maybe, without our knowledge. We spoke to all those [Gabonese officials] and then you'd find that when we are coming back [to the hotel] they've made a table, [told] us to sit there and start now reporting for them to send the report file [sic]. At one time, me and Davey, we just said, "Ah … we'll just go into our room and sleep," because they were being lazy. But we did almost everything.'

Mungonge's recollection – Davey Sakala had died in June 2006 – begs the question: if the Zambian officials tasked to investigate the crash spent most of their brief time in Libreville at their hotel, who was out there talking to the Gabonese aviation authorities and gathering information about the crash? If picking the brains of the four journalists and receiving a briefing or two from the Gabonese was the extent of the Zambian investigation, it makes sense then that no official Zambian report has been released.

In November 2003, a decade after the catastrophe, Gabon's Ministry of Defence released their official report on the crash of the Zambia Air Force DHC-5D Buffalo. The 60-page report suggested that once the Buffalo's port (left) engine had caught fire shortly after take-off, the pilot shut down the starboard (right) engine, causing the plane to lose all thrust and plunge to its doom. It surmised that this fatal error was made by Colonel Fenton Mhone, noting that he was tired, having just flown back from Mauritius the previous day.

However, identifying Mhone as the pilot flying the Buffalo when it crashed was speculative at best by the Gabonese. There were two other vastly experienced pilots on the Buffalo, Lt Cols Victor Mubanga and James Sachika, with some 40 years of flying experience between them. And according to erstwhile ZAF sources, it was Mubanga and Sachika at the controls when the Buffalo went down, and not Mhone. This inference was presumably based on the condition of the two pilots' bodies, retrieved from the cockpit almost intact (on account of the harness seat belts strapping them) compared to the other remains in the plane. So that undermines the Gabonese conclusion that a tired, fatigued Mhone had ultimately doomed the Buffalo by switching off its only remaining source of thrust after its port engine had exploded.

At any rate, shortly after the Gabonese report came out, the Zambian government released what was construed as its crash finding. Vice-president Nevers Mumba read from the report in parliament. It was basically a summary of the Gabonese account to a tee.

On Friday, 28 November 2003, under the headline '"Faulty plane" killed Zambia team', the BBC's Lusaka correspondent Kennedy Gondwe filed an article.

It read: 'An official report into the 1993 plane crash which killed 18 members of Zambia's football team has blamed a mechanical fault in the left engine. Then the pilots switched off the still functioning right engine by mistake because of a "poor indicator light bulb" causing the plane to lose all power and crash, the report said.

'The first report was released on Friday – ten years after the national tragedy. A lawyer for the victims' families accused the government of "gross negligence" for using a faulty plane. Sakwiba Sikota, who is also an opposition member of parliament, urged the government to issue a public apology and increase the compensation payment to the victims' relatives. The report, released in parliament by vice-president Nevers Mumba, said that the loss of power and lift indicated the failure of both engines but said the government may wish to have this confirmed by experts. It also said that the pilot was tired, having just flown back from Mauritius the previous day.

'Mr Mumba said the government would make an official statement on the report at a later date. The BBC's Kennedy Gondwe in Lusaka says that Zambians are angry that it took so long for the report to be released.

'The Zambian Air Force plane crashed near Gabon on 28 April 1993, as it was taking the football team to play a World Cup qualifier in Senegal. Thirty people died in total, including some of Zambia's most talented players. They were buried just outside Independence Stadium in Lusaka, at a special monument called "Heroes' Acre".'

In March 2023, Kennedy Gondwe said, 'I remember in parliament, [Mumba] promised that that was a provisional report – it was inconclusive, but then there was a promise to release a final one and to the best of my recollection nothing ever followed what he had promised. All I can remember is the very report that I based the BBC report on.'

Mumba served as vice-president from 29 May 2003 to 4 October 2004.

Epilogue

THE FLAMING Buffalo that plunged into the dark Atlantic took with it two legends from Zambian football's glorious past, most of its contemporary aces and the best of its emerging stars. The two coaches on board, Godfrey 'Ucar' Chitalu, 45, and Alex Chola, 36, represented the glorious past. They'd both go down in African football folklore as two of the continent's all-time greatest players.

Chitalu's 79 goals from 111 Zambia appearances earned him the distinction as Africa's greatest scorer at the international level. In comparison, Didier Drogba and Samuel Eto'o, both recent strikers of world-class calibre, rank fourth and fifth, with their respective tallies of 65 from 105 caps, and 56 from 118 for Ivory Coast and Cameroon respectively. Chola's 43 goals from his 86 caps place him tenth to this date.

Nineteen years after his death, world football would hear Chitalu's name again. This following a Lionel Messi brace in a Barcelona win against Real Betis on 9 December 2012 that brought the Argentine great's tally that year to 86 – breaking Gerd Müller's presumed record of 85 goals for a calendar year set in 1972. Zambia protested. 'Der Bomber' Müller may have netted 85 times in 1972. But Ucar had struck an eye-popping 107 times in that same year, as any Zambian football lover above the age of five then can recall. There was that newspaper photograph, captured for perpetuity back in December 1972, of a dapper, smiling Chitalu holding a white football with '107' emblazoned on it in celebration of his unprecedented feat. Zambian football historian Jerry Muchimba would later detail Chitalu's goals in his biography on the goal machine.

In a 13 December 2012 article for Bleacher Report titled 'Lionel Messi V Godfrey Chitalu: Why Zambia's Case for Goals Record Is Legitimate', Andrew Jordan wrote, 'The brilliance Chitalu exhibited in 1972 cannot be ignored. The accounts, which have been published online, do hold merit. Considering very little is known about Zambian football, Godfrey Chitalu, not Lionel Messi, could reasonably hold the record for most goals scored in a calendar year.'

In addition to the two coaches, there was a collection of other talent aboard the doomed plane, many in their prime and a few precocious. Efford Chabala, 33; Derby Makinka, 27; Eston Mulenga, 25; Kelvin 'Malaza' Mutale, 23; and the 19-year-old Patrick 'Bomber' Banda. Gerald Mulwanda, *Times of Zambia* deputy sports editor in 1993, was attending a workshop in Zimbabwe on 28 April when he heard about the crash. At the *Times* since 1986, he'd covered all the players on that fateful flight at one time or another, including at AFCON 92 in Senegal. Following are his reminisces of the other players killed in the crash of the Buffalo:

Wisdom Mumba Chansa, 29:

One of the three Zambian players at South Africa's Lenasia Dynamos at the time of the Gabon tragedy, attacking midfielder Chansa was the elder statesman of that ill-fated squad. He had made a name for himself playing for his boyhood club Power Dynamos in Kitwe and then blossomed into a goalscoring machine for the national team where he, Charles Musonda and Kalusha Bwalya formed a near-telepathic understanding. His characteristic run-stop-turn routine would have the fans roaring 'WHIIZZ!' as he surged into the box. One of the best of his generation.

Whiteson Changwe, 28:

You hardly ever heard left-back Changwe's voice on the team bus and he was just as reticent when approached by journalists, but you could never fault him for effort on the field where he dutifully stuck to his script, whatever the opposition, for club or country. He was a mainstay of Kabwe Warriors' backfield for years, and kept his place in the national team as long as he was fit. Good in the tackle, he was efficient at orchestrating attacks from that side of the field and creative with his final ball. He scored a couple of brilliant, long-range goals for Warriors.

Moses Chikwalakwala, 23:

Chikwalakwala had made the meteoric rise from promotion side Chambishi FC to nail down a place on the right wing for Zambia's dominant club side of the 1990s, Nkana, and the national team in the months before the Gabon tragedy. A line-hugging, direct player in the tradition of the best of his predecessors like Moses Simwala and Bizwell Phiri, Chikwalakwala had pace to burn, loads of double-footed trickery and the kind of final ball from the flanks that strikers fantasise about.

Samuel Chomba, 29:

Chomba was the defensive bedrock of the Kabwe Warriors side moulded by Zambia legend Bizwell Phiri in his first stint as coach in 1987, a side bristling with talent deploying an enchanting attacking style of football as they swept well-nigh everything before them that season. Well built, strong in the tackle, he was also a great reader of the game and brilliant at setting up attacks from the back, thanks in large measure to his being comfortable on the ball. He had lost a yard of pace by 1993, and was being deployed in a more defensive midfield role where his ball-playing skills had assumed greater value for the team. He was also on the books of Johannesburg-based Lenasia Dynamos, alongside Wisdom Chansa and Robert Watiyakeni, at the time of the crash.

Godfrey Kangwa, 29:

Nicknamed 'Dunga' after the outstanding Brazilian midfielder, Kangwa had made his name in the blue-and white of Kabwe Warriors before being snapped up by Moroccan side Olympique Casablanca. Not exactly fleet-footed, his greatest attributes were vision and range of passing. Allied to his brilliant hold-up play, he had the ability to dictate the pace of the game, as he so expertly did for Warriors as the club romped to the 1987 league title. Sadly, his role for Zambia away to Mauritius in the Africa Cup of Nations qualifier would be his first and last for the national team.

Moses Masuwa, 21:

An all-action attacking midfielder, Masuwa was another member of this tragic ensemble who came to national prominence under the tutelage of Bizwell Phiri at Kabwe Warriors, where he won the 1987 league title and the 1991 BP Cup. He packed a powerful shot and always looked to find the shortest way to goal.

Winter Mumba, 23:

Mumba was another product of Power Dynamos, where he'd starred since his days as a youth international. A left-back, he'd been part of the Dynamos side that had bagged the African Cup Winners' Cup in 1991, upsetting holders BCC Lions of Nigeria 5-4 on aggregate. His form in Power's remarkable continental victory earned him a call-up to the senior Zambia squad where he established himself as Whiteson Changwe's backup. The two were of almost similar personality and both steady, enterprising and dependable footballers.

Timothy Mwitwa, 24:

Mwitwa ranked among Zambia's most technically gifted players ever – right up there with the revered Alex Chola, Kalusha Bwalya and Charles Musonda. The fans called him 'Teacher' for his technical brilliance, and there are few Zambian defenders of his era who could say they had not been taught a lesson in dribbling and deception. Mwitwa emerged as a right-winger for Kabwe Warriors but could operate with the same efficiency and menace on the opposite flank, as well as in midfield. As mesmerising with the left foot as with his favoured right, he was a defender's nightmare, scoring some sumptuous goals for club and country. He had a stint with top Czechia side Sparta Prague before returning home to Kabwe, and then breaking the hearts of Warriors fans by moving to arch rivals Nkana early in 1993.

Numba Mwila, 21:

Diminutive, speedy, direct and armed with great dribbling skills, the left-footed Mwila was hard to dispossess when in full flight. That meant a raft of free kicks and spot kicks for Nkana as desperate defenders struggled to contain the little man. Alongside Kenani Simambe, Winter Mumba, Patrick Banda, Moses Masuwa and Moses Chikwalakwala, Numba had recently been blooded into the national squad and he was generating quite some excitement among the fans with his Maradona-like runs at defenders.

Richard Mwanza, 33:

Born on 5 May 1959, Mwanza was a few days short of his 34th birthday, and the oldest player on the doomed Buffalo. He'd been the peerless Efford Chabala's backup goalie since 1983, but would finally get to don the gloves in his absence at the Confederation of East and Central African Football Association tournament in November 1992, where Zambia fielded a team of home-based players. Mwanza's agility, leadership qualities and shot-stopping skills had helped Kabwe Warriors land the 1987 league title.

Kenani Simambe, 18:

Another pint-sized menace from Power Dynamos injected into the national team for his pace and trickery, Simambe was always a handful for defenders. The little forward had already given Zambian fans a preview of his enormous potential in the choking atmosphere of a high-pressure game by netting the fourth and final goal against Namibia in Lusaka, in a match Zambia needed to win by a four-goal margin to stay alive in the World Cup. At age 18, he was the youngest victim in the crash.

John Soko, 24:

The team's chief jester off the field, the lightweight Soko was an absolute terrier on it. In man-marking situations, the right-back stuck to his duties with the resolve of a famished tick at meal time. When a reporter pointed out to him that he had been given a rather torrid time for 90 minutes by Ghana's dribbling wizard Ali Ibrahim at the 1992 Africa Cup of Nations finals in Senegal, Soko responded, 'He didn't score. He can turn me any which way he wants as many times as he can, my duty is to stop him scoring or creating for others.' He was no less feisty in training sessions. One local Zambia coach said Soko was the only player he had seen dismissed in training for his overzealous play. 'When he gets on the pitch, I don't think he understands there is a difference between a training match and a competitive one,' said Brightwell Banda.

Robert Watiyakeni, 23:

Rangy Watiyakeni had always promised much during his early days at Nchanga Rangers and Power Dynamos, but it was at South African side Lenasia Dynamos that he really began to come into his own, his performances earning him a call-up to the national side coached by Godfrey Chitalu and Alex Chola. With a penchant for overlapping, Watiyakeni could rely on the experience of compatriot Samuel Chomba to cover for him when he yielded to the temptation at Lenasia. That forward-driving urge was on display in what would be his last match on Zambian soil – against Zimbabwe. Frozen in the memory of many a fan is the image of Watiyakeni's gangly 6ft 4in frame suspended horizontally in mid-air as he attempted an acrobatic overhead kick that just sailed over the bar.

* * *

Three decades later, wistful memories of his young brother Kelvin Mutale and enduring thoughts of what might have been continue to haunt Michael Chanda, 'We had a lot of hope in Kelvin. That's why for us as a family it was not just one funeral, it was a multi-faceted funeral because it's like you have this hope and before you even finish celebrating it's gone. He loved family and put it first all the time. For example, he never bought a house for himself – but [from] the contract that saw him into Saudi Arabia he bought a plot and gave money to my parents to build a house. Now, that is something that's quite rare for a young man of his age, because most people when they make money, they'd rather enjoy their money, but that wasn't the case. This guy was going to make it big and we, the family, would have really been elevated financially.'

And that might have happened sooner rather than later. Although in the Saudi league for just a few months, Kelvin's scoring form had evidently earned him suitors in Europe. 'If he had returned from Senegal [on the Buffalo], there was a move to Portugal that I was aware of,' said Michael. 'He didn't mention [the club], he just said when I come back, because apparently, we should have gone back [to Saudi Arabia] together. He said, "OK, I will come and fill you in on the details when I get back."' Of course, he never did.

Michael recalled the last time he saw his brother. It was before Kelvin flew to Mauritius for what would be his last match. He'd net his second international hat-trick there, making it 14 goals in just 13 appearances for Zambia.

He also remembered that there was something unusual about Kelvin's last trip to the family's Kafue home, 'It's like he had a premonition, because all the times that he visited from Saudi Arabia, he'd just come with a few things. But that [last] time around, he came with a whole lot of luggage like he was not going back. He left it in Kafue. So, it only began to add up after the crash. We just appreciate God really for allowing us that short time with him.'

Kelvin Mutale left more than his Saudi household goods with his family in Kafue. Simataa Simataa – the banker, sometimes football scout, and, briefly, interim FAZ chairman after the crash – had served as Mutale's de facto financial adviser during the prodigy's tragically short top-flight career. Simataa's strategy was simple: invest Mutale's earnings from his international allowances and let him live off his club wages. A little while after the crash, and after the public open-air funeral that had paralysed a nation and saddened the football universe, Simataa met with Mutale's family. His sombre mission was to notify them of the investments he'd made on behalf of Kelvin during his brief professional career and their value. They amounted to US$12,000 – a princely sum in 1993 Zambia.

Postscript

IN THE three decades since the Gabon Disaster, there's only been one aviation accident involving a team of athletes – the 28 November 2016 crash of a charter flight taking Brazilian club side Chapecoense to a Copa Sudamericana game in Medellín, Colombia. That's good and bad. Good because, of the thousands of flights annually ferrying athletes to sporting events globally, only one has resulted in fatalities in 30 years. And bad because even that one tragedy occurred, killing 19 players among the 71 fatalities. There were 77 passengers aboard the British-made Avro RJ85 jet that, two weeks earlier, had reportedly ferried Lionel Messi and the Argentine national side. 'Fuel exhaustion' was the reported cause of the crash, according to the official report from Colombia's civil aviation agency.